Growth Product Manager's Handbook

Winning strategies and frameworks for driving user acquisition, retention, and optimizing metrics

Eve Chen

Growth Product Manager's Handbook

Group Product Manager: Alok Dhuri

Publishing Product Manager: Uzma Sheerin

Senior Editor: Nithya Sadanandan

Book Project Manager: Manisha Singh

Technical Editor: Jubit Pincy

Copy Editor: Safis Editing

Indexer: Pratik Shirodkar

Production Designer: Nilesh Mohite

Developer Relations Marketing Executives: Deepak Kumar and Mayank Singh

Business Development Executive: Puneet Kaur

First published: January 2024

Production reference: 1120124

Published by Packt Publishing Ltd.

Grosvenor House,

11 St Paul's Square,

Birmingham,

B3 1RB.

ISBN 978-1-83763-595-5

www.packtpub.com

To my beloved daughter, Maya, whose creativity and spirit motivate me to build a better future through innovation. And to the intrepid product innovators challenging the status quo every day to uplift humanity—may we have the courage to transform visions of progress into realities of hope. Onward!

- Eve Chen

Contributors

About the author

Eve Chen is a best-selling author, coach, serial entrepreneur, veteran growth marketer, and change driver with extensive experience from several global organizations. In 2015, she developed the Revenue Generation Value Chain (RVC) and a maturity framework to guide organizations to transform into high-performing systems with a methodical approach and align their resources to build a robust growth engine to exceed their goals. Currently, she leads The Growth Engine, a revenue performance consulting firm that focuses on helping business leaders accelerate their revenue results, and holds the position of Growth Experience Officer (GXO) for MOD Commerce, a global solution provider that helps retailers do more and sell faster. Eve has an MBA from the Macquarie Graduate School of Management and is on the boards of several tech startup companies.

About the reviewer

David Allinson started his career in IT as a Technical Author and has since held a number of roles including Product Management, Product Marketing, Channel and Alliance Management, Sales and Marketing both as a professional and as a leader. His experience has mainly been with IT vendors such as Microsoft, Dell, Autodesk, and Splunk. However, he once took a short break that ended up being 3 years during which he worked in retail with IKEA. He has worked and lived in the UK, Singapore and now calls Australia home. David got his MBA from the Open University in the UK.

Table of Contents

3

Understanding Your Customers   43

Part 2: Demonstrating Your Product's Value

4

Unlocking Success in Product Strategy and Planning   65

5

Setting the Stage for a Powerful Product-Led Enterprise   85

8

Define, Monitor, and Act on Your Performance Metrics   143

9

Guiding Your Clients to the Pot of Gold   165

Part 4: Winning the Battle and the War

10

Maintaining High Customer Retention Rates   187

11

Unlocking Wallet Share through Expansion Revenue   209

12

The Future of a Growth Product Manager   233

Preface

The discipline of growth product management has witnessed explosive demand in recent years, with over 400% annual growth in hiring for this critical role. As companies adopt product-led strategies and customer-centric business models, the need for specialized growth product managers has intensified dramatically. This meteoric rise spotlights the immense value growth PMs bring to organizations across all industries.

Growth product managers play a pivotal role in unleashing the potential of products by combining a strategic understanding of markets and customers with a relentless focus on growth. They drive **retention, acquisition, and customer development** (**RAD**), as well as customer activation, by optimizing the customer journey and experience. Their specialized skill set, which bridges product design, marketing, analytics, and commercial strategy, enables data-driven delivery of customer value.

This book provides a comprehensive playbook to excel as a growth product manager in the era of product-led growth. It equips traditional product managers, founders, and business leaders with the strategies, frameworks, and best practices required to thrive in this highly dynamic domain. From conducting user research to developing buyer personas, and mapping the customer journey to driving viral product features, this definitive guide unlocks the essential knowledge and capabilities for customer-centric product success.

By mastering the art and science of putting users first, listening to customer feedback, and pursuing growth opportunities with discipline, product managers can maximize impact, career growth, and organizational value. This book serves as an indispensable reference for anyone operating at the intersection of product, growth, and leadership.

Who this book is for?

This book is intended for traditional product managers, product marketing managers, product leaders, and start-up founders of product-led organizations. To fully benefit from this playbook, a basic understanding of core product management principles across the product development life cycle is necessary. This includes processes such as ideation, roadmap planning, requirements analysis, and go-to-market. Professionals in product roles focused on execution, rather than strategic leadership, will also derive immense value from the frameworks outlined to evolve into growth drivers.

Additionally, some knowledge of marketing strategies related to positioning, messaging, and campaigns is helpful to contextualize the growth tactics discussed in the book. A data-driven mindset and analytical approach will further allow you to comprehend and apply the data-centric methods for customer understanding and product optimization. Whether leading full-cycle development or specialized aspects such as customer research or life cycle engagement, this guide will equip those with foundational PM experience to transition into the emerging domain of product-led growth.

What this book covers

Chapter 1, Introduction to Growth Product Management, defines growth product management and outlines why it is an essential strategic capability in today's evolving business context. It summarizes the key responsibilities of a growth product manager, deconstructs core processes such as experimentation and stakeholder collaboration, and explores common challenges that teams face. This foundational overview equips you with an understanding of the growth product manager's crucially distinctive role in driving scalable business success through relentless user focus.

Chapter 2, Understanding Product-Led Growth Management Models, explores product-led growth management strategies and models that growth product managers leverage to attract and retain users effectively. It outlines the differences between product management approaches, analyzes engagement frameworks such as freemium and free trials, examines viral and expansion growth models, discusses key considerations for strategy selection, and summarizes future PLG trends to leverage. This comprehensive analysis equips you to make informed decisions regarding PLG techniques for your product and market.

Chapter 3, Understanding Your Customers, focuses on strategies to deeply understand customers and users to drive product growth. It covers conducting user research through methods such as interviews, surveys, usability testing, and data analysis. Creating detailed customer personas for key segments is discussed, including the differences between B2B and B2C personas. Identifying customer pain points using techniques such as social listening and analyzing support interactions is emphasized. Finally, methods for leveraging persona knowledge to optimize customer acquisition, retention, and development are explored, such as targeted marketing campaigns, personalized onboarding, and customer success programs tailored to persona needs. The key takeaway is equipping product managers with frameworks to gain customer insights that fuel growth.

Chapter 4, Unlocking Success in Product Strategy and Planning, provides an overview of the fundamental components of a product strategy and planning required for growth and business value. It emphasizes learnings around continuously gathering customer insights, embracing iterative design with rapid testing, and prioritizing features based on customer value.

Best practices for developing **minimum viable products** (**MVPs**), crafting product roadmaps, executing go-to-market plans, and proactively addressing typical challenges are covered. You will learn the importance of positioning products and pricing strategies effectively. Appropriate distribution channels, marketing campaigns, and managing the entire product life cycle are additionally discussed.

Chapter 5, Setting the Stage for a Powerful Product-Led Enterprise, covers the capabilities required of growth product managers to spearhead successful product-led transformations. Key learnings include establishing an insightful product vision based on research and then communicating it persuasively across a company. Additional responsibilities span fostering cross-functional collaboration around shared objectives, promoting rapid experimentation and continuous learning using customer feedback, championing customer centricity by facilitating immersive user research, and implementing supporting processes such as agile that enable product excellence. By mastering this expansive set of leadership, culture, and execution skills, growth product managers can transform organizations into product-led enterprises, fueled by delivering exceptional customer value and experience.

Chapter 6, Defining and Communicating Your Product Value Proposition, explains how clearly articulating the unique value a product delivers to customers is critical to driving adoption and growth. Key learnings include dedicating significant effort to understanding target customers and their needs through extensive research, gaining insights into motivations, frustrations, and decision-making considerations. With deep customer empathy, companies can define differentiated value propositions by identifying capabilities that address user needs and highlight tangible improvements over alternatives. Concise, benefit-driven messaging that captures the essence of the value proposition becomes a North Star. Companies must communicate it consistently across owned, earned, and paid channels, with each interaction reinforcing advantages. Frameworks aim to equip teams to compellingly convey why their solution is the superior choice.

Chapter 7, The Science of Growth Experiments and Testing for Product-Led Success, provides a comprehensive guide to leveraging experimentation for driving product-led growth. Key learnings include formulating clear, measurable hypotheses connected to goals, choosing appropriate success metrics, designing controlled experiments to isolate variables, planning tests comprehensively, and securing adequate resources. Various experiment types are explored, including A/B testing funnel analysis, cohort analysis, and multivariate testing. Analytics tools to gather qualitative and quantitative data are discussed. Finally, best practices for sound analysis such as examining statistical significance, assessing alignment with hypotheses, and continuously iterating experiments based on insights are covered. By internalizing disciplines around rigorous testing, analytics, and iteration, product managers can systematically optimize customer experiences, accelerate product-market fit, and drive sustainable business growth.

Chapter 8, Define, Monitor, and Act on Your Performance Metrics, provides a strategic framework to define, monitor, analyze, and act on performance metrics to maximize product success. Key concepts covered include connecting metrics to business objectives, automating insightful dashboards, segmenting users, identifying trends and outliers, running cohort analysis, and connecting data to user outcomes. Best practices for establishing a metrics-driven culture are shared by securing executive buy-in, creating a data roadmap, evangelizing a metrics mindset, democratizing data access, and incentivizing aligned behaviors. As growth product managers play a pivotal role in spearheading cultural transformation through metrics initiatives, an enduring metrics focus fuels agility and customer centricity and sustains competitive advantage.

Chapter 9, Guiding Your Clients to the Pot of Gold, explores the strategies and best practices to achieve customer success and long-term growth. Key concepts covered include laying the groundwork for retention through effective onboarding, adoption, and nurturing initial relationships. Strategic scaling of customer success teams is discussed by defining roles and the required skills, and fostering collaboration. Building strong customer relationships through engagement, delivering value-added services, and driving expansion are also emphasized. Finally, the pivotal role of a performance-driven culture centered on metrics, transparency, and customer-centric rituals is underscored to cement enduring loyalty.

Chapter 10, Maintaining High Customer Retention Rates, outlines the playbook to cement credibility and transform transient transactions into lifelong customer partnerships. Key learnings involve cultivating customer empathy through research to align experiences to evolving needs, and setting realistic expectations with transparent messaging. Driving advocacy while enhancing value requires care to nurture symbiotic relationships grounded in trust. Sparking meaningful connections between users through community builds affinity and organic growth. Customized predictive models assess signals to address emerging vulnerabilities proactively. By leaning on insights into marketing glam, teams enable fulfilled expectations instead of disappointed hopes to earn enduring loyalty.

Chapter 11, Unlocking Wallet Share through Expansion Revenue, equips growth product managers with a strategic playbook to sustainably scale revenue, by responsibly nurturing greater wallet share from loyal user bases. Key concepts span essential metrics, exposing expansion opportunities, data-backed decision frameworks, controlled experimentation capabilities that tie tactics to revenue, and considerations around ethical practices that nurture trust while delivering ongoing value, to responsibly scale customer lifetime value.

Chapter 12, The Future of a Growth Product Manager, explores the rapidly evolving role of growth product managers in the digital age to steer cross-functional teams, optimizing product-market fit and user experiences. We discuss essential attributes such as customer empathy, analytics fluency, strategic vision, communication abilities, leadership capabilities, and systems thinking that distinguish elite growth PMs. The chapter also delves into the dynamic contexts these leaders must traverse, including ethical tech challenges, emerging technologies, omnichannel consumption, and shifting consumer behaviors, to continue driving sustainable innovation.

To get the most out of this book

To get the most value out of this book, resist the urge to skip sections—the chapters deliberately build on one another. Immerse yourself in the key frameworks and examples. Brainstorm creative ways to apply the learnings to your unique context. Experiment relentlessly with the growth tactics recommended. Chart your progress quantitatively, be ready to tweak the formula regularly, and keep the end user front and center through it all. With commitment and rigor, the frameworks here can unlock transformational business outcomes.

Let this book be the catalyst to place users in the driver's seat to accelerate your product-led growth journey. The knowledge within is designed to serve both as your comprehensive roadmap and loyal companion along the route to sustainable commercial success.

Conventions used

There are a number of text conventions used throughout this book.

Bold: Indicates a new term, an important word, or words that you see onscreen. For instance, words in menus or dialog boxes appear in **bold**. Here is an example: "The concept of **RAD**, which stands for **Retention, Acquisition, and Development**, plays a pivotal role in leveraging buyer persona profiles to optimize your strategies."

> **Tips, important notes, or real-world examples**
> Appear like this.

Get in touch

Feedback from our readers is always welcome.

General feedback: If you have questions about any aspect of this book, email us at customercare@ packtpub.com and mention the book title in the subject of your message.

Errata: Although we have taken every care to ensure the accuracy of our content, mistakes do happen. If you have found a mistake in this book, we would be grateful if you would report this to us. Please visit www.packtpub.com/support/errata and fill in the form.

Piracy: If you come across any illegal copies of our works in any form on the internet, we would be grateful if you would provide us with the location address or website name. Please contact us at copyright@packt.com with a link to the material.

If you are interested in becoming an author: If there is a topic that you have expertise in and you are interested in either writing or contributing to a book, please visit authors.packtpub.com.

Share Your Thoughts

Once you've read *Growth Product Manager's Handbook*, we'd love to hear your thoughts! Scan the QR code below to go straight to the Amazon review page for this book and share your feedback.

https://packt.link/r/1837635951

Your review is important to us and the tech community and will help us make sure we're delivering excellent quality content.

Download a free PDF copy of this book

Thanks for purchasing this book!

Do you like to read on the go but are unable to carry your print books everywhere?

Is your eBook purchase not compatible with the device of your choice?

Don't worry, now with every Packt book you get a DRM-free PDF version of that book at no cost.

Read anywhere, any place, on any device. Search, copy, and paste code from your favorite technical books directly into your application.

The perks don't stop there, you can get exclusive access to discounts, newsletters, and great free content in your inbox daily

Follow these simple steps to get the benefits:

1. Scan the QR code or visit the link below

https://packt.link/free-ebook/9781837635955

2. Submit your proof of purchase
3. That's it! We'll send your free PDF and other benefits to your email directly

Part 1:
A User-Centric
Management Strategy

Part 1 has three chapters that focus on establishing a user-centric foundation. The introductory chapter defines growth product management and explains why it is critical in today's dynamic business landscape. It is followed by an overview of various product-led growth models and a detailed exploration of understanding user needs.

The following chapters will be covered in this part:

- *Chapter 1, Introduction to Growth Product Management*
- *Chapter 2, Understanding Product-Led Growth Management Models*
- *Chapter 3, Understanding Your Customers*

1

Introduction to Growth Product Management

In today's dynamic and continuously changing business landscape, growth product management has emerged as a critical subject. As a **growth product manager** (**GPM**), you will face obstacles that distinguish you from traditional product managers. However, by arming yourself with the necessary knowledge and tactics, you will be able to successfully navigate these stumbling blocks and generate outstanding growth in your company.

Whether you are about to embark on your journey as a GPM or are thinking about upskilling to take your career to the next level as a traditional product manager, this chapter will provide you with valuable insights into the key concepts, principles, necessary skills, and some of the effective methodologies you can use to achieve success. We will also delve thoroughly into the challenges of growth product management and give thoughts on how to overcome them.

We will cover the following main topics:

- The emergence of growth product management and its importance in today's business environment
- Key processes of growth product management
- Challenges of implementing growth product management processes

As competition intensifies, combining professionalism with a personable attitude allows you to confidently face obstacles and accomplish extraordinary outcomes. Let's find out how to become a successful GPM!

The emergence of growth product management and its importance in today's business environment

To handle the difficulties of today's corporate environment, growth product management has become a strategic discipline that blends product management, marketing, and data-driven experimentation with a single objective in mind: to drive business growth!

Traditional product management is no longer adequate to meet market demands. The administration of growth products is more iterative and holistic, emphasizing constant experimentation, data analysis, and user-centricity.

One of the most important reasons why growth product management is replacing traditional product management is its ability to negotiate the continually changing world of technology and consumer behavior. Technological improvements have transformed how organizations communicate internally as well as externally with their clients. GPMs play an important role in exploiting these improvements to improve consumer experiences across several channels.

Another critical area where growth product management excels is staying ahead of the competition. Companies must constantly innovate and differentiate themselves in the face of the rise of startups and disruptive actors. GPMs are at the vanguard of this innovation, always looking for new ways to improve products, engage customers, and gain market share.

Key responsibilities and skills of a GPM

As stated in the introduction, a GPM is responsible for driving a company's growth and success by strategically managing and optimizing its product portfolio. Their duties include a variety of activities such as product strategy, user research, data analysis, experimentation, and cross-functional collaboration. Let's take a closer look at each of these tasks of a GPM and how they differ from those of a traditional product manager. Then we'll look at a GPM's day-to-day duty to give you a clear picture of what it's like to be a successful GPM.

Product strategy

A GPM adds value to product strategy by concentrating on driving sustainable and scalable growth outside the purview of traditional product management. They look beyond traditional product characteristics and customer needs to include a broader perspective that includes market dynamics, business objectives, and upcoming prospects.

A traditional product manager will gather user feedback, do market research, and prioritize features based on consumer demand when designing a new feature for an existing product. While this strategy is critical, a GPM would provide value by looking at the big picture.

A GPM would begin by researching the market, detecting trends, and assessing competition pressures. They would concentrate on client demands and look for new alternative markets, unexplored user categories, or emerging technology that could provide prospects for expansion. They can discover new opportunities for growth that were previously ignored by undertaking extensive market research and considering broader market dynamics.

A GPM also collaborates closely with business and senior stakeholders to align product strategy with the overall growth objectives of the firm. They would be intimately familiar with the business concept, revenue streams, and **key performance indicators (KPIs)**. This broader understanding enables them to see how the product strategy can contribute to the company's growth objectives and design a roadmap that is consistent with the overall strategy.

A GPM, unlike a traditional product manager, combines data-driven decision-making in their product strategy. They employ data analytics, insights into user behavior, and performance indicators to support their decisions and validate theories. They may optimize the product offering, find areas for improvement, and make educated judgments that maximize growth potential by using data to drive their strategic choices.

GPMs prioritize growth experiments and programs that strive to test and validate new ideas and embrace an experimentation and learning culture. They may swiftly iterate on product features, pricing structures, marketing campaigns, and user acquisition tactics by planning and executing experiments. This iterative methodology allows them to identify scalable growth strategies and pivot as needed based on real-world data.

User research

User research is a vital responsibility of both traditional product managers and GPMs. GPMs, however, contribute value and differentiation in their approach to user research.

GPMs go beyond traditional product managers in terms of data-driven user insights by building a holistic understanding of customer needs. While traditional product managers concentrate on gathering input and performing research on existing products, GPMs look at the big picture. They investigate users' motivations, pain areas, and goals in order to find unmet needs and growth potential. This broad understanding enables them to create creative solutions that more effectively answer user needs.

For GPMs, experimentation is a critical component of user research. They plan and carry out experiments such as A/B tests, usability tests, and/or focus groups to gather input and validate assumptions. These trials provide useful information about user preferences, behaviors, and pain spots. GPMs improve the user experience and drive growth by iterating on the product based on these results. This iterative method ensures that user research is a continuous and dynamic process that allows them to respond swiftly to changing user needs and market circumstances.

GPMs add substantial value by focusing on scalable and sustainable growth. Through extensive user research, they uncover growth prospects and optimize the product experience to attract and keep consumers. They establish strategies to extend the user base, enhance engagement, and drive revenue development by understanding user needs, motivations, and pain areas. This user-centric strategy ensures that product decisions are in line with consumer expectations and preferences, resulting in the company's long-term growth.

Successful GPMs actively prioritize collaboration and cross-functional alignment. To incorporate user research insights into product development, they must work closely with designers, engineers, marketers, and data scientists. They promote collaboration and ensure that the product roadmap and feature priority address customer needs effectively. Because of this active cross-functional collaboration, they are able to translate user research findings into meaningful product enhancements.

While both traditional product managers and GPMs perform user research, GPMs differentiate themselves by focusing on scalable and sustainable growth through a comprehensive understanding of user demands, data-driven insights, and experimentation. Their user-centric strategy, along with collaboration and cross-functional alignment, enables them to identify growth opportunities, optimize the user experience, and generate improved company growth outcomes.

Data analysis

GPMs mine data for meaningful insights that influence decision-making and improve product performance. GPMs differ from standard product managers in the depth and breadth of their data analysis. While traditional product managers may focus on fundamental indicators such as user engagement and revenue, GPMs analyze data in a more complete and sophisticated manner.

To find hidden patterns and trends in user behavior, GPMs use techniques and methodologies such as cohort analysis, user segmentation, and predictive modeling. This enables them to look beyond surface-level analytics and gain a better understanding of the underlying elements that influence user **retention, acquisition, and development (RAD)**.

GPMs place a high value on data-driven decision-making. Data analysis is used to inform and validate product strategies, feature prioritization, and experimentation. They decrease biases and make better-informed judgments that are more likely to create growth by relying on objective data rather than subjective opinions.

Another key difference between GPMs and traditional product managers is their experience in hypothesis testing and data-driven experimentation. They plan and carry out multivariate tests and other experiments to assess the effect of modifications and iterations on KPIs. This rigorous testing methodology enables them to iteratively refine the product based on data-driven insights.

Additionally, GPMs contribute value by effectively synthesizing and communicating data insights. They convert complex data analysis into practical recommendations that cross-functional teams can comprehend and implement. This talent is critical for driving alignment, influencing stakeholders, and fostering an organization-wide data-driven culture.

GPMs examine data at the product and macro levels, benchmarking against market trends, competitive environments, and industry benchmarks. This larger perspective enables them to recognize possibilities for growth, assess market shifts, and make strategic product decisions that position the organization for long-term success.

Experimentation and iteration

GPMs differ from traditional product managers in that they use a systematic and deliberate approach to testing and iteration. While traditional product managers may undertake limited testing or rely on intuition, GPMs place an emphasis on experimentation as a key component of their technique.

GPMs, for example, support a culture of innovation and encourage a philosophy of continual learning. They look for opportunities to put theories to the test, validate assumptions, and get data-driven insights. GPMs promote a culture of experimentation and build an environment in which failure is not viewed as a setback but rather as a chance to learn and iterate.

The volume and scope of exploration is another unique feature. GPMs are more likely to run large-scale, data-driven experiments, such as A/B tests, multivariate tests, or user studies, to assess the impact of changes on key KPIs. They construct experiments in a systematic manner to isolate factors, test the effectiveness of various techniques, and make educated judgments based on the results.

GPMs are also skilled in analyzing and interpreting experimental outcomes. They have a thorough understanding of statistical principles and data analysis procedures, allowing them to derive relevant conclusions from data obtained during trials. They can iterate on product innovations, user experiences, and growth strategies more effectively by exploiting these insights, generating incremental changes, and optimizing for better outcomes.

Additionally, they contribute value by integrating experimentation with the overall product plan. They coordinate experiments with strategic goals and efforts to ensure that each experiment serves a defined purpose in driving growth. They prioritize trials that have the potential to make a substantial impact while also aligning with the company's growth goals.

It is critical for GPMs to excel at synthesizing and applying experimentation insights. They use data and customer feedback to discover improvements and iterate on the product roadmap. This iterative strategy allows them to consistently improve the user experience, fix pain spots, and generate long-term growth.

Real-world example

When PayPal aimed to boost customer acquisition, the payments pioneer leveraged rapid experimentation to optimize signup conversion. Rigorous A/B testing examined the sensitivity of reductions in form fields and faster credit approvals. By instrumenting key funnels and iteratively trying variations, PayPal determined the minimal yet sufficient data requirements to reduce fallout. Promising tests were incrementally expanded to larger groups with control groups continually validating improvements. Despite risks of lower data capture, conversion lift is persistently overshadowed. Continued measurement some months later showed double-digit gains, upon which further signup refinements were launched. Through disciplined testing cadences, PayPal fostered cycles of data-driven innovation.

A typical day for a GPM is dynamic and multifaceted, involving a variety of activities focused on driving growth and optimizing the product experience. While specific tasks may vary depending on the company and the stage of the product life cycle, here is a glimpse into what a day in the life of a GPM might look like.

A GPM's day

Typically, the day begins with a perusal of emails, messages, and notifications from productivity tools. The GPM sets objectives and goals for the day based on active initiatives, metrics, and forthcoming deadlines.

A large portion of the day is spent evaluating user data and developing insights. To uncover trends, patterns, and opportunities for improvement, the GPM delves into user behavior analytics, conversion funnels, and other relevant data sources. They collect useful information to inform decision-making and prioritize prospects for growth.

GPMs meet and collaborate with cross-functional teams on a regular basis. They engage with designers, engineers, marketers, data scientists, and other stakeholders to discuss current initiatives, provide direction, solicit input, and assure alignment. Collaborative meetings may include brainstorming new ideas, debating experiment results, or dealing with technical issues.

They collaborate closely with the team to design A/B testing, usability tests, and other experiments to validate hypotheses and assess the impact of product changes. They track the progress of experiments, assess the outcomes, and iterate based on data-driven ideas.

Strategic planning and product roadmap development take up a portion of the day. To refine the product strategy, the GPM analyzes market trends, the competitive landscape, and customer wants. They work with the team to create new initiatives, prioritize feature improvements, and match product direction with the company's growth goals.

A GPM must communicate effectively. They plan meetings with CEOs, team members, or other stakeholders to deliver updates on growth efforts, exchange insights, and discuss goals progress. They collect input, address issues, and ensure that stakeholders are informed and on board with the product vision.

Continuous learning is vital as the field of growth product management evolves. The GPM spends time reading industry blogs, attending webinars, and taking appropriate training courses. They stay current on emerging trends, best practices, and new tools that can help them improve their abilities and advance their careers.

The GPM takes time at the end of the day to reflect on the day's activities, review progress toward targets, and document insights and learnings. They may be responsible for updating project planning, documenting experiment results, or preparing reports for distribution to the team or stakeholders.

Key processes of growth product management

The core processes of growth product management encompass a range of activities that contribute to driving sustainable growth. To fulfill the key responsibilities of a GPM, there are several common processes that help to facilitate their day-to-day activities. Let's dive into the details of the steps involved in each of these processes.

Strategy development

GPMs use this process to do strategic planning in order to determine the broad goals and direction of the product. They analyze market trends, the competitive landscape, and customer preferences to find growth prospects. They establish a distinct product vision and strategy that are in line with the goals of the business and its target audience.

There are various phases that are commonly involved while creating a growth product management plan:

1. **Set clear objectives**: Setting explicit objectives for your product, such as increasing user engagement, making money, or expanding the user base, is the first step in the growth product management process. These goals provide the ensuing actions with a defined direction.

2. **User research**: To get a thorough grasp of the target market, substantial user research is carried out at this phase. This entails tasks including conducting user interviews, surveys, and careful observation of user behavior. Finding insights and figuring out user wants and preferences as well as where market opportunities are located are the objectives.

3. **Competitive analysis**: After doing user research, it is critical to analyze the competitive environment and define KPIs. This research enables the discovery of existing applications' strengths and weaknesses as well as potential for innovation and distinction. To assess success, KPIs are created. These KPIs include **average revenue per user** (**ARPU**) and retention rates.

4. **Feature prioritization**: Prioritizing features involves making a list of prospective features or upgrades while considering the objectives, user research, competitive analysis, and KPIs. The viability and potential effects of these concepts are then categorized. Setting feature priorities guarantees efficient resource allocation.

5. **Concept confirmation and experimentation**: This stage entails idea validation and information collecting about user behavior and preferences through methodical experimentation. In order to determine the most efficient strategies, different features, designs, or user flows are tested using a rigorous methodology such as A/B testing.

6. **Data analysis and insights**: In this stage, it is essential to carefully study and analyze the data gathered through tests and user interactions. Important insights are gathered through analyzing patterns, trends, and user preferences, which guide subsequent iterations and advancements.

7. **Refinement and enhancement**: It is crucial to continuously improve the application based on findings from user research, testing, and data analysis. To enhance user experience and foster development, upgrades and additions are made. The product will continue to be competitive and relevant thanks to this iterative approach.

By following these phases, GPMs can effectively manage the product's growth trajectory, align it with user needs, and drive continuous improvement.

Real-world example

As an emergent player in the online dating industry, Tinder leveraged rigorous growth product management processes to rapidly capture market share and engagement. Setting clear objectives, Tinder aimed to expand its user base exponentially while making the dating experience mobile-first, easy, and enjoyable to drive retention. Extensive user interviews and surveys yielded pivotal insights into preferences and frustrations surrounding existing dating platforms. Competitive analysis of early apps informed key areas of differentiation for Tinder—namely the gamified, card-swipe matching mechanic.

Armed with these strategic insights, Tinder astutely prioritized feature development around streamlined signup, smart mutual matching algorithms, and delightfully fluid user interfaces. Ongoing experimentation with elements such as UI design, chat functionality, and tiered pricing plans enabled Tinder to continuously refine and tailor experiences using meticulous A/B testing protocols. By relentlessly analyzing user behavior and response data, Tinder sharpened its onboarding, monetization, personalization, and retention capabilities over time. This laser focus on understanding target users, combined with agile product testing, data-informed iterations, and enhancements catalyzed Tinder's meteoric rise. Leveraging growth product management methodologies proved instrumental for Tinder to disrupt an industry and cement phenomenal market leadership.

User research and insights

Once the strategy is developed, it is critical for GPMs to conduct in-depth user research. This is important as it enables GPMs to gain a comprehensive understanding of customer demands and preferences. Key phases of this process include the following:

1. **Goal definition**: The user research processes' aims and objectives should be made very clear. Choose the specific knowledge you wish to gain and consider how it fits into your larger growth strategy. This action determines how the study will be conducted.

2. **Research question formulation**: Once the objectives are identified, develop research questions that will yield the needed insights. Pay close attention to the needs, problems, preferences, and actions of the user. Choose the best research approach, such as questionnaires, interviews, usability testing, user observation, or data analysis.

3. **Target audience identification**: Choose participants who represent the user base or certain user subgroups to reflect the research's target audience. To achieve a representative sample, consider elements such as user behavior, demographics, and product usage.

4. **Data collection**: Utilize the research approaches selected to get information and insights. This might entail gathering information through surveys or interviews, watching people at work or play, or looking at how they use the product. To obtain a thorough understanding, collect abundant and varied facts.

5. **Data analysis and insights**: Analyze the study data to find trends, patterns, and important conclusions. Combine statistical analysis with qualitative and quantitative research techniques,

such as affinity mapping and thematic analysis. Create user personas that illustrate various user types and their traits. To see the user experience, pain points, and places for improvement, create user journey maps.

6. **Communication of findings**: Put the research's conclusions and key takeaways together to form sensible suggestions. Inform the appropriate parties, such as the marketing teams, product managers, designers, and engineers, of these observations. Utilizing visual aids and narrative strategies, deliver the findings in a clear and interesting manner.

7. **Integration into product development**: It is imperative that you include the research outcomes in product development reviews. Also, it is important to include the suggestions in the product plan, iterations of the design, and feature prioritization. Verify the answers put forth by doing more testing and utilizing feedback loops. Create continuing user feedback channels to gather information and validate product improvements.

8. **Stakeholder collaboration**: Encourage stakeholder involvement in decision-making to promote collaboration and cross-functional alignment. Encourage honest and open dialogue while using the study findings to inform data-driven decision-making.

Real-world example

Spotify conducted in-depth user research to understand how its music streaming app was utilized in various mobile contexts. The key goal was to uncover specific usage insights that could inform enhanced mobile experiences to drive increased engagement and retention. Formulating exploratory research questions was critical, focused specifically on contextual mobile use cases, user needs, and pain points, and how behaviors may differ from desktop environments. Spotify interviewed and directly observed a diverse sample of users including students, professionals, commuters, and so on, from both free and paid subscriber tiers. Researchers employed ethnographic techniques, such as user diaries of daily mobile behaviors, as well as shadowing users executing real-world routines.

Analyzing the qualitative data uncovered a key insight – the very tight coupling of music integration into mobility contexts such as driving, exercising, and getting energized before a night out. Journey maps, personas representing user types, and highlight reels conveyed the textured findings. Spotify's engineers and designers actually took part in the field research, collaboratively aligning priorities. Leveraging these human-centered insights, Spotify built into their apps context-aware, adaptive playlists that react intelligently to situations the user is in, such as unwinding after work or powering through an intense workout. This research-fueled, user-driven mobile product innovation was crucial for Spotify's growth and cementing market leadership. The processes and methodologies of user research proved integral to transforming user insights into design, experience, and business impact.

By following these phases, GPMs can gain a deep understanding of customer demands and preferences. This empowers them to make informed decisions and drive product growth effectively.

Experimentation and iteration

GPMs support an experimental and iterative improvement culture. They plan and carry out experiments, including A/B tests, to determine how changes affect important metrics. They optimize the product for better results and sustainable growth by methodically iterating on product features, user experiences, and growth plans based on data-driven insights. Phases of experimentation and iteration in growth product management include the following:

1. **Hypothesis development**: Making assumptions based on user expectations, pain spots, and growth potential is the first step. Create hypotheses that explicitly identify the issue to be solved, the suggested fix, and the predicted effect on important metrics.

2. **Metric definition**: Select the key metrics that will be used to assess the success of the trial. These measures have to be in line with the growth goals and offer important information about how well the suggested remedy works.

3. **Experiment design**: Describe the precise changes or adjustments that the experiment will test. Changes to user interfaces, feature implementations, price policies, or marketing tactics may be involved. Create the experiment with accuracy, measurability, and the capacity to quickly compare many versions.

4. **Experiment execution**: Implement the required adjustments to the product or marketing strategies to put the trial into effect. Make sure that the right tracking and measuring techniques are being used. Gather information on user interactions, behavior, and experiment results. To acquire pertinent insights, make use of analytics tools, user feedback, and other data sources.

5. **Data analysis and insights**: Analyze the collected information to evaluate how each variant performed in relation to the given metrics. Analyze whether the experiment confirms or disproves the basic hypothesis. Make inferences and learn from the results of the experiment. Understand user behavior and preferences in response to the factors that affected the success or failure of each version.

6. **Data-driven decision-making**: Based on the results and insights from the trial, decide, using data, whether to iterate, refine, or pivot the product plan. To optimize the potential for progress, decide the next course of action. Improve user experiences, alter pricing, or change marketing tactics as appropriate, basing your decisions on the knowledge you gained from the experiment.

7. **Monitoring and scaling**: As time passes, track and assess how the applied modifications affect the given KPIs. Keep tabs on user activity, engagement levels, and conversion rates to determine how well the changes are working. To spur growth, iterate, test, and enhance the product continuously. Increase the scope of effective tests to reach more users.

8. **Collaboration and learning**: Promote cooperation among cross-functional teams, including product managers, designers, engineers, and marketers, to preserve alignment and shared learning from experimentation. To aid in informed decision-making, notify stakeholders of the findings and insights from trials.

By following these phases, GPMs can leverage experimentation and iteration to validate hypotheses, enhance product offerings, and improve user experiences, leading to long-term, sustainable growth for the product and the business.

Real-world example

Experimentation and rapid iteration were critical to Tinder's ability to accelerate growth while enhancing user experiences over time. When hypothesizing ways to facilitate more connections on Tinder, product managers put forth the assumption that displaying potential matches' shared Facebook friends and common interests on profiles could lead to higher match conversion rates. To test this, Tinder designed an experiment showing this extended contextual profile data to a sample user group, while retaining minimal profiles for the control group. The key metric of match rate would indicate whether the hypothesis proved true.

Tinder tracked and measured match rates rigorously over a 2-week period as the experiment ran in the wild. When analyzing the resulting data, however, the product team found negligible differences in critical conversion metrics between the control and test groups. Given these unexpected results from the data, Tinder decided not to launch the feature at scale, and instead went back to the drawing board to explore other innovation opportunities. This exemplifies Tinder's commitment to hypothesis-driven testing guided by user behavior insights.

While this experiment did not yield fruitful results, Tinder persisted in running rigorous tests on enhancements such as the UI design of the card stack and smart photo sequencing algorithms. The processes of rapid experimentation, user analysis, and data-informed iteration were integral to Tinder's ability to continuously evolve the app experience to changing user needs. By collaborating closely across product engineering and design, Tinder was able to scale successful experiments, learn from results, and fuel ongoing cycles of innovation.

Data analysis and insights

Data analytics are used by GPMs to derive important insights and make defensible choices. To find patterns and trends, they examine user behavior, conversion funnels, cohort analysis, and other pertinent information. They get a greater understanding of user engagement, retention, and conversion through data synthesis and interpretation, which enables them to spot growth possibilities and promote evidence-based decision-making.

Typically, there are multiple phases in the data analysis and insights process for growth product management:

1. **Goal definition**: Setting clear objectives for the data analysis process is the first stage. Identify the most crucial issues and metrics that must be dealt with in order to gather information and make wise decisions.

2. **Data collection**: Assemble pertinent information from a variety of sources, such as user interactions, website analytics, client feedback, polls, and market research. Make sure the data is accurate, thorough, and reflective of the intended user base.

3. **Data cleansing and preprocessing**: Preprocess and clean up the gathered data to get rid of any conflicts, mistakes, or missing numbers. Maintain data integrity while transforming the data into a format that is appropriate for analysis.

4. **Exploratory data analysis**: Utilize tools such as data visualization and summary statistics to explore the data and better comprehend its characteristics. Utilize statistical methods to generate hypotheses and test them in light of early findings and organizational objectives.

5. **In-depth data analysis**: Use cutting-edge statistical techniques and models to analyze the data to uncover important insights. Interpret the analysis's results and come up with useful conclusions. To successfully explain the findings, make use of charts, graphs, and visual aids, and use dashboards to automate live intelligence for the right person at the right time.

6. **Decision-making and implementation**: Work together with cross-functional teams to set priorities, create action plans, make data-driven choices, and put changes or enhancements into the product strategy in response to the findings and suggestions. Monitor and evaluate the effects of the adjustments you've made on a regular basis to spot long-term trends and patterns.

7. **Continuous learning and development**: By incorporating the knowledge gained from data analysis into subsequent product revisions and experiments, you may foster a culture of continual learning and improvement. Maintain suitable data governance procedures to guarantee data security, privacy, and legal compliance.

By following these phases, GPMs can effectively utilize data analysis and insights to make informed decisions, improve product strategies, and foster long-term product growth.

Real-world example

When Nike launched its activity tracking app, Nike+ Run Club, the athletic giant aimed to provide personalized fitness recommendations fueled by user data and progress insights. Extensive data from sensors and community usage allowed Nike to deeply analyze behavior patterns—from running terrains to workout frequency—at scale. Initial data cleansing uncovered gaps between Nike's assumptions and the reality of key categories such as beginners. Exploratory studies revealed surprising engagement friction points post-signup that churned new runners.

These insights led Nike to introduce adaptive training plans dynamically calibrated to each runner's demonstrated commitment and capability levels. In-depth statistical models ensured plan adjustability to evolving user stamina over time. While initially risky, continual measurement showed these customized plans boosted retention dramatically across beginner cohorts. Additional app refinements were spurred by further analysis into social motivation and competition triggers.

Ultimately, the processes of hypothesis-based experimentation guided by data-driven insights enabled Nike to transform Nike+ Run Club's capabilities to include not just activity logging but also intelligent planning. Feeding real-world usage patterns back into app improvements fueled sustainable consumer engagement growth. For Nike, leveraging analytics translated user research into increased brand loyalty and market leadership in the fitness tech revolution. Data analysis continuously informs their vision to motivate athletes of all skill levels.

Cross-functional collaboration

To match product development efforts with corporate goals, GPMs collaborate with cross-functional teams. They work together with marketers, data scientists, designers, engineers, and other stakeholders to make sure that product features and improvements are carried out successfully. Collaboration is encouraged, which makes it easier to incorporate technical know-how, market feedback, and user insights into the product development process. The key phases to achieve best practice cross-functional collaboration include the following:

1. **Identifying key stakeholders**: Finding the key stakeholders who are crucial to the product's success is the first step. These stakeholders include members of a variety of teams, such as data analytics, engineering, design, marketing, customer support, customer success, sales, and external partners such as resellers and alliance partners.

2. **Establishing clear communication routes**: Establishing clear communication channels can help cross-functional teams collaborate more effectively. Effective information sharing may be facilitated through regular meetings, project management software, shared papers, and other communication channels.

3. **Aligning goals and objectives**: The aims and objectives of the product should be understood by all teams. This guarantees that everyone is in agreement on the targeted results and creates a common understanding of what success is.

4. **Fostering a collaborative culture**: Transparency, open communication, and an atmosphere that enables team members to openly express opinions, critiques, and insights are necessary for developing a collaborative culture. This makes it possible for everyone to participate in a welcoming environment.

5. **Encouraging active participation**: The process of developing a product should involve team members of many different roles. They may provide their unique viewpoints to brainstorming meetings, user research initiatives, and decision-making processes.

6. **Planning and coordination**: Product development activities need to be planned and coordinated by cross-functional teams. This makes sure that everyone is informed of their own responsibilities, positions, and due dates. All stakeholders are kept informed through frequent updates and progress reporting.

7. **Regular progress meetings**: Set up frequent meetings to evaluate progress, go through problems, and decide what to do next. These meetings offer a chance to talk about new advances, get feedback, and resolve any problems or worries that may come up.

8. **Collaborative problem-solving and decision-making**: Participating in the design and development process with individuals from various teams promotes group problem-solving and decision-making. This guarantees that many viewpoints are considered and incorporated into the finished product.

9. **Incorporating input from cross-functional teams**: At each stage of the product development process, suggestions from members of the cross-functional team should be solicited. Their

recommendations must be considered, and the finished item ought to be enhanced in light of their experience and understanding.

10. **Joint testing and validation**: With feedback from many teams, the product should be collaboratively tested and verified. This guarantees that the product satisfies the necessary quality standards and meets the expectations of many stakeholders.

11. **Continuous contact and alignment**: Throughout the entire lifespan of a product's development, cross-functional teams should be in regular communication and alignment. Success depends on regular collaboration, getting feedback, and handling any changes or difficulties that may occur.

12. **Acknowledging and celebrating accomplishments**: Cross-functional efforts and triumphs should be honored and celebrated. Continuous development and progress are enabled through fostering a culture of learning from errors and converting them into chances for improvement.

GPMs may encourage productive cross-functional cooperation, tap into the combined knowledge of many teams, and guarantee a smooth and effective product development process by adhering to these guidelines.

Real-world example

When Uber sought to transform urban mobility, close cross-functional coordination was critical in scaling operations globally. Early on, Uber's product leaders identified domain experts spanning marketing, data science, engineering, and driver operations. Weekly workshops and quarterly hackathons established tight collaboration rhythms even as hypergrowth continued. Yet tensions inevitably emerged amid complexity—data teams grappling with marketplace dynamics felt overwhelmed by endless feature requests, while engineers fixated on technical debt felt misunderstood.

To nurture empathy, Uber fostered job shadowing so teams could walk in others' shoes. Gradually, psychological safety enabled healthy debate without politics. People managers encouraged knowledge sharing across domains so insights could inform decisions company-wide. For example, analytics models forecasting rider demand were integrated with driver app features to enhance supply positioning. Through joint priority setting sprints, Uber aligned around pragmatic solutions balancing contrasting constraints.

Creative friction was catalyzed by encouraging interdisciplinary teams to rapid-prototype consumer promotions or operations tools. By perpetually synthesizing diverse inputs, Uber tapped collective intelligence to pioneer a new economy. Engineers created vastly scalable cloud infrastructure while data scientists delivered the pricing algorithms that defined the category. Ongoing communal testing and controlled experimentation ensured reliability and positive user experiences.

The integrated orchestration of technology, analytics, and user-centric design was made possible through persistent coordination pursued with discipline. At Uber, cross-functional harmony, connecting strategy to architecture to delivery, has been foundational in revolutionizing consumer transportation amid complexity at scale.

Performance measurement and optimization

KPIs and metrics are set up by GPMs to gauge product performance and monitor growth objectives. To determine how product changes and efforts will affect consumers, they regularly monitor and analyze data. They discover opportunities for improvement through continual optimization work and put plans into place to promote ongoing growth and improvement. The following describes the key phases to achieve best practices for performance measurement and optimization:

1. **Identifying essential metrics**: The first step is to choose important metrics and indicators that align with the product's aims and objectives. These KPIs must be SMART-specific—in other words, measurable, relevant, time-based, and directly correlated with the product's efficacy.

2. **Assessing current performance**: Collect and analyze relevant data to assess the product's current performance levels. This can serve as a baseline against which future enhancements and optimizations are compared.

3. **Data collection methods**: Set up procedures for gathering data on the KPIs you've chosen. It can be essential to make use of analytics tools, user monitoring systems, surveys, or other data collection techniques. Make sure that data is consistently and accurately collected over time.

4. **Data analysis**: Analyze the acquired data to discover more about the product's functionality. Identify trends, patterns, and potential areas for improvement. You may track your progress toward the set objectives by comparing performance indicators with the given baseline.

5. **Identifying optimization opportunities**: Determine whether certain aspects or properties of the product need to be optimized in light of the inquiry. This may mean improving user experience, adding new features, increasing conversion rates, or exploring further optimization options.

6. **Hypothesis development**: Create hypotheses or offer solutions to the optimization opportunities that you have found. These assumptions should be supported by data and derived from analysis-related insights. Sort the hypotheses based on their viability and potential outcomes.

7. **Experimentation and A/B testing**: To assess the validity of the hypotheses and determine the efficacy of the suggested optimizations, conduct design studies or A/B testing by splitting the user base into a control and an experimental group, and then applying the alterations to the experimental group.

8. **Monitoring and analysis**: Monitor the results of the tests and assess the impact they have on the KPIs that have been selected. Analyze the results to assess the effectiveness of the optimizations and look for any unexpected results or effects.

9. **Iterative improvement**: Improve the product optimizations through iteration based on the trial results. Keep or change inefficient improvements while adding effective ones to the finished product. Continue iterating while taking into consideration the data-driven learnings gained through testing. It is important to note that sometimes stepping back and taking a new direction can also be an option when iterative development leads you to a dead end. For example, the Mercedes F1 car was developed for 2022 without sidepods for air intake while all nine other

teams had them. Mercedes pursued this approach and encountered a dead end. However, three months into 2023, it adopted sidepods and is now making massive improvements in performance.

10. **Stakeholder communication**: Regularly update stakeholders on performance metrics and optimization results. Talk about the outcomes of the experiments and the impact of the advancements. Visual and concise arguments are necessary for effectively explaining the findings.

11. **Continuous optimization and monitoring**: Maintain a continual procedure for monitoring and optimizing performance. Track performance metrics, get user feedback, and discover new areas that might require improvement. Take corrective actions and improve the product iteratively using input from customers and data-driven insights.

GPMs can successfully gauge the performance of their products, spot chances for optimization, and make ongoing improvements to the product to promote growth and success by following these procedures.

Real-world example

As Amazon rapidly scaled its Amazon Prime business, continuous performance monitoring and optimization were imperative to managing explosive growth. To gauge Prime's developing traction, product leaders established conversion rates, retention levels, and subscriber engagement as key tracking metrics against internal targets. Rigorous instrumentation was implemented for near real-time data flows—from signup funnel analysis to usage pattern tracking across video, shipping, and other Prime entitlements. Still, early readings showed lackluster renewal rates despite steep subscriber acquisition levels due to post-purchase drop-off issues.

Diagnosing optimization hypotheses involved intense strategy sprints synthesizing insights from executives down. Hypothesized fixes for renewal fall-off included more prominent media content offerings and streamlining cancellation flows. A series of meticulously instrumented A/B experiments were launched to validate assumptions—novel shows were exposed to subsets of users while redesigned account management screens reduced friction for another group. Control groups helped isolate signals from noise. After monthly reviews, certain tests proved inconclusive and were retooled while others showed promise through lift on engagement metrics and were expanded incrementally.

However, continued measurement some months down the line indicated that while sticky, content investments had limited impact on renewals. UX refinements conversely lifted renewal conversions notably across initial regions. As such, redesigns were progressively rolled out globally while content budgets were reassessed. This example shows how Amazon rigorously leveraged data, research, and controlled testing to distill signals from noise to guide executive resource allocation for Prime's growth and retention gains over time. Measurement enabled disciplined incrementation toward overarching customer lifetime value optimization.

Stakeholder communication

GPMs are skilled communicators with team members, customers, and executives. They provide updates on growth initiatives and outcomes while outlining the product's vision, strategy, and development. They develop trust, solicit input, and guarantee alignment throughout the organization by encouraging open and transparent communication. Key phases of best practice stakeholder communication include the following:

1. **Identifying important stakeholders**: Finding the important parties with a stake in the outcome of the project is the first stage. Internal teams, executives, clients, users, investors, and other pertinent external stakeholders are all included in this. Developing a **Responsible, Accountable, Consulted, and Informed (RACI)** chart can significantly help with this process.

2. **Understanding stakeholder requirements**: To effectively interact with stakeholders, GPMs must have a thorough understanding of their needs, goals, and expectations. Conduct focus groups, surveys, or feedback sessions to learn more about their particular requirements and difficulties.

3. **Establishing communication goals**: For each set of stakeholders, establish clear communication objectives. Establish the information that must be communicated, and the goals and main statements that must be provided.

4. **Selecting communication methods**: Select the most effective communication channels to include and speak to each stakeholder group. Meetings, presentations, emails, newsletters, project management tools, and collaboration platforms may all fall under this category. When choosing communication mediums, take stakeholders' preferences and accessibility into account.

5. **Crafting clear and concise messages**: Create messages that are precise and targeted at each stakeholder group. In your communications, speak to their particular objectives, issues, and interests. To guarantee effective communication, speak in plain words.

6. **Developing a communication plan**: For each stakeholder group, create a thorough communication strategy that outlines the frequency, timing, and substance of messages. Make sure the approach fits with the timetable and significant milestones for product development.

7. **Sharing relevant information and updates**: Inform stakeholders on a regular basis with relevant information, product innovations, and development updates. Inform them of the project's accomplishments, setbacks, and any other developments that may affect them.

8. **Soliciting user input**: Direct user feedback on the features, direction, and any other matters that require attention should be sought. When making judgments, consider their suggestions and wherever feasible, include them. Be transparent and swift in your response to criticism.

9. **Responding to stakeholder inquiries**: Respond quickly to stakeholder questions, concerns, or requests for further information. Answer any queries or issues customers may have in a fast and accurate manner.

10. **Encouraging two-way communication**: Encourage the use of open, transparent channels for two-way communication. Adopt smart collaboration tools to give interested parties the

chance to express their ideas and ask questions. Talk in depth with them and carefully examine their recommendations.

11. **Adapting communication strategies**: Adapt communication strategies and approaches depending on input from stakeholders and evolving needs. To guarantee engagement and understanding, constantly assess how successful existing communication tactics are and make the necessary adjustments.

12. **Evaluating communication initiatives**: Review stakeholder communication activities on a regular basis. Keep an eye on how communication affects cooperation and decision-making, stakeholder satisfaction, and participation levels. Use statistics and customer feedback to inform future communication efforts.

These steps may be taken to produce effective stakeholder communication that encourages comprehension, alignment, and collaboration. Communication that is clear and consistent increases stakeholder participation, fosters trust, and helps the product succeed.

Real-world example

When Instagram introduced advertising into its popular photo-sharing app, frequent communication with diverse stakeholders was imperative amid monetization concerns. Surveys and interviews highlighted serious user worries about disruptive, intrusive ads degrading experiences. Meanwhile, investors pushed aggressively for lucrative revenue streams given massive consumer reach. Upon careful deliberation, Instagram pursued subtle promotions preserving core utility first. Ongoing dialogue with advocacy groups shaped thoughtful guardrails and disclosures for emerging ad formats over time.

Despite some inevitably negative reactions, sincere explanations grounded in user benefits eased tensions. Instagram convened a council between advertisers, activists, and technologists, addressing trade-offs transparently to forge acceptable policies amid complexity. The sustained willingness to listen, learn, and adapt built lasting trust and unlocked sustainable monetization aligned with societal needs. By communicating respectfully despite competing incentives, Instagram continues advancing interests collectively. Its journey shows stakeholder connections enable better decisions, even on thorny monetization. Dialogue yields creative solutions that address value equitably.

GPMs face a range of difficulties, including limited resources, conflicting objectives, organizational resistance, and the complexity of data analysis. Realizing the full potential of growth product management and attaining long-term success in today's dynamic and competitive business environment depends on comprehending these issues and developing strategies to solve them.

GPMs may use the power of these processes to make wise decisions, deliver outstanding user experiences, and advance their businesses in their pursuit of success by overcoming these challenges. In the section after this, we'll examine some of the strategies used by effective GPMs to address these issues.

Challenges of implementing growth product management processes

Many problems can arise when using growth product management systems. The following are some of the biggest problems and their possible solutions.

Challenge 1 – Limited resources

The efficient application of growth product management techniques may be hampered by a lack of resources, including time, money, and labor.

Solution

Find and concentrate efforts on high-impact areas to strategically distribute resources and set priorities. Utilize technology, streamline processes, and automate repetitive tasks to maximize resource usage. Showcase the benefits and potential ROI of growth product management tactics to acquire more resources.

Challenge 2 – Organizational resistance

CEOs, team members, and other departments within an organization may be averse to change and the adoption of novel approaches.

Solution

Make a compelling argument for growth product management by highlighting its advantages and tying it to corporate goals. Key stakeholders should be informed of the justification and any positive effects to win their support. To promote a culture of experimentation and ongoing growth, encourage open communication, the sharing of success stories, and the celebration of victories.

Challenge 3 – Complex data analysis

It can be challenging to analyze and produce usable insights from vast amounts of data, especially when working with several data sources and sophisticated analytics software.

Solution

To facilitate efficient data collection, storage, and analysis, invest in data infrastructure and analytics. To assist the team in developing its data analytic capabilities, train and hire experts. Utilize techniques for data visualization to deconstruct complex information and effectively share findings with stakeholders.

Challenge 4 – Uncertainty and risk

The testing and calculated risks involved in managing growing products can cause uncertainty and failure-related fear.

Solution

Establish a fail-safe environment where failure is accepted as a learning opportunity and experimentation is encouraged. Establish a structure for risk evaluation and mitigation to lessen potential drawbacks. Encourage a growth mindset that values trying new things, failing, and iterating on concepts.

Challenge 5 – Cross-functional collaboration

Due to competing priorities, communication gaps, and divergent opinions, collaboration within functional teams, such as product, design, engineering, marketing, and sales teams, can be challenging.

Solution

To promote a culture of cooperation and open communication, schedule frequent cross-functional meetings, workshops, and feedback sessions. Encourage team collaboration on information exchange and idea generation. Develop effective facilitation and project management skills and adopt tools and processes such as RACI to encourage effective cross-functional collaboration.

> **Real-world example**
>
> "In my tenure at Medcan, it was abundantly clear how essential cross-functional collaboration was to the successful implementation of our growth product management strategies. For instance, when we were pioneering the launch of video consultations in Canada, we had to gain buy-in from across the organization. This meant crafting comprehensive presentations to engage everyone from the doctors to the reception staff, underlining the benefits and addressing potential concerns.
>
> We also faced a significant challenge following the introduction of new legislation banning private healthcare. We had to reframe the way we talked about our services, making it clear that our offerings supplemented rather than replaced their existing OHIP coverage. This shift involved training staff at all levels, from sales to medical professionals, to effectively communicate this change to our clients.
>
> When we launched a family plan for our Year-Round Care membership, we encountered difficulties with user research and insights. We found a solution by using the renewal process for individual plans as an opportunity to gather feedback about potential interest in a family plan. This required coordination across multiple departments, from marketing to customer service, to ensure a seamless and efficient process."
>
> *- David Cyrus, MBA, Head of APAC Marketing at Staffbase, and former Product Marketing Manager at Medcan*

In each of these situations, maximizing touchpoints across the organization and engaging in innovative problem-solving proved critical in overcoming the challenges GPMs faced.

By identifying these issues and implementing appropriate solutions, organizations can get beyond barriers and maximize the promise of growth product management. Adopting a development mindset, promoting cooperation, making the most of resources, and effectively utilizing data are essential strategies for putting growth product management techniques into practice.

Summary

This chapter introduces growth product management as a strategic discipline in the dynamic business world of today. GPMs confront particular difficulties, including the need to collaborate with cross-functional teams, adapt to change, comprehend various customer wants, and analyze complicated data. Growth product management is necessary for managing changes in consumer and technological behavior, remaining one step ahead of rivals, and attaining long-term success through innovation and user-centricity. Strategic product management, user research, data analysis, and cross-functional cooperation are among the duties of GPMs. Understanding growth processes is essential because they entail data-driven decision-making, adaptive behavior, and holistic product development. GPMs need to foresee and solve challenges, manage risks, efficiently evaluate data, and promote teamwork. In general, this chapter gives professionals the tools they need to be successful in promoting growth.

GPMs can develop excellent solutions that meet user expectations and promote business growth by effectively overcoming these hurdles, maximizing the potential of growth product management, and driving real results. Next chapter, we will dive into the different product-led growth management models.

Questions

1. What are some key differences between traditional product managers and GPMs?
2. What are some best practices when conducting user research as a GPM?
3. How can GPMs leverage experimentation and iteration?
4. What are some challenges GPMs face and their potential solutions?
5. Why is cross-functional collaboration important for GPMs?

Answers

1. GPMs have a broader perspective beyond just product features to encompass market dynamics, business objectives, and future opportunities. They utilize more rigorous data analysis, experimentation, and an iterative approach to drive sustainable and scalable growth.

2. Best practices include defining clear goals, formulating insightful research questions, identifying representative target users, collecting abundant behavioral data, analyzing for key insights, effectively communicating findings, and ensuring research integration into product development.

3. GPMs can plan rigorous experiments to validate assumptions, assess ideas, understand user behaviors, make data-driven decisions on product iterations, and optimize the customer experience and product offering over time through this cycle.

4. Challenges include organizational resistance, complex data, uncertainty from experiments, and collaboration difficulties. Solutions involve compelling arguments, investing in infrastructure, encouraging a growth mindset, and facilitating open communication.

5. Collaboration across teams such as engineering, design, and marketing teams helps GPMs gain holistic perspectives, tap into specialized expertise, and ensure alignment when translating research into product development. This enables effective implementation.

2

Understanding Product-Led Growth Management Models

In the previous chapter, we explored the distinction between conventional product managers and growth product managers. While both types prioritize the product roadmap by considering the needs of the business and customers, growth product managers particularly concentrate on optimizing for **product-led growth** (**PLG**). Their primary objective is to ensure that the product attracts and retains customers effectively. Therefore, we must familiarize ourselves with various **growth product management** (**GPM**) strategies and models associated with PLG.

We will cover the following main topics:

- Difference between GPM and PLG
- Key GPM models and frameworks
- Types of PLG strategies
- Distinction between demo, free trial, and freemium models
- Utilizing PLG techniques – pros and cons
- Other considerations when deciding what techniques to use
- Future trends of PLG management

By the end of this chapter, you will have acquired a comprehensive knowledge of the role of growth product managers and their focus on PLG. By comparing the roles of traditional product managers and growth product managers, you will have grasped the distinct role of growth product managers in optimizing products to attract and retain customers. You will also have delved into multiple strategies and models associated with PLG, encompassing various PLG strategies and discerning the differences between demo, free trial, and freemium models. Additionally, readers will have explored the advantages and disadvantages of PLG techniques, empowering them to make well-informed decisions when implementing these strategies. By the end of the chapter, you will be adequately prepared to navigate the realm of GPM and leverage the principles of PLG to drive success within your organization.

Difference between growth product management (GPM) and product-led growth management (PLGM)

It's crucial for Growth Product Managers to understand the differences between GPM and **product-led growth management (PLGM)** before we delve into product-led growth models.

GPM and PLGM are two techniques used by growth product managers to drive growth in product-driven companies. Although they are very similar, there are some differences.

Utilizing techniques including user acquisition, activation, retention, and revenue growth, GPM focuses on maximizing product growth. PLGM places a strong emphasis on using the product as the main engine of development by providing a smooth user experience that encourages organic growth.

While PLGM uses a self-serve strategy to reduce friction in user acquisition, GPM works with marketing teams to acquire users. PLGM strategically works to ensure client success for the purpose of upselling and cultivating growth prospects, aiming to enhance overall revenue streams. In contrast, GPM is dedicated to the precise optimization of these income sources, emphasizing a targeted approach to maximizing financial outcomes.

Therefore, while PLG strategies may be a part of both GPM and PLGM, PLGM places a greater focus on this strategy, whereas GPM covers a wider variety of development methods and responsibilities than just PLG.

Understanding the differences between GPM and PLGM can help growth product managers determine which approach is best suited for their company's goals and needs. For example, if the company's goal is to maximize revenue growth, then GPM may be the better approach. On the other hand, if the company's goal is to foster organic growth through a seamless user experience, then PLGM may be the better approach.

Moreover, understanding the differences between GPM and PLGM can help growth product managers collaborate more effectively with other teams, such as marketing and monetization teams. By understanding the different strategies and focuses of GPM and PLG, growth product managers can better communicate their goals and priorities to these teams and collaborate to achieve their company's growth objectives.

	Traditional Product Managers	**Growth Product Managers**
Focus	Balance business and customer needs in product roadmap	Maximize product growth
Technique	Collaborate with marketing teams for user acquisition	Use self-serve strategy for user acquisition

	Traditional Product Managers	Growth Product Managers
Strategies	Various development methods and responsibilities	Primary focus on PLG
Revenue Optimization	Optimize income sources	Promote upselling and growth prospects through client success

Table 2.1 - Differences between traditional product managers and growth product managers

Understanding these differences can assist growth product managers in determining the most suitable approach for their company's goals and needs. It can also facilitate effective collaboration with other teams, such as marketing and monetization teams, by aligning goals and priorities.

Key GPM models and frameworks

GPM is a discipline that focuses on driving user and revenue growth for digital products and services. Several key models and frameworks are commonly used in GPM to help product managers and teams achieve their growth goals. Here are some of the key models:

- **Pirate metrics (AARRR framework)**: Pirate metrics (acquisition, activation, retention, referral, and revenue) is a framework that helps product managers analyze and optimize different stages of the user journey to drive growth. It provides a structured way to measure and improve **key performance indicators** (**KPIs**) during each stage.

- **North Star metric**: The North Star metric is a single, key metric that represents the core value a product delivers to its users. Product managers focus on this metric to align the entire team's efforts toward achieving sustained growth. It helps maintain clarity and direction in the pursuit of growth.

- **RICE framework**: RICE (reach, impact, confidence, and effort) is a prioritization framework that helps product managers and teams decide which growth initiatives to tackle first. It quantifies the potential impact of a project or feature by considering reach (how many users it affects), impact (how much it benefits users), confidence (how sure you are about the estimates), and effort (how much work it requires).

- **HEART framework**: HEART (happiness, engagement, adoption, retention, and task success) is a user-centric framework for measuring user experience and product success. It helps product managers assess the holistic impact of product changes on user satisfaction and engagement.

- **Pareto principle (80/20 rule)**: The Pareto principle suggests that 80% of your outcomes result from 20% of your efforts. In GPM, this principle is often applied to identify the most critical features or actions that drive the majority of user growth or revenue.

- **Retention funnel**: Similar to the sales funnel, the retention funnel focuses on user retention. It breaks down the user journey into stages related to continued engagement and retention, helping product managers identify where users drop off and take action to improve retention rates.

- **OKRs (objectives and key results)**: OKRs are a goal-setting framework that many product teams use to align their efforts with growth objectives. Product managers set clear objectives and key results that are measurable and time-bound to track progress and success.

- **Customer life cycle framework**: This framework divides the customer journey into various stages, such as awareness, consideration, conversion, retention, and advocacy. Product managers use this model to tailor growth strategies and initiatives to specific stages of the customer life cycle.

- **Funnel analysis**: Funnel analysis involves tracking how users move through the conversion funnel, from initial awareness to taking desired actions (e.g., signing up, making a purchase). It helps identify where users drop off and allows product managers to optimize the funnel for improved growth.

- **Cohort analysis**: Cohort analysis groups users based on specific characteristics or behaviors and tracks their performance over time. This helps product managers understand how different user segments contribute to growth and how changes affect user behavior.

These models and frameworks provide valuable tools and methodologies for growth product managers to strategize, prioritize, and measure the success of their efforts in driving user and revenue growth for digital products and services. The choice of which model to use often depends on the specific goals and challenges faced by the product team.

Types of product-led strategies

As mentioned in the previous section, PLG and GPM are two different but related methodologies that may be used to create a variety of PLG strategies. It is significant to note that these solutions include methods that follow the GPM and PLG tenets.

In this section, we will explore the various models of product-led strategies and examine how they align with the principles of GPM and PLG. It is crucial for our readers to grasp these models, as they offer practical frameworks that utilize GPM and PLG principles to drive successful PLG. By understanding these models, readers will gain actionable strategies that they can apply within their own organizations.

Product engagement model

"Freemium," "free trial," and "product demo" all refer to methods of presenting and promoting a product. First of all, each of the three tactics aims to provide potential buyers a chance to experience the product for themselves. The objective is to enable people to investigate and comprehend the worth of the product, whether through a free version with restricted capabilities (freemium), a time-limited trial period with full access (free trial), or a guided demonstration (product demo). Additionally, by raising awareness, stoking interest, and perhaps even turning users into paying clients, these tactics work well as marketing tools. They all provide a look into the features of the product, showcasing its distinctive selling propositions and attending to client demands.

Freemiums and free trials are self-service models that allow customers to explore on their own. With the self-service models, consumers may autonomously onboard and use the product without a lot of help thanks to a flawless and intuitive user experience. By removing friction from the user acquisition and activation process, this strategy promotes quick product acceptance and expansion. A product demo, on the other hand, often entails more direct coaching and engagement with a representative. We will talk more about how these models differ in the *Distinction between demo, free trial, and freemium models* section and when best to use these techniques.

Viral loop model

The viral loop model uses the user base already in place to promote organic growth. The product is intended to encourage users to invite others, resulting in a cycle of user growth that reinforces itself. Referral programs, social sharing, and word of mouth all help the product become viral.

The product itself becomes a major motivator in the sales process under the product-led sales model. This strategy seeks to persuade potential consumers to make a purchase without heavily relying on conventional sales techniques by offering value and letting them feel the product's worth directly.

Dropbox's referral program serves as an example of the viral loop model. Users are rewarded for inviting friends to sign up for the service with more storage for both the referrer and the new user. As more users sign up thanks to referrals, which in turn prompt further referrals and possible signups, this viral loop of user acquisition promotes organic growth. Dropbox uses its user base to accelerate quick development and widen its clientele by automating the referral process and providing incentives. The viability of the Dropbox referral program serves as evidence of the viral loop model's ability to use user networks and word-of-mouth marketing for PLG.

Expansion model

The expansion model puts a strong emphasis on fostering expansion within the current clientele. It places a strong emphasis on providing value, assuring customer satisfaction, and boosting product adoption and usage inside the company. This then opens up options for upselling, cross-selling, and deepening the relationship with the consumer.

An example of the expansion model in action could be a SaaS company that offers a project management tool. After successfully acquiring customers and achieving initial product adoption, the GPM team identifies an opportunity to expand within the existing customer base. It conducts user research and identifies that many customers are also in need of document collaboration features. Leveraging this insight, the product team enhances the product by adding robust document collaboration capabilities. This expansion of product functionality encourages customers to increase their usage, leading to upselling opportunities and revenue growth.

Platform ecosystem model

The platform ecosystem model entails establishing an ecosystem around the product so that technology partners or outside developers may produce related goods and services. Through the network effects produced by the ecosystem, this technique improves the product's value proposition, draws in more users, and promotes growth.

The platform ecosystem model is best shown by the CRM platform Salesforce. Third-party developers are able to create supplementary products that interface with Salesforce through its AppExchange marketplace. By doing this, the platform's value proposition is increased, a larger user base is attracted, and innovation is encouraged. As additional partners and developers join the ecosystem, network effects drive growth and improve the overall offering and user experience. By utilizing the skills and capabilities of outside developers and partners, Salesforce's platform ecosystem has positioned it as a CRM leader.

Depending on the company's goals, target market, competitive landscape, and growth ambitions, these product-led strategies are frequently mixed. A company may develop a user-centric strategy and achieve scalable and sustainable growth by utilizing these methods.

Distinction between demo, free trial, and freemium models

While freemium and free trials are self-service models that allow customers to explore on their own, it's vital to keep in mind that a product demo often entails more direct coaching and engagement with a representative.

Which business model to use—whether "freemium," "free trial," or "product demo"—depends on a number of variables, including the nature of the product, the target market, and the corporate goals. Here is a description of each model and when it would be appropriate to use it:

- **Freemium**: When your product offers distinctive premium features that clearly differentiate it from competitors and add value, the freemium business model makes sense. It may work well for growing a sizable user base, raising brand recognition, and producing network effects. When your product has a collaborative or viral component that profits from widespread user adoption, freemium is very helpful. The conversion rate from free users to paying customers must be high enough to support the business model.

- **Free trial**: The free trial approach is worth taking into consideration if your product requires people to fully experience its features in order to appreciate its value. It gives prospective consumers the chance to try the product in real-world situations and determine whether it is a good fit for their requirements. Most software, SaaS, and subscription-based products provide free trials. The trial time must be lengthy enough for users to thoroughly investigate the product and make an educated buying choice for it to be effective.

- **Product demo**: The product demo format is frequently selected for sophisticated or high-value items that require explanation, customization, or personalization. This strategy is frequently employed in B2B sales when a sales engineer walks prospective clients through the features and advantages of the product. Demonstrations of products are useful for showcasing their features, addressing particular consumer needs, and fostering partnerships. The decision-making process of the customer can be significantly influenced by a customized and engaging demonstration, which often evolves into a paid **proof of concept** (**POC**) where professional services are engaged to run for an extended time with the client at the end of the demo.

The distinctive qualities of your product, the target market you're addressing, the duration of the sales cycle, and your income-generating plan ultimately determine which model you should choose. To choose the most appropriate model, it is critical to assess the customer journey, value proposition, and desired balance between user acquisition and revenue generation. In order to determine which model or mix of models is best for its particular product and market, a business may also experiment.

Now that we understand different types of product-led strategies, let's have a look at the pros and cons of each of these strategies.

Utilizing PLG techniques – pros and cons

In this section, we will explore further the application of PLG techniques and examine how businesses can utilize them to drive their growth strategies. We will discuss four key models of PLG: the product engagement model, the viral loop model, the expansion model, and the platform ecosystem model. Each model has its own set of advantages and challenges, and understanding these can help a business make informed decisions about which approach is most suitable for its specific circumstances.

Product engagement model

The product engagement model, which incorporates freemium, free trials, and product demo techniques, has both benefits and drawbacks for businesses.

On the plus side, these approaches give users a compelling user experience by enabling direct product interaction with potential buyers. Users are better able to comprehend the value and advantages of the product because of this first-hand experience, which boosts user engagement and conversion rates. For instance, Spotify provides a freemium model where users may use a restricted version of the music streaming service for free. This increases the possibility that customers will upgrade to a paying membership by allowing them to explore the platform and experience its features.

By decreasing entrance barriers, these models also function as efficient client acquisition channels. A larger user base is drawn to the free or trial versions since they tempt people to explore the product without making an upfront purchase. In order to increase the likelihood that customers will subscribe to the full version, Adobe Creative Cloud provides free trials of its software programs, including Photoshop and Illustrator, enabling users to explore the product's capabilities throughout the trial time.

The product engagement model also offers the potential for upselling. Users are more inclined to upgrade to a premium version or buy more features if they are happy with the free or trial version. For instance, HubSpot provides a free CRM with constrained functionality so customers may evaluate its advantages before deciding whether to subscribe to its premium marketing or sales software for more sophisticated functionalities and/or product support. It is important to note that product and technical support is only offered with the paid version, not the free version.

On the other hand, there are certain disadvantages to take into account. A free or trial version may have an immediate negative impact on income creation, especially if a sizable percentage of consumers do not become paying customers. Conversion rate monitoring and improvement are necessary for this. Due to difficulties in monetizing its enormous user base, Evernote changed from a freemium to a paid-only model, which had a negative impact on its income.

Allocating resources for product creation, maintenance, and customer service for both free and paid users can also put a strain on resources, especially for businesses with tight budgets or complex products. For example, teams can utilize Slack's collaboration platform capabilities for free but with some limitations. This requires Slack to maintain a large enough unpaid user base while still offering efficient assistance to paying customers to sustain its business model.

Additionally, consumers who utilize the free or trial version could form specific expectations regarding the features or cost of the product. It might be difficult to meet those expectations while maintaining a viable company strategy. In certain areas, Netflix ended its free trial period after taking user behavior and the effect on new subscriber acquisition into account.

In conclusion, the product engagement model presents potential for user experience, upselling, and customer acquisition. To choose the best model and successfully deal with the related issues, businesses must carefully evaluate their unique circumstances, business objectives, and target audiences.

Viral loop model

As a PLG approach, the viral loop model offers both benefits and drawbacks.

On the plus side, the viral loop model may boost brand recognition through word-of-mouth advertising and provide quick, organic growth. A company may take advantage of network effects and establish a self-reinforcing cycle of customer acquisition by rewarding users who refer other people to the product or service. Uber is a well-known example of a service that incentivizes customer referrals by giving both the referrer and the new user discounts or free trips. Uber was able to increase its user base and establish a solid market presence because of its viral growth technique.

In addition, the viral loop model might be more affordable than conventional marketing avenues. A business may lower its client acquisition expenses and rely on the credibility and confidence built via personal connections by utilizing user-generated referrals and recommendations. Dropbox, a platform for cloud storage and file sharing, successfully developed a referral program that gave customers extra storage space in exchange for recommending friends to sign up. The quick rise of Dropbox was facilitated by this encouraged sharing, which also lessened the demand for expensive advertising efforts.

Dropbox also allows people to share files through a link that brings the viewers to its platform online. The user experience of easy cloud storage and sharing then drives organic/viral growth.

There are certain disadvantages to think about, though. To keep the viral cycle going, it might be difficult to maintain a high level of user involvement. Viral growth may stagnate if the product or service fails to provide value or motivate customers to invite others. Assuring a pleasant user experience and ongoing product upgrades are necessary for this. Due to changing user tastes and heightened competition, Facebook, for example, struggled to retain user engagement and continue its viral growth in some demographics.

Companies also need to take care to control any risks related to data security and privacy in the viral loop model. Personal information may be shared through user recommendations; thus, businesses must build trust and uphold stringent data protection standards. The well-known social media site TikTok came under fire for data privacy issues, which it had to solve in order to maintain user confidence and continue its viral development.

The viral loop model might not be appropriate for all goods or sectors, as well. Some goods or services might not naturally lend themselves to viral sharing or might have a small target market, which limits the viral loop's potential reach. To examine the feasibility of the viral loop model, it is critical to evaluate the product-market fit and the dynamics of the target audience.

The viral loop model presents the possibility of organic development that provides quick and inexpensive marketing through user-generated recommendations. To fully realize its potential, a business must pay attention to user involvement, manage privacy issues, and carefully consider the model's suitability to its offering and target market.

Expansion model

The expansion model is a strategy for PLG that also has its advantages and disadvantages. One advantage is that it allows a company to increase growth within its current customer base by concentrating on providing value and ensuring customer success. This can lead to higher customer satisfaction, stronger customer relationships, and opportunities for upselling, cross-selling, and expanding accounts. Salesforce, a top CRM platform, uses the expansion model effectively by offering additional modules, integrations, and advanced features to current customers, allowing them to expand their CRM capabilities as their business grows.

In addition, the expansion model has the potential to create lasting customer loyalty and retention. Companies can build strong relationships with their customers by continuously providing value and supporting their success. This can lead to repeat purchases, customer referrals, and decreased churn rates. Amazon, a large e-commerce company, uses the expansion model by introducing programs such as Amazon Prime. By providing a premium subscription with perks including free shipping, streaming services, and exclusive discounts, Amazon promotes customer loyalty and motivates customers to continue utilizing its platform for various purposes.

Nonetheless, there are some factors to consider. One obstacle with the expansion model is the requirement for continuous customer engagement and assistance. A company must allocate resources to the customer success team to ensure that customers are utilizing the product or service to its fullest potential. This necessitates a thorough understanding of customer needs, proactive communication, and consistent product updates and enhancements. Slack, a well-known team communication platform, concentrates on customer success by providing extensive documentation, tutorials, and a dedicated support team to help users optimize their productivity and collaboration within the platform.

Furthermore, the expansion model may have certain limitations in terms of market saturation or restricted growth potential within a particular customer base. A company must evaluate the scalability of its product and target market to ensure that it can continue to expand within existing accounts. Microsoft Office 365, for instance, has accomplished significant expansion within organizations by offering a collection of productivity tools and cloud-based services. However, its growth potential may be restricted within organizations that have already extensively adopted its products.

Additionally, the expansion model necessitates a thorough understanding of customer needs and the ability to customize products or services. A company must be capable of tailoring its product or service to meet the unique needs of various customers or industries. This can be resource-intensive and may require additional investments in research and development. SAP, an **enterprise resource planning (ERP)** software provider, employs the expansion model by offering industry-specific solutions that cater to the unique requirements of different sectors, such as manufacturing, healthcare, and finance.

As illustrated, the expansion model presents opportunities for customer loyalty, upselling, and account expansion. However, a company must prioritize customer success, invest in ongoing engagement, and evaluate the scalability of its product to maximize the potential of this model. By focusing on delivering value and customization, a company can foster long-term relationships and achieve sustainable growth within its existing customer base.

Platform ecosystem model

The platform ecosystem model, as a growth strategy based on product, has its advantages and disadvantages as well.

On the plus side, the platform ecosystem model allows a company to create a network of products and services around its product, which enables third-party developers or partners to create complementary products or services. This expands the product's value proposition, attracts a wider user base, and drives growth through the network effects generated by the ecosystem. An excellent example of this is Apple's App Store, which has created a vibrant ecosystem that enhances the value and functionality of Apple products by providing a platform for developers to create and distribute applications for Apple devices.

Moreover, the platform ecosystem model can lead to increased innovation and accelerated product development. By opening up their platforms to external developers, companies can leverage the diverse expertise and creativity of the developer community. This results in a wider range of innovative applications, integrations, and extensions that enhance the overall user experience. Salesforce's

AppExchange is a prime example of a platform ecosystem that offers a vast marketplace of apps and integrations developed by third-party providers, allowing Salesforce customers to customize and extend their CRM capabilities.

Additionally, the platform ecosystem model can drive customer lock-in and loyalty. Once users become heavily invested in a platform and rely on its ecosystem of products and services, they are less likely to switch to a competitor. This creates a strong competitive advantage and can result in long-term customer relationships. **Amazon Web Services (AWS)** is an example of the success of the platform ecosystem model. By offering a comprehensive suite of cloud computing services, AWS has built a robust ecosystem that attracts developers, startups, and enterprises, fostering customer loyalty and making it challenging for competitors to replicate the breadth and depth of their offerings.

However, there are some factors to consider. One challenge with the platform ecosystem model is maintaining the quality and security of third-party products or services within the ecosystem. Companies need to establish rigorous standards, developer guidelines, and certification processes to ensure that the offerings from external developers meet the required quality and security standards. The Google Play Store, for example, has faced challenges with malicious or low-quality applications slipping through their review process, requiring continuous monitoring and improvement of their ecosystem's integrity.

Another factor to consider here is the technical skills needed for applications and integration into a platform such as Salesforce. As developers create modules that integrate with it, we begin to see the development of skills in the marketplace that further drive product use and adoption. Cisco is a great example of this as it offers a lot of free or subsidized training, which encourages developers to invest in these skills and leads to an increase in the skill base and product usage.

Furthermore, the success of the platform ecosystem model depends on its ability to attract and retain developers or partners. Companies need to provide robust developer tools, documentation, support, and incentives to encourage developers to build on their platforms. Microsoft's Azure platform has successfully attracted developers through its comprehensive set of development tools, extensive documentation, and partnerships with technology companies, allowing it to build a thriving ecosystem around its cloud computing services.

Moreover, the platform ecosystem model may face challenges related to platform dominance and potential antitrust concerns. Companies with dominant platforms may be subject to regulatory scrutiny and pressure to ensure fair competition and prevent monopolistic practices. Facebook is an example of this, as it faces ongoing debates and investigations regarding its control over user data and its impact on competition within the social media ecosystem.

The platform ecosystem model offers opportunities for expanded functionality, innovation, and customer lock-in. However, companies must establish robust standards, nurture developer relationships, and address regulatory considerations to ensure the success and sustainability of their ecosystems. By fostering a thriving developer community and maintaining the quality and security of its ecosystem, a company can leverage the collective power of its platform and drive growth through network effects.

To select the appropriate product-led strategy, it is recommended that you adhere to the following best practices

- **Define your company's goals**: Clearly state your business's aims and objectives. Identify the goals you have for your product-led approach, such as increasing user engagement, promoting viral growth, gaining market share, or developing a platform ecosystem.

- **Know your target audience**: Conduct extensive market research to fully comprehend your target market and its wants, preferences, and pain points. Determine the essential traits of your ideal clients and how they use and interact with your products.

- **Analyze the product/market fit**: Examine how effectively your product satisfies the demands and expectations of your intended audience. Determine whether your product has the potential to encourage user adoption and engagement and whether it delivers a compelling value proposition.

- **Understand the competitive landscape**: Conduct research and analysis to learn about the product-led tactics of your rivals and how effective they have been. Identify market insufficiencies and opportunities for your product to stand out from the competition.

- **Use data and analytics to your advantage**: Utilize data and analytics to gain insights into user behavior, product usage trends, and performance metrics. Identify areas for improvement, any obstacles, and potential opportunities for product enhancement.

- **Implement a continuous process of testing and iteration**: Conduct small-scale tests to verify assumptions and ideas on various product-led strategies. Obtain user feedback, track outcomes, and adjust your strategy based on the newfound knowledge.

- **Examine scalability and sustainability**: Consider the scalability and long-term viability of any product-led approach. Analyze the long-term impact on your infrastructure, resources, and ability to meet the needs of your user base as it expands and grows.

- **Align with your resources and capabilities**: Take into account the resources, knowledge, and talents that your organization has to offer. Choose a product-driven approach that leverages your strengths and ensures successful implementation and maintenance.

- **Consult industry experts and benchmarks**: Seek guidance from mentors or work with consultants who have expertise in product-led initiatives to obtain benchmarks. Look to success stories and industry benchmarks for knowledge and inspiration.

After deciding on a product-led approach, pay close attention to how it is carried out and the outcomes. Measure and analyze important indicators over time to assess the strategy's efficacy. Be ready to modify your strategy in response to criticism and shifting market realities.

Other considerations when deciding what techniques to use

Growth product managers can make the most of PLG strategies by understanding their advantages and disadvantages and following the best practices outlined in the previous section. This knowledge helps them make informed decisions that align with their product and growth objectives, and choose the most suitable tactics for their specific product and market. Additionally, it enables them to identify potential risks and challenges and proactively mitigate them. They can also optimize resource allocation by allocating budget and team efforts effectively, and adjust strategies based on evolving needs to ensure alignment with business goals. Evaluating outcomes and iterating the approach contributes to continuous improvement.

To make an educated selection when selecting a product-led strategy for their firm, growth product managers must consider a number of extra considerations. First and foremost, it's crucial to think about time to value, which entails assessing how fast consumers can enjoy the advantages and value of the product following onboarding. Users' time to value may be accelerated via an easy-to-use and efficient onboarding process that helps them interact with key features and comprehend the product.

Customer service and self-service resources are also very important. Strong customer service channels and self-help tools enable consumers to solve issues on their own, increasing their happiness and engagement. Higher retention rates may be attained with a solid support system that fosters customer confidence in the brand and the product.

It is also crucial to assess the likelihood of network effects. The value of products that benefit from network effects rises as more customers utilize the platform. Examining how a product encourages user interaction, cooperation, and communication can encourage organic development through beneficial network effects.

The chosen PLG strategy should be in line with the price and monetization model. To ensure that the plan meets revenue goals without degrading the user experience, careful thought should be given. This can entail investigating various pricing levels, freemium models, or other revenue techniques that encourage adoption and growth.

When expanding internationally, there are two important factors to consider: internationalization (i18n) and localization (l10n). i18n refers to the development and engineering of the product itself to be used in other languages. This includes adapting the user interface and documentation. It is relatively easier with Latin and Arabic-based languages, but much harder with double-byte languages such as Japanese. On the other hand, l10n involves the translation of sales, marketing, and service materials that surround the product and its adoption. Further, the likelihood of the product being adopted successfully in new markets rises when it is modified to meet the demands of various cultures, languages, and market niches.

Growth that is driven by products can also benefit greatly from strategic alliances and mergers. Finding and working with complementary goods or services may improve the value offer for customers and promote growth for both parties. This strategy increases the product's capabilities and reach, bringing in more users and boosting engagement.

It is crucial to take the target market's maturity into account since it determines the best PLG approach. While methods that stress distinctiveness, customer retention, and stealing market share from rivals may be necessary in developed countries, an emphasis on education and awareness may be necessary in emerging areas.

Another important consideration is long-term sustainability. The organization's selected PLG strategy should be compatible with its vision and long-term objectives and flexible enough to change along with the market, users' expectations, and the competitive environment.

The secret to success is to promote experimentation and adaptability. The PLG approach can be continuously improved and fine-tuned with the help of a culture that values trying new things, monitoring outcomes, and learning from both triumphs and mistakes.

Growth product managers may choose a PLG strategy that fits their goals, target market, and organizational environment by carefully weighing these elements and making educated decisions.

Future trends of PLG management

PLG strategies are evolving in response to several future trends. The emphasis on personalization and a customer-centric strategy is one notable trend. By customizing onboarding, recommendations, and user journeys, businesses are delivering highly customized experiences that increase engagement and conversion.

The fusion of automation and **artificial intelligence (AI)** is another trend. Automation enabled by AI can speed up user onboarding, provide informed suggestions, and automate customer care, allowing businesses to grow their operations yet provide tailored experiences.

Virtual and augmented reality are emerging, and are influencing PLG strategies. Users may be able to perceive items, interact with virtual settings, and make wise purchase decisions by combining AR and VR technology.

Companies are implementing voice-activated interfaces into their PLG plans as they become more and more popular. Voice commands for product discovery, onboarding, and support improve accessibility and user comfort.

Another tendency is expanding to new platforms and channels. To reach and engage people across several touchpoints, businesses are utilizing developing social media platforms, messaging applications, voice assistants, and linked products.

Security and data privacy are becoming increasingly crucial factors in PLG strategies. To establish trust and maintain strong connections with users, it is essential to prioritize data protection, open communication, and legal compliance. It is important to note that legal compliance and regulations are constantly changing, varying from country to country. For instance, in Australia and Thailand, digital data standards and regulations are currently hot topics.

The importance of constant experimentation and iteration is growing. Businesses adopt a culture of constant experimentation, using user feedback, data insights, and A/B testing to improve their goods, onboarding procedures, and conversion funnels.

PLG methods are increasingly relying on partnerships and collaboration. Companies are able to tap into existing user bases, take advantage of network effects, and promote mutual growth through shared ecosystems thanks to strategic partnerships with similar goods or services.

Companies that embrace and adapt to these trends as they develop will be well-positioned to promote sustainable growth and keep up with the competitive environment of PLG strategies.

Summary

To create effective development plans, growth product managers must have a thorough awareness of the different PLG methods, their benefits and drawbacks, and when to apply them. Product managers may decide which methods to use to achieve scalable and sustainable growth by taking into account elements such as target market, corporate goals, competitive landscape, and growth aspirations.

Additionally, staying ahead in the shifting market requires being informed of the upcoming trends in PLG methods. The future of PLG is being shaped by trends such as customization, AI and automation, AR and VR, voice-activated interfaces, expansion into new platforms and channels, data privacy and security, constant iteration and experimentation, collaboration, and partnerships.

By adopting these trends, growth product managers may take advantage of new technology, enhance user experiences, and promote growth via creative and client-focused strategies. In order to maintain competitiveness and satisfy changing consumer needs, it is essential to react to these trends and incorporate them into development initiatives.

Overall, growth product managers can create effective growth strategies that deliver value, encourage user adoption, and support sustainable growth in the dynamic and constantly changing environment of the PLG paradigm with a solid understanding of PLG strategies, their advantages and disadvantages, consideration of key factors, and awareness of future trends.

Questions

1. What are the main distinctions between GPM and PLG management?
2. What are the various types of PLG strategies?
3. What are the major differences between freemium, free trial, and product demo models?
4. What are the pros and cons of each type of PLG model?
5. What are some of the considerations you should factor in when considering which model to use for your organization?
6. What are some of the future trends of PLG strategies, and why is it critical that you understand and explore them?

Answers

1. GPM oversees growth strategy, metrics, and cross-functional teams, while PLG management focuses on creating a product that delivers value upfront for organic user adoption and expansion.

2. Self-service, viral loops, and product-led sales.

3. Freemium offers a basic version for free and premium features for a paid subscription, free trials provide complete access to premium features for a limited period, and product demos offer a guided walkthrough to demonstrate the product's value.

4. Pros and cons of PLG models:

   A. Product Engagement Model

      i. Pros: Enables direct product interaction, lowers barrier to entry, potential for upselling, good for user acquisition

      ii. Cons: Can negatively impact revenue, strains resources, managing user expectations

   B. Viral Loop Model

      i. Pros: Boosts brand recognition, low-cost user acquisition, takes advantage of network effects

      ii. Cons: Hard to sustain engagement, privacy/security risks, not suitable for all products

   C. Expansion Model

      i. Pros: Increases customer loyalty/retention, opportunities for upselling, deeper customer relationships

      ii. Cons: Requires extensive customer support, potential market saturation, need for customization

   D. Platform Ecosystem Model

      i. Pros: Expands functionality/value proposition, accelerated innovation, customer lock-in

      ii. Cons: Maintaining quality/security, need to attract developers, platform dominance concerns

5. Some of the key considerations you should factor in when choosing a PLG model for your organization include your company goals and target audience to ensure alignment, conducting product/market fit and competitive analysis to identify opportunities, evaluating available resources and capabilities to successfully execute the strategy, assessing scalability and sustainability of the model, determining time to value and self-service/support needs to drive adoption, analyzing the potential for network effects and how they can accelerate growth, ensuring alignment with your pricing and monetization strategy, considering localization and international expansion needs if relevant, identifying strategic partnerships opportunities to expand reach, understanding market maturity and growth potential to select the optimal strategy, and factoring in long-term

vision and flexibility to adapt the model over time. Carefully weighing these elements enables informed decision making in selecting a PLG approach that fits your organizational context and growth objectives.

6. Some of the key future trends shaping product-led growth strategies include a focus on personalization to deliver tailored user experiences, the infusion of AI and automation to streamline processes like onboarding and support, adoption of emerging technologies like virtual/augmented reality to enable more immersive product interactions, expansion to voice-based interfaces and new platforms to reach users through multiple touchpoints, an emphasis on security and privacy to build user trust, constant experimentation and iteration utilizing user feedback and data to drive refinements, strategic partnerships and collaboration to leverage network effects, and adaptability to evolving consumer expectations and market landscapes. Staying updated on these trends and exploring how to leverage them allows growth product managers to future-proof strategies, capitalize on technology shifts, continuously enhance user value, sustain competitiveness, and achieve scalable growth amidst the dynamic product-led growth environment. Understanding and incorporating these trends is critical for continued success.

Understanding Your Customers

In the competitive world of business today, grasping your customers' needs is essential to the success of a product manager in driving growth. As companies adopt product-led strategies, the importance of gaining a deep understanding of the target market and its customers becomes more critical. A product-led approach that emphasizes the value and usefulness of the product itself as the primary driver of customer acquisition and retention can provide significant gains when executed effectively.

To leverage the power of a product-led approach, it is vital to have a comprehensive understanding of the nature of your company's market and audience. If your target market is filled with customers who have various alternatives, opting for a product-focused strategy is imperative. However, if your product is a pioneer in the market, consider combining elements of sales and product-centric strategies to reinforce your hold on the market.

In this chapter, you will embark on a journey to deepen your understanding of customers and elevate your capabilities as a growth product manager. You will explore a range of essential skills and strategies that will empower you to excel in your roles.

We begin by delving into the world of user research and analysis. By adopting various research methods such as interviews, surveys, usability testing, and data analysis, you will unlock valuable insights into the needs and behaviors of your customers. Armed with this knowledge, you will be better equipped to make informed decisions and drive product growth.

You will then venture into the realm of buyer personas. By segmenting your target audience and crafting detailed personas, you will gain a deep understanding of the diverse customer groups you serve. These personas provide a framework for tailoring product development, marketing strategies, and customer experiences to meet the specific needs and preferences of different customer segments.

Building upon the foundation of buyer personas, you will explore advanced techniques for creating more refined and intricate buyer persona profiles. By incorporating best practices, you will gain a deeper understanding of customer pain points, aspirations, and motivations. Armed with this deeper understanding, you will be able to develop targeted strategies that truly resonate with your customers.

Finally, you will dive into the realm of customer acquisition and retention strategies. You will explore a range of approaches, including personalized onboarding experiences, strategic marketing campaigns, referral programs, and customer success initiatives. By adopting these proven techniques, you will be able to attract new customers, foster long-term relationships, and drive sustainable growth.

We will cover the following main topics:

- Conducting user research and analysis
- Creating customer personas
- Unveiling buyer pain points – crucial insights for B2B and B2C persona profiles
- Applying buyer persona profiles in your customer acquisition and customer retention strategy

As you progress through this chapter, you will gain invaluable insights and develop a skill set that enables you to leverage customer understanding for driving growth and achieving success as a growth product manager. You will emerge equipped with the knowledge, strategies, and techniques needed to navigate the dynamic landscape of customer-centric product management.

Conducting user research and analysis

User research and analysis play a crucial role in the responsibilities of a growth product manager. They provide you with invaluable knowledge about customer behaviors, needs, and preferences. By utilizing various techniques, understanding key success factors, and addressing challenges, growth product managers can unlock a wealth of insights about their users. Furthermore, embracing a continuous improvement mindset ensures that businesses remain informed and stay current with the latest user insights.

To gain a comprehensive understanding of customers, growth product managers employ a diverse range of techniques that capture both qualitative and quantitative insights. These techniques shed light on user motivations, pain points, and preferences, enabling data-driven decision-making. Now, let us explore some commonly utilized techniques:

- **Interviews**: By conducting interviews, growth product managers can directly interact with users and gather qualitative data. One-on-one interviews provide an opportunity to ask thought-provoking questions, unearth deep insights, and comprehend the underlying reasons behind user behaviors and opinions. Open-ended questions encourage participants to provide detailed feedback, while follow-up questions add clarity and context.

- **Surveys**: Surveys offer a quantitative approach to collect a larger sample of user opinions and preferences. By designing well-structured questionnaires, growth product managers can obtain demographic information, measure user satisfaction levels, identify product usage patterns, and more. Surveys facilitate data analysis and help detect trends, patterns, and correlations, providing a broad perspective on user sentiments.

- **Usability testing**: Usability testing allows for a hands-on evaluation of a product's usability and pinpoints areas for improvement. It involves observing users as they interact with the product, recording their actions, and noting any difficulties or frustrations they encounter. Usability testing uncovers user pain points, evaluates the intuitiveness of the product's design, and validates or refines user workflows.

- **Data analysis**: Analyzing user behavior, engagement metrics, and conversion rates through data analysis provides valuable quantitative insights. Growth product managers can leverage tools such as Google Analytics, heatmaps, and user tracking to understand how users engage with the product. This data-driven approach helps pinpoint popular features, usage patterns, and areas where users drop off, enabling optimization of the product experience based on concrete data.

Critical success factors

User research and analysis techniques such as interviews, surveys, usability testing, and data analysis provide invaluable qualitative and quantitative insights into customer behaviors, needs, and preferences. To get the most value out of these techniques, growth product managers must consider several critical success factors:

- **Clear research objectives and questions**: It is vital to establish precise research objectives and develop clear research questions to maintain focus and guide the research process effectively. This clarity enables the efficient collection and analysis of data.

- **Well-defined target audience**: Understanding the target audience is of utmost importance. By identifying specific user segments, growth product managers can tailor research to meet their unique needs, preferences, and behaviors, resulting in more accurate insights.

- **Diverse sample**: Including a diverse range of users helps in obtaining a comprehensive understanding of the customer base. By considering variables such as demographics, user roles, and product usage, the research becomes more representative and reflects the entire user population more accurately.

- **Confidentiality and privacy**: Respecting the confidentiality and privacy of participants is essential in building trust. Growth product managers should communicate clearly and ensure that participant data remains confidential, as this fosters an environment where users feel comfortable sharing their honest feedback.

Real-world example

"As a Growth Product Manager, my success in user research was rooted in the recognition and implementation of critical success factors. By defining clear research objectives and questions, I ensured focused data collection and analysis, unlocking valuable insights. Understanding the importance of a well-defined target audience allowed me to tailor the research to their needs and behaviors, leading to accurate user insights. Embracing participant confidentiality and privacy fostered trust, encouraging candid feedback. Through a diverse sample of users, I gained a comprehensive understanding of the customer base. These critical success factors empowered me to uncover deep user motivations, pain points, and preferences, enabling data-driven decision-making and driving growth with precision." (*Craig Maconnachie, Founder, CTO and Head of Product Development, MOD Commerce*)

Challenges when conducting user research and analysis

Effective user research and analysis is critical for the success of a product. It enables growth product managers to identify user needs, preferences, and pain points and develop solutions that meet those needs and enhance customer satisfaction. However, conducting user research and analysis comes with its own set of challenges, including participant recruitment, time constraints, data analysis complexity, and the often-overlooked aspect of uncovering assumptions ingrained in product development. When product managers are too close to the product, there is a risk of overlooking or not questioning assumptions, which can impact the accuracy and effectiveness of the research findings.

In this section, we will detail various strategies to address these challenges and provide growth product managers with actionable recommendations to conduct comprehensive and efficient user research and analysis. By implementing the following suggestions, growth product managers can ensure they have diverse and representative participants, manage their time effectively, and analyze data accurately, leading to informed decision-making and product growth.

Participant recruitment

Finding participants that accurately represent the target audience is a challenging aspect of user research and analysis. Growth product managers need to ensure they have a diverse group of participants that meet specific demographic or behavioral criteria. This requires reaching out to a broad range of individuals through various channels. Leveraging user communities, such as online forums or social media groups, can aid in identifying potential participants with a genuine interest in the product or industry. Partnering with user research agencies or recruiting platforms can also provide access to a wider pool of participants with diverse backgrounds, ensuring a comprehensive understanding of the target audience.

To overcome the challenge of finding participants who accurately represent the target audience, growth product managers can employ several strategies, including these:

- **Diverse recruitment channels**: Expand the reach by utilizing various channels such as online platforms, social media groups, industry-specific forums, or communities. This helps tap into a wider pool of potential participants and increases the likelihood of finding individuals who align with desired demographics and behaviors.

- **User research agencies**: Collaborate with specialized agencies that excel in participant recruitment. These agencies have established networks and databases, making it easier to find qualified individuals quickly. Working with professionals who understand the research process can streamline participant recruitment and ensure a more diverse pool.

- **Incentives and rewards**: Offer incentives or rewards to participants as a token of appreciation for their time and feedback. This can motivate individuals to participate and provide more honest and valuable insights.

Time constraints

Conducting thorough user research and analysis requires a significant investment of time and resources. Balancing the need for comprehensive data collection and analysis with project timelines can pose a challenge. Growth product managers must carefully manage their time and prioritize activities to optimize the research process. Setting realistic timelines and milestones, breaking down research tasks into manageable chunks, and using project management tools can streamline the process. Delegating responsibilities and collaborating with cross-functional teams can also ease the workload and ensure efficient utilization of resources.

Effectively managing time and balancing research activities with project timelines can help overcome time constraints in user research and analysis. Here are some of the strategies growth product managers can employ to address the time constraint challenge:

- **Prioritization and focus**: Clearly define research objectives and prioritize activities based on impact and importance. Focus on collecting key data points that align with research goals, ensuring efficiency without compromising the quality of insights.

- **Agile research approach**: Adopt an agile approach by breaking down the process into smaller iterations or sprints. This allows for more flexibility in adjusting research plans, incorporating feedback, and making iterative improvements within shorter timeframes.

- **Resource allocation**: Allocate resources strategically, considering the availability of team members, tools, and technologies. Streamline processes and workflows, leveraging collaboration tools and automation to reduce administrative overhead and maximize productivity.

Data analysis complexity

Interpreting and analyzing the data collected during user research and analysis can be intricate. Growth product managers need to synthesize qualitative and quantitative data to obtain meaningful insights and actionable recommendations. It requires analytical skills, domain knowledge, and an understanding of statistical methods. Growth product managers should invest time in developing their data analysis skills or collaborate with data analysts or researchers who can help extract valuable insights. Utilizing tools and software that enable data visualization, such as spreadsheets, data analytics platforms, or **business intelligence (BI)** tools, can aid in analyzing and interpreting complex datasets, facilitating informed decision-making.

To address the complexity of data analysis and derive meaningful insights, growth product managers should consider the following antidotes:

- **Skill development**: Invest in developing data analysis skills or collaborate with data analysts who can assist in interpreting and analyzing the collected data. Attend training programs, online courses, or workshops to enhance data analysis capabilities and gain proficiency in statistical methods, visualization tools, and data interpretation techniques.

- **Utilize data analysis tools**: Leverage data analysis tools and software to streamline the process and extract valuable insights more efficiently. Spreadsheet applications, data analytics platforms, and visualization tools can assist in analyzing large datasets, identifying patterns, and conveying findings effectively.

- **Iterative analysis and validation**: Perform iterative analysis, continuously revisiting and validating the data to ensure accuracy and reliability. Cross-reference qualitative and quantitative findings to gain a comprehensive understanding of user behaviors and preferences.

Recognizing these challenges and implementing strategies to overcome them enables growth product managers to conduct user research and analysis effectively. Effective participant recruitment, efficient time management, and proficiency in data analysis contribute to obtaining actionable insights that improve product growth and customer satisfaction.

Creating customer personas

Conducting user research provides invaluable insights into customer needs and behaviors. To make practical use of these insights, growth product managers can develop detailed customer personas that represent key user segments. Crafting realistic and nuanced personas is a proven technique for keeping the end-user perspective front and center throughout product development and marketing.

Whether you are a B2C or a B2B company, product-led businesses seeking to deeply understand their target audience consider creating user personas as a fundamental practice. User personas, which are also referred to as buyer or customer personas, are fictional representations of the ideal customers that provide useful insights into the needs, behaviors, goals, and preferences of distinct user segments. These insights empower product-led companies to customize their approaches, products, and messaging to cater to the specific requirements of their target audience. To create accurate and detailed user personas, it is helpful to learn best practices and techniques that enable growth product managers to make data-driven decisions and drive growth with a customer-centric approach.

Before we delve into developing best-practice customer persona profiles, it is essential to understand the difference between B2C and B2B customer personas, as they can vary considerably.

Difference between a B2C and a B2B customer persona

B2C buyer personas focus on understanding the personal motivations and preferences of individual consumers, while B2B buyer personas delve into collective decision-making processes within organizations and the relevant business objectives. In this section, we will explore the significant disparities between B2C and B2B buyer personas, emphasizing unique aspects to consider when creating these personas to inform marketing strategies, customer engagement approaches, and product development in their respective contexts. By fully grasping these disparities, businesses can customize their approaches to effectively connect with their target audiences and drive meaningful engagement and conversions. The following table sums up the key differences:

	B2C Buyer Persona	B2B Buyer Persona
Decision Makers	Individual consumer who is the primary decision-maker for personal purchases.	Collective decision-making unit within an organization. The buyer persona needs to be defined for each individual role involved.
Motivation	Focus on personal motivations, aspirations, and pain points.	Prioritize organizational objectives, challenges, and desired outcomes.
Complexity	Simpler and more transactional, with fewer stages and a more direct path to purchase.	Involves multiple stages, research, evaluations, negotiations, and approvals.
Target Audience Roles	Individual consumers with personal preferences, needs, and desires.	Executives, managers, users, and influencers with specific needs and priorities.
Industry Knowledge and Expertise	Generally, does not require the same level of industry knowledge and expertise.	Requires a deeper understanding of the industry, market trends, and challenges.
Relationship Building	Focuses on shorter-term interactions.	Emphasizes long-term relationships and partnerships based on trust and credibility.
Communication Channels and Preferences	A wider range of communication channels, including social media and direct marketing.	Formal communication channels within the organization.

	B2C Buyer Persona	B2B Buyer Persona
Solution Fit and Customization	May require less customization in purchasing decisions.	Requires a higher level of customization and solution fit.
Decision-Making Factors	Prioritizes factors such as price, convenience, features, and brand perception.	Considers **Budget, Authority, Need, and Timeline (BANT), return on investment (ROI)** analysis, **Metrics, Economic Buyer, Decision Criteria, Decision Process, Paper Process, Identify Pain, Champion, and Competition (MEDDPICC)**, vendor reputation, solution fit.

Table 3.1 – Key differences between a B2C buyer persona and a B2B buyer persona

Developing effective buyer personas – process and steps for B2B and B2C contexts

Although the ultimate objective of developing B2B and B2C buyer personas is to obtain insights into the target market, their processes differ in some ways. However, there are also similarities in their overall approach. In this section, we will discuss the steps involved in establishing buyer personas for both B2B and B2C contexts. By analyzing the differences and similarities, we can acquire a comprehensive understanding of how to create effective personas that inform marketing strategies, product development, and customer engagement efforts. Understanding the nuances of developing buyer personas in different situations will enable businesses to customize their approaches and reach their target audiences more efficiently.

Let us delve into the specifics of the best-practice processes involved in creating B2B and B2C buyer personas.

To create a B2B buyer persona, a systematic approach that blends research, analysis, and stakeholder feedback is necessary. The following steps are involved:

1. **Determine key stakeholders**: Identify the relevant stakeholders in the B2B buying process, including decision-makers, influencers, users, and so on.

2. **Conduct internal interviews**: Interview internal stakeholders such as sales representatives, customer success teams, and product managers to get insights into the target audience.

3. **Gather external data**: Use methods such as surveys, interviews, market research, and so on to acquire data about your target audience's challenges, goals, decision-making factors, and preferences.

4. **Analyze customer data**: Analyze existing customer data to look for patterns and trends that can help create the buyer persona.

5. **Identify relevant information**: Collect demographic and firmographic data about the target audience.

6. **Define goals and pain points**: Identify the target audience's goals, aspirations, and pain points.

7. **Identify decision-making factors**: Determine the factors that influence buying decisions.

8. **Create a narrative and description**: Use the gathered information to create a persona with a name, job title, responsibilities, demographics, goals, challenges, decision-making factors, and so on.

9. **Validate the persona**: Share the persona with internal stakeholders to obtain feedback and ensure its accurate representation of the target audience.

10. **Use the persona for decision-making**: Use the developed B2B buyer persona as a reference for marketing strategies, product development, customer engagement, and sales efforts.

It is important to remember that buyer personas should be kept up to date as your target audience and market dynamics evolve. Continuously obtaining feedback and research will keep the buyer personas relevant and help guide B2B marketing strategies.

Developing a B2C buyer persona also requires a systematic approach that involves research, data analysis, and a deep understanding of the target consumer. Here are the steps involved in creating a B2C buyer persona:

1. **Define your target market**: Identify specific market segment(s) within the B2C space that you want to focus on. Consider factors such as age, gender, location, interests, income, and other demographic information relevant to your target audience.

2. **Conduct market research**: Gather external data and conduct market research to understand the needs, behaviors, and preferences of your target market. Use surveys, interviews, social media analysis, and other research methods to collect data on consumer preferences, pain points, motivations, and buying behaviors.

3. **Analyze customer data**: Analyze existing customer data, such as purchase history, website analytics, customer support interactions, and social media engagement. Look for patterns, trends, and commonalities to gain insights into your current customer base.

4. **Identify demographic and psychographic information**: Define the demographic and psychographic characteristics of your target consumers. Consider factors such as age, gender, occupation, income level, interests, lifestyle, values, and attitudes.

5. **Understand goals and pain points**: Identify the goals, aspirations, and pain points of your target consumers. Understand what they aim to achieve or solve, and the challenges they face in relation to your product or industry. This understanding will help tailor your marketing and messaging.

6. **Determine decision-making factors**: Identify factors that influence the consumer's decision-making process. This can include price sensitivity, brand perception, product features, convenience, social proof, and customer reviews.

7. **Create a persona narrative**: Compile all the gathered information and create a persona narrative that represents the target consumer. Create a fictional character with a name and describe their demographics, interests, goals, challenges, and decision-making factors.

8. **Validate the persona**: Share the persona with internal stakeholders and obtain feedback to ensure its accuracy and resonance. Validate the persona against market research findings, customer insights, and experiences of those who interact with your target consumers.

9. **Use the persona for marketing strategies**: Utilize the developed B2C buyer persona to inform your marketing strategies, content creation, messaging, and advertising efforts. Ensure that your marketing efforts align with the goals, pain points, and decision-making factors of the persona.

10. **Continuous refinement**: Regularly revisit and refine your buyer persona as new data and insights emerge. Consumer preferences and behaviors evolve, so it's important to stay updated and adjust your strategies accordingly.

By following these steps, you can create a comprehensive B2C buyer persona that represents your target consumers, their motivations, and their decision-making processes. This persona will serve as a guide for crafting effective marketing strategies and delivering personalized experiences that resonate with your target audience.

Real-world example

At IKEA, the process of developing a B2C buyer persona involves a meticulous approach to cater to diverse consumer needs. For instance, when considering an inner-city store, the focus is on individuals living in small spaces, such as apartments, with an emphasis on students facing budget constraints. This insight is derived from a thorough understanding of the local demographic, achieved through research and analysis conducted in collaboration with Mosaic, a reputable company specializing in consumer profiling.

Conversely, for out-of-town stores, the strategy shifts to accommodate families with children, spanning various age groups, or elderly couples. This approach is informed by in-depth research conducted in those specific locations to capture the unique preferences and lifestyles of the target audience. The global growth product manager at IKEA utilizes this information to analyze growth potential and tailor product placement strategies, ensuring a more targeted and effective approach to meet the diverse needs of different store profiles.

Unveiling buyer pain points – crucial insights for B2B and B2C persona profiles

Understanding the challenges faced by your target buyers is vital in both B2B and B2C scenarios. This understanding allows businesses to develop effective marketing strategies and provide solutions that meet their specific needs. By identifying and addressing these pain points, businesses can deliver tailored experiences, enhance customer satisfaction, and foster meaningful engagement.

In this section, we will discuss the importance of identifying buyer pain points, explore methods to uncover them and highlight key considerations when uncovering pain points for your target personas. Whether your target audience is businesses or individual consumers, this knowledge will empower you to create impactful strategies and deliver valuable solutions.

Identifying buyer pain points serves multiple important purposes. Firstly, it allows for a customer-focused approach by concentrating on understanding customers and their obstacles, which enables companies to develop bespoke solutions that truly address their issues and fulfill their requirements. This approach demonstrates a sincere commitment to customer satisfaction and cultivates stronger customer relationships. Recognizing pain points also helps align the value proposition with the specific needs of the target buyers. By addressing their difficulties, businesses can effectively communicate the unique benefits of their products or services, setting themselves apart from competitors. Lastly, comprehending pain points provides guidance for product development efforts, which enables companies to identify gaps or annoyances experienced by buyers.

This knowledge can assist in the development of features or enhancements that specifically aim to alleviate those pain points, resulting in a better product-market fit and increased customer satisfaction. By actively identifying and addressing buyer pain points, businesses can enhance their customer focus, value proposition, and product development strategies.

How to effectively identify buyer persona pain points?

So, how do you identify buyer pain points? The following list describes the four main methods of effectively identifying your buyer pain points, whether you are in the B2B or B2C space:

- **Conducting customer surveys and interviews** is an effective way to identify pain points. Companies can ask open-ended questions related to their customers' frustrations, challenges, and areas for improvement. By actively listening to the responses, businesses can observe recurring pain points. Customer and partner advisory boards have now become popular ways to establish ongoing dialogues to continuously identify customer pains so that businesses can address them in a timely manner. These strategic forums are integral to the key facets of customer and partner retention, fostering a profound sense of value among stakeholders. Members of these advisory boards feel significantly more valued by the seller, sensing a heightened degree of influence on the direction of product development. This collaborative engagement ensures that products evolve in resonance with the nuanced requirements articulated by these vital stakeholders, consequently fortifying the likelihood of sustained alignment with their specific needs as the products undergo development and refinement.

- **Social listening** is another method to identify pain points. By monitoring social media platforms, industry forums, and online communities where the target audience discusses their experiences, businesses can recognize conversations, comments, and reviews related to their industry or product. Companies should pay attention to common pain points raised in these interactions.

- **Gathering feedback from customer support** is a valuable method to identify pain points. Businesses should communicate with their customer support teams to understand common customer issues and challenges. Analyzing customer support tickets, emails, and chats can help identify patterns and recurring pain points.

- **Analysis of customer data** is an additional method to identify pain points. By examining customer data such as usage patterns, behavioral analytics, and purchase history, companies can identify patterns and drop-off points that may indicate pain points in the customer journey.

After familiarizing yourself with the techniques to uncover buyer pain points, it is crucial to consider certain factors during the process. By being mindful of these considerations, you can ensure a thorough and efficient identification of pain points that resonate with your target audience.

Considerations while uncovering pain points

Understanding the intricacies of pain-point identification will allow you to gather valuable insights and prioritize the areas that will have the most significant impact for improvement. Let us delve into the key elements when uncovering pain points for your target personas:

- **Quantitative and qualitative data**: Combining quantitative and qualitative data sources is necessary to obtain a thorough understanding of pain points. While quantitative data offers statistical insights, qualitative data provides context and narratives behind the pain points.

- **Variability within segments**: Keep in mind that pain points may vary even within the same target segment. Factors such as job roles, industries, demographics, and personal preferences must be considered to identify unique pain points for different subsets of the target audience.

- **Hidden or unexpressed pain points**: Be aware that some pain points may be latent or not explicitly expressed by customers. To uncover hidden pain points, actively listen, use probing questions and recorded/observed user testing, and empathetically understand the customers.

- **Prioritization**: Prioritize pain points based on their impact and frequency. Address pain points that have the most significant effect on customer satisfaction and the potential to drive meaningful improvements in your offerings.

Recognizing buyer pain points is an essential aspect of devising impactful marketing strategies and delivering customer-centric solutions. Whether your focus is on B2B or B2C personas, comprehending the obstacles and frustrations experienced by your buyers enables you to customize your messaging, offerings, and services to deliver optimal value. Utilizing techniques such as customer surveys, social listening, and data analysis empowers businesses to gain valuable insights into pain points and leverage them to foster innovation, enrich customer experiences, and gain a competitive advantage. It is crucial to continuously monitor and adapt to evolving pain points to ensure continual customer satisfaction and long-term success.

Applying buyer persona profiles in your customer acquisition and customer retention strategy

Understanding customer pain points is vital and must be paired with actionable solutions. An impactful next step is to develop detailed buyer persona profiles that encapsulate key customer segments. With realistic and nuanced personas guiding strategy, businesses can optimize their customer acquisition and retention approaches to establish deeper engagement.

In this section, we will delve into how you can utilize buyer persona profiles to optimize your customer acquisition, development, and retention efforts, attract the appropriate customers, and strengthen customer retention by nurturing existing relationships. By integrating these profiles into your strategies, you can create customized experiences that align with the needs of your customers, foster loyalty, and drive sustainable business growth. The concept of **RAD**, which stands for **Retention, Acquisition, and Development**, plays a pivotal role in leveraging buyer persona profiles to optimize your strategies. It involves a comprehensive approach to customer engagement that focuses not only on acquiring new customers but also on retaining and developing existing ones. Here is how you can integrate RAD into your customer acquisition and retention efforts using buyer persona profiles.

Customer retention

Establishing long-lasting, solid relationships with customers is the core of a thriving business. In the customer retention segment, we will analyze how buyer persona profiles can be employed to improve customer retention strategies. By comprehending the requirements, predilections, and pain points of your present customers, you can devise customized approaches that encourage gratification, loyalty, and advocacy. From tailored communication to individualized product updates and proactive customer involvement, we will investigate effective methods that leverage buyer persona profiles to ensure customer retention and stimulate sustainable growth:

- **Personalized communication**: Utilize the information from buyer persona profiles to personalize your communication with current customers. Customize your emails, provide exclusive offers, and offer content that aligns with their interests and needs. By demonstrating that you understand and care about their specific challenges, you enhance the customer relationship.

- **Tailored product updates**: Utilize the insights derived from buyer personas to inform product updates and improvements. Continuously monitor customer feedback, pain points, and evolving needs. This enables you to proactively address their concerns and offer solutions that meet their evolving requirements.

- **Customer success programs**: Devise customer success programs that align with the goals and desired outcomes of each buyer persona. Provide resources, training, and support that assist customers in achieving success with your product or service. By enabling their success, you increase customer satisfaction, loyalty, and retention.

- **Proactive customer engagement**: Maintain a connection with your customers by reaching out to gather feedback, conduct satisfaction surveys, or offer assistance. By proactively engaging with them, you demonstrate that you value their input and are dedicated to their success. This enhances the customer relationship and reduces the chances of customer attrition.

Customer acquisition

In the customer acquisition domain, realizing the significance of utilizing buyer personas is essential to designing efficient strategies. These personas provide valuable insights into the pain points, motives, and preferences of your target audience. By utilizing this understanding, businesses can create focused marketing campaigns, select suitable communication channels, position their products or services proficiently, and encourage leads throughout the buyer's journey. Let's explore four different applications to enhance customer acquisition utilizing buyer personas. Here are four major tactics:

- **Targeted marketing**: Utilize the insights derived from buyer personas to devise focused marketing campaigns. Develop messages, content, and advertisements that reflect the pain points, motivations, and preferences of each persona. By providing personalized and pertinent content, you can captivate and interact with the appropriate audience.

- **Channel selection**: Determine the favored communication channels and platforms of each buyer persona. Concentrate your marketing endeavors on those channels where your intended audience is most involved. This facilitates effective communication and enhances your chances of acquiring new customers.

- **Product positioning**: Strategically position your product or service to tackle the specific needs and challenges of each buyer persona. Emphasize the unique value propositions and benefits that align with their pain points. By showcasing how your offering addresses their predicaments, you augment the possibility of attracting new customers.

- **Lead nurturing**: Develop strategies to nurture leads that align with the purchasing journey of each persona. Provide relevant information, educational content, and individualized experiences at each phase of the buyer's decision-making process. This engenders trust, establishes credibility, and brings prospects closer to making a purchase.

By aligning your approach with the specific requirements of your target personas, you can draw in the appropriate customers, boost conversions, and drive business growth. The insights gained from buyer persona profiles are equally valuable when it comes to customer retention, enabling businesses to nurture existing relationships and foster long-term loyalty.

Customer development

In the context of customer development within the RAD model, it's crucial to understand how buyer persona profiles can be instrumental in guiding strategies that foster growth, satisfaction, and lasting relationships with customers. Here, we explore how buyer personas can be effectively applied to customer development, focusing on nurturing existing relationships and maximizing their potential:

- **Persona-based customer journey enhancement**: Begin by leveraging buyer personas to enhance the customer journey for existing customers. Analyze each persona to identify pain points and opportunities for improvement in their ongoing experience with your product or service. Tailor touchpoints, content, and interactions to meet their evolving needs, ensuring a smooth and satisfying journey.

- **Upselling and cross-selling strategies**: Utilize buyer personas to identify upselling and cross-selling opportunities tailored to the specific preferences and interests of each persona. Craft offers and recommendations that align with their evolving requirements, providing additional value while increasing revenue and **customer lifetime value (CLV)**.

- **Personalized customer engagement**: Implement personalized customer engagement strategies based on the insights from buyer personas. Reach out to customers with relevant content, offers, and interactions that demonstrate your commitment to their individual success. This personal touch fosters deeper relationships and increases the likelihood of repeat business.

- **Feedback-driven product development**: Continuously gather feedback from customers based on their personas to inform product or service improvements. Monitor their evolving needs, pain points, and expectations. By proactively addressing their concerns and providing solutions that align with their personas, you can ensure that your offerings remain valuable and relevant.

Incorporating RAD principles into your customer development strategy, guided by buyer persona profiles, empowers your business to create a holistic and highly effective approach to both customer acquisition and retention. By focusing on retention, acquisition, and development simultaneously, you can achieve sustainable growth, nurture customer loyalty, and drive long-term success for your business. This leads to better customer acquisition, improved customer satisfaction, and increased customer loyalty, resulting in long-term success for the business.

> Real-world example
>
> "During the early years of developing and growing a SaaS business, we relied heavily on live customer conversations and insight to shape the med-long range product roadmap and prioritize investment in feature development in the short-med term.

We were operating in a niche and capitalizing on a wave of market interest in our area, which presented both problems and opportunities.

We knew our core users and our 2-3 closest competitors well; however, we did not have much visibility to grow beyond them. We were also aware that the market would move on and we needed to be able to move with it to stay alive (i.e., go beyond only solving one tactical problem to become an embedded part of a sales or Martech stack).

Through a combination of always on customer feedback in conversations (using Intercom), market research in demos, competitor monitoring, and A/B testing in the platform itself, we built a continuous flow of feedback from our customers.

This unlocked key insights that directly informed our plans:

1. Which markets were most open to our solution and which were not

2. Identified two new high value customer segments we were previously unaware of

3. Categorized our feature development into two buckets ("Exciters" that attract new customers) and a retention bucket ("Essentials" that improved QoL and kept users with us).

4. Realized we had a much bigger customer education burden than we originally suspected

This always-on listening, discussion, and the associated insights allowed us to structure our energy, investment, and team around real growth drivers led by customer demand.

It also translated into brand-associated value as people let us know they chose us because we actually listened." (*Stuart P. Turner, Managing Director, Flow State*)

Harnessing the power of customer persona knowledge for product-led businesses

Understanding and meeting the needs of the target audience is crucial for product-led businesses, and having knowledge about customer personas is incredibly powerful in achieving this. Customer persona knowledge serves as the basis for comprehending the target audience and their requirements.

Through a thorough understanding of the characteristics and preferences of their buyer personas, product-led businesses can create products that effectively meet the needs of their target audience. Customer persona knowledge aids in identifying pain points, desired features, and user expectations, enabling businesses to develop products that offer value and address specific problems. This targeted approach enhances the likelihood of product success and customer satisfaction.

Product-led businesses can provide a personalized and customized user experience with the help of customer persona knowledge. By comprehending the goals, preferences, and behaviors of the target audience, businesses can create intuitive user interfaces, simplify workflows, and optimize features. Prioritizing user experience drives greater engagement, adoption, and customer loyalty.

Last but not least, having knowledge of pain points, issues, and anticipated needs of the target audience enables businesses to create comprehensive support systems, documentation, and resources that resolve common problems and offer prompt assistance. This proactive strategy strengthens the overall customer experience, cultivates satisfaction, and minimizes customer churn.

As presented in this chapter, customer persona knowledge is an invaluable asset for product-led businesses. It plays a crucial role in directing product development, improving the user experience, shaping marketing strategies, optimizing customer acquisition, and facilitating proactive customer support. By leveraging this knowledge, growth product managers can align their products, marketing efforts, and customer support with the unique requirements and preferences of their target audience. This, in turn, leads to heightened customer satisfaction, loyalty, and sustainable growth.

Summary

This chapter explored techniques for conducting effective user research and analysis to gain insights into customer needs and behaviors. Key methods discussed include interviews, surveys, usability testing, and data analysis. Critical success factors for user research were outlined, such as having clear research objectives, understanding the target audience, ensuring participant diversity, and respecting privacy. Common challenges were examined, including recruiting representative participants, managing time constraints, and analyzing complex data.

We then covered creating customer personas to represent key user segments and inform product decisions. Differences between B2B and B2C personas were highlighted. Steps for developing detailed B2C and B2B personas through research, interviews, data analysis, and narrative building were provided.

Identifying customer pain points was emphasized as crucial for devising targeted marketing strategies and tailored solutions. Methods for uncovering pain points include surveys, social listening, analyzing customer support interactions, and evaluating usage data. Considerations such as prioritizing high-impact pain points were noted.

Finally, applications of persona knowledge for customer acquisition and retention were explored. For acquisition, tactics such as targeted marketing, channel selection, product positioning, and lead nurturing were discussed. For retention, personalized communication, tailored product updates, customer success programs, and proactive engagement were highlighted.

In summary, this chapter provided a comprehensive overview of conducting user research, developing data-driven personas, uncovering pain points, and leveraging insights to optimize customer acquisition and retention strategies. The goal is to equip growth product managers with the knowledge to drive growth through deep customer understanding.

Questions

1. What are some commonly utilized techniques for user research and analysis?
2. To achieve the best outcomes for user research and analysis, what are some critical success factors that growth product managers must consider?

3.   What are some common challenges when conducting user research and analysis and what are some of the solutions?

4.   What are the key differences between a B2B buyer persona profile and a B2C buyer persona profile?

5.   How to identify buyer persona pain points effectively?

Answers

1.   Some commonly utilized techniques for user research and analysis include surveys, interviews, usability testing, ethnographic research, and analytics data analysis.

2.   Some critical success factors that growth product managers must consider for achieving the best outcomes in user research and analysis include setting clear objectives, selecting appropriate research methods, ensuring representative and diverse user samples, conducting regular and iterative research, involving cross-functional teams, effectively analyzing and interpreting data, and translating insights into actionable improvements.

3.   Some top challenges when it comes to user research and analysis include participant recruitment, time constraints, and data analysis complexity. Solutions to these challenges are:

   I.   *Participant recruitment*:

      i.   Utilize diverse recruitment channels such as online platforms, social media groups, and industry-specific forums.

      ii.   Collaborate with user research agencies that specialize in participant recruitment.

      iii.   Offer incentives or rewards to motivate participants.

   II.   *Time constraints:*

      i.   Prioritize research activities based on impact and importance.

      ii.   Adopt an agile research approach with shorter iterations or sprints.

      iii.   Strategically allocate resources and leverage collaboration tools and automation.

   III.   *Data analysis complexity:*

      i.   Invest in developing data analysis skills or collaborate with data analysts.

      ii.   Utilize data analysis tools and software for efficient analysis and interpretation.

      iii.   Perform iterative analysis and validation to ensure accuracy and reliability.

4. The main distinctions between a B2B buyer persona profile and a B2C buyer persona profile are as follows:

    I.   B2B involves multiple stakeholders, whereas B2C is driven by individual consumers.

    II.   B2B purchases are larger and more intricate, while B2C purchases are smaller and simpler.

    III. B2B relationships are long-term, while B2C relationships are transactional.

    IV.   B2B decisions consider ROI and business impact, while B2C decisions prioritize price and personal preferences.

        i.   B2B purchase decisions take longer, while B2C decisions can be more impulsive.

        ii. B2B marketing utilizes industry-specific channels, while B2C marketing employs broader channels.

5. Irrespective of B2B or B2C focus, there are four primary approaches to determine buyer pain points. These include surveys and interviews, social listening, customer support feedback, and customer data analysis. Survey and interview strategies enable the collection of direct feedback. Social listening includes tracking social media and online communities. Customer support feedback entails analyzing support tickets and communication channels. Customer data analysis involves assessing usage, behavior, and purchase history. These methods provide insights into buyer pain points, allowing businesses to address customer needs effectively.

Part 2: Demonstrating Your Product's Value

Part 2 is about demonstrating and communicating your product's value. It starts by outlining product strategy frameworks for growth and lays the groundwork to build a product-led organization. A crucial chapter explains how to clearly articulate and market the unique value proposition of your offering.

This part covers the following chapters:

- *Chapter 4, Unlocking Success in Product Strategy and Planning*
- *Chapter 5, Setting the Stage for a Powerful Product-Led Enterprise*
- *Chapter 6, Defining and Communicating Your Product Value Proposition*

4
Unlocking Success in Product Strategy and Planning

To succeed in today's competitive market, having a well-defined product strategy and plan is crucial for any organization. This chapter goes beyond exploring market research methods and delves into the vital components of product strategy and planning, which are product development and **product lifecycle management (PLM)**. The aim is to provide you with the necessary skills to transform customer insights and market research into successful product offerings.

The chapter covers essential areas such as product design, feature prioritization, developing a **minimum viable product (MVP)**, and PLM, all of which are crucial for effective product development. Additionally, the chapter highlights the significance of product positioning, pricing strategies, and developing a comprehensive product roadmap to ensure that your product remains relevant and adaptable to the changing needs of your target audience.

The chapter includes best practices and strategies for effective **go-to-market (GTM)** planning, as well as addressing common challenges that organizations face in executing their product strategies.

We will specifically cover the following main topics:

- Turning customer insights into products—product development and MVP development
- Developing a product roadmap—PLM, product positioning, and pricing strategies
- Fueling growth—mastering GTM planning for growth product managers
- Navigating the pitfalls of product planning

By the end of the chapter, you will have gained a solid understanding of key elements of product strategy and planning and the skills required to develop a comprehensive product roadmap and execute an effective GTM plan. This journey will enable you to develop a winning product strategy that will shape the future of your organization and give you a competitive edge in today's dynamic market.

Turning customer insights into products – product development and MVP development

Creating a product that satisfies customer needs has always been at the heart of businesses, but how can organizations ensure that they are creating products that meet and exceed customer expectations? This is where customer-centric product development comes into play. By taking a customer-centric approach to product development, organizations can ensure that their products meet the unique needs of their target market. This approach is based on the idea that the customer should be the main focus when developing a product, rather than the product itself.

One important factor in customer-centric product development is understanding the importance of customer insights. In *Chapter 3*, we talked about some effective techniques to gain customer insights. Before starting product development, it is essential to first understand the target market and the unique needs and pain points of potential customers. This information allows organizations to develop products that will be successful in the market by satisfying customer needs. By taking a customer-centric approach, organizations increase the likelihood of developing successful products, leading to improved sales and customer retention.

Conducting user research and gathering customer feedback is an important part of understanding customer insights. User research involves engaging with potential customers to gather data on their preferences, behaviors, and needs. This data can be collected through surveys, interviews, product reviews, limited releases, alpha and beta programs, or focus groups. Customer feedback can also be gathered through social media platforms, online reviews, or email campaigns. This information provides valuable insights into the unique requirements and preferences of the target market and can help in designing products that meet their needs.

Once this data has been collected, it is then important to identify the pain points and unmet needs of the target market. This can be achieved by carefully examining the data to understand common issues and problems faced by customers. These pain points and unmet needs can then be used to inform product development decisions. This was covered extensively in *Chapter 3*. I suggest you familiarize yourself with the best-practice techniques of understanding those buyer pain points to ensure your knowledge of the customers you serve is current and accurate so that product design and prototyping will be highly relevant from a demand standpoint. Now, let us dive into the practice areas growth product managers must focus on to develop customer-centric products or MPVs.

Product design and prototyping – creating user-centric products

The concept of customer-centric product development goes hand in hand with effective product design and pre-release programs or prototyping. To create products that truly resonate with the target audience, businesses must not only translate customer insights into design principles but also follow an iterative design process that involves prototyping and usability testing.

By incorporating user feedback at every stage of the **product development life cycle (PDLC)**, businesses can ensure that their products meet customer expectations and deliver a seamless user experience. In this way, the principles of customer-centric product development and the practices of product design and prototyping form a powerful combination that drives the creation of successful, user-centric products. Now, let's dive into the details of applying customer insights to product design practices.

Translating customer insights into product design principles

Designing products that meet customer needs is the foundation of successful product development. To achieve this, businesses must start with a deep understanding of their target customers. This understanding comes from translating customer insights into product design principles. By analyzing customer research and feedback, businesses can discern the desires and pain points of their target audience.

Customer insights can be gathered through various methods, including surveys, interviews, and direct observation. This data provides valuable information about customer preferences, motivations, and behaviors. By synthesizing this information, businesses can identify common themes and trends that are key in developing design principles that align with customer expectations.

For instance, if customer insights reveal a preference for improved ease of use, product design principles can focus on simplifying the user interface and reducing complexity. By translating these customer insights into design principles, businesses ensure that their products are tailored to meet the specific needs and expectations of their target market.

Iterative design process and prototyping techniques

Iterative design process and prototyping techniques are fundamental to developing user-centric products. Rather than relying on a linear approach where design decisions are made upfront and little room is left for modification, the iterative design process allows for continuous refinement and improvement.

Prototyping is a critical part of the iterative design process. It involves creating physical or digital representations of the product that allow for testing and validation. By prototyping early and often, businesses can obtain valuable feedback from users and stakeholders, leading to the refinement of design concepts and the identification of potential issues.

Prototyping techniques can range from low-fidelity paper mock-ups to high-fidelity interactive prototypes. Low-fidelity prototypes are quick and inexpensive to produce, allowing for faster iterations and more frequent user testing. High-fidelity prototypes, on the other hand, provide a more realistic representation of the final product and can be used to gather more detailed feedback from users.

By embracing the iterative design process and prototyping techniques, businesses can uncover design improvements, validate product concepts, and reduce the risk of developing products that do not meet user expectations.

Usability testing and incorporating user feedback

Usability testing and incorporating user feedback are crucial steps in the product design and prototyping process. Usability testing involves observing users as they interact with the product prototype and collecting data on their experience and satisfaction. This testing helps identify usability issues, fine-tune design elements, and improve overall user experience.

When conducting usability testing, it is important to involve representative users from the target market. By watching and listening to users, businesses gain valuable insights into their behaviors, preferences, and pain points. This feedback can then be incorporated into the iterative design process, resulting in product enhancements and a better user experience.

Incorporating user feedback also helps build a sense of ownership and adoption among customers. When users feel that their opinions are valued and integrated into the product, they develop a deeper connection and are more likely to become loyal customers.

To effectively incorporate user feedback, businesses should establish feedback channels such as online surveys, feedback forms, or user communities. These channels provide a platform for users to share their thoughts and suggestions, ensuring that their voices are heard and considered throughout the PDLC.

Growth-centric product managers understand that product design and prototyping should be driven by customer insights. By translating these insights into design principles, embracing an iterative design process and prototyping techniques, and incorporating user feedback through usability testing, businesses can create user-centric products that meet the needs and expectations of their customers. This approach leads to higher customer satisfaction, improved product adoption, and, ultimately, business success in today's customer-centric market.

Feature prioritization – building the right product

The process of feature prioritization is an integral part of the larger framework of product design and prototyping. Once customer needs and market demands have been assessed, prioritizing the right features becomes essential to create a user-centric product. Techniques such as the value versus effort matrix and the Kano Model help in making informed decisions about feature prioritization. Additionally, defining an MVP allows for quick validation and iterative improvements. With a clear roadmap for feature development and release cycles, businesses can effectively integrate feature prioritization into the overall product design and prototyping process. Together, these practices form a cohesive approach toward building products that resonate with customers, boosting user satisfaction and driving business success.

This section explores techniques for prioritizing product features, the concept of an MVP, and the importance of creating a roadmap for feature development and release cycles.

Techniques for prioritizing product features

Prioritizing product features requires a systematic approach that considers customer needs and market demand. Here are a few techniques commonly used to prioritize features:

- **Value vs. effort matrix**: This technique involves plotting features on a matrix based on their perceived value to customers and the effort required for implementation. Features that offer high value and can be implemented with limited effort are prioritized.

- **Kano Model**: The Kano Model categorizes features into three types: basic, performance, and delight. Basic features are necessities, performance features provide differentiation, and delight features exceed customer expectations. Prioritization is done by ensuring a balance of all three types.

- **Impact vs. effort matrix**: Similar to the value vs. effort matrix, this technique involves evaluating features based on their potential impact on customer satisfaction and the estimated effort required for implementation. High-impact, low-effort features are given priority.

By using these techniques, businesses can make informed decisions about which features to prioritize, creating a product that delivers maximum value to customers.

Defining MVP and its benefits

In the world of product development, the concept of MVP has gained significant popularity. An MVP is a version of a product with only the essential features required to fulfill its primary purpose. The idea behind an MVP is to deliver a core set of functionalities to customers quickly and gather feedback for further iterations.

Defining an MVP has several benefits. It allows businesses to do the following:

- **Validate assumptions**: By releasing an MVP, businesses can test their assumptions about customer needs and preferences early on. Gathering user feedback helps refine the product roadmap and prioritize future feature development.

- **Reduce time to market (TTM)**: Instead of investing resources in building a fully-featured product, an MVP allows businesses to launch quickly and start capturing market share. This accelerated TTM provides a competitive advantage and helps generate early revenue.

- **Mitigate risk**: By focusing on essential features, an MVP reduces the risk of investing time and resources in developing a product that may not meet customer expectations. This lean approach helps identify and address potential flaws or hurdles before committing to full-scale product development.

Creating a roadmap for feature development and release cycles

To ensure a systematic approach to feature development, businesses should create a roadmap that outlines the planned features and their release cycles. A roadmap acts as a strategic guide, aligning the business's vision, customer needs, and technical feasibility.

When creating a roadmap, businesses should consider factors such as market trends, customer feedback, resource availability, and business goals. By prioritizing features based on these factors, the roadmap ensures that the most important features are developed and released in a timely manner.

A well-designed roadmap also aids in managing stakeholder expectations and facilitating communication across teams. It provides a shared understanding of the product's future development direction and allows stakeholders to track progress toward feature implementation and release.

As you can see, feature prioritization is a crucial aspect of product development. By using techniques such as the value vs. effort matrix and the Kano Model, businesses can prioritize features based on customer needs and market demand. Defining an MVP helps validate assumptions, reduce TTM, and mitigate risk. Creating a roadmap ensures a systematic approach to feature development and release cycles, aligning the product's evolution with market trends and business goals. By effectively prioritizing features, businesses can build the right product that meets customer expectations and achieves success in a competitive market.

Developing an effective MVP

After identifying the most impactful product features, the next step is to develop an MVP. An MVP is a powerful tool for validating product-market fit, understanding customer needs, and reducing development costs. In this section, we will discuss strategies for developing an effective MVP, utilizing lean development methodologies, and launching and gathering feedback on the MVP.

Strategies for developing an effective MVP to validate product-market fit

One of the primary objectives of an MVP is to validate the product-market fit. For that, it is important to develop a core set of features that satisfies immediate customer needs and aligns with the business goals. Here are some strategies for developing an effective MVP:

- **Focus on the core value proposition (VP):** An MVP should primarily focus on delivering the core VP of the product. The MVP should only include essential features that solve a key customer problem and differentiate the product from competitors.

- **Keep it simple:** Simplicity is key when developing an MVP. Businesses should aim to create a product that is easy to use and understand, with minimal complexity.

- **Use existing tools and frameworks:** Using existing tools and frameworks helps reduce development time and effort. Popular frameworks such as React or Ruby on Rails provide a solid foundation for MVP development.

By following these strategies, businesses can develop an MVP that delivers value to customers and aligns with their product vision.

Utilizing lean development methodologies

Lean development methodologies are an essential part of MVP development. These methodologies support rapid experimentation, early validation, and iterative improvements. Here are some key principles of lean development:

- **Fail fast, fail cheap**: The idea behind lean development is to experiment quickly and fail fast. Businesses should embrace a culture that encourages rapid experimentation and learning from failures with minimal impact.

- **Build, measure, learn**: Developing an MVP involves a continuous loop of building, measuring, and learning. Businesses should measure user feedback and use it to inform further development.

- **Iterate frequently**: Lean development emphasizes frequent iteration, allowing businesses to make improvements to the product based on user feedback. Through rapid iteration, businesses can fine-tune the product to meet customer needs and preferences.

By utilizing these methodologies, businesses can build an MVP faster, validate assumptions sooner, and refine the product to deliver a better user experience.

Launching and gathering feedback on the MVP

Once the MVP is developed, the next step is to launch it and gather feedback. Launching an MVP involves releasing a beta version of the product to early adopters to understand their reactions and identify issues. Gathering feedback is a crucial part of this process, and this feedback can be used to improve the product.

To effectively launch and gather feedback on the MVP, businesses should do the following:

- **Recruit early adopters**: To get meaningful feedback, businesses should conduct user research and recruit early adopters who fit the target audience

- **Set specific objectives**: Set specific objectives for the MVP launch and define key metrics to measure the success of the MVP

- **Collect user feedback**: Collect qualitative and quantitative user feedback to understand the user experience and identify areas for improvement

By launching and gathering feedback on the MVP, businesses can validate their product idea, gain early traction, and make necessary improvements to the product before releasing it to a wider audience.

Developing an effective MVP is a critical step toward building a successful product. By focusing on the core VP, using lean development methodologies, and launching and gathering feedback on the MVP, businesses can build a product that meets customer needs and achieves success in a competitive market. Developing an MVP requires a systematic approach, a willingness to experiment and learn, and a sound understanding of the target audience and product vision. With these factors in mind, businesses can develop an MVP that sets the foundation for a successful product and moves the business in the right direction.

Iterative development and continuous improvement

To effectively apply iterative development and continuous improvement, it is important to understand how to develop an effective MVP and utilize lean development methodologies. This section will explore the application of Agile development principles to iterate and improve the product, the importance of collecting and analyzing user feedback to inform future iterations, and the need to balance innovation and stability throughout the PDLC.

Applying Agile development principles to iterate and improve the product

Agile development principles provide a framework for iterative development and continuous improvement. By embracing Agile methodologies such as Scrum or Kanban, businesses can break down the product development process into smaller iterations known as **sprints**. Here are some ways to apply Agile principles to iterate and improve the product:

- **Collaborative cross-functional teams**: Agile promotes the formation of collaborative cross-functional teams comprising developers, designers, and other stakeholders. This allows for better communication and alignment throughout the development process.

- **Sprints and iterations**: Agile advocates for shorter development cycles called sprints, typically lasting 1-4 weeks. Each sprint focuses on delivering a specific set of features, allowing for quicker iterations and feedback loops.

- **Prioritization and backlog management**: Agile emphasizes the importance of prioritizing features based on customer needs and business value. By actively managing a product backlog, teams can continually reassess and reprioritize features to ensure alignment with user needs.

By implementing these Agile development principles, businesses can steadily and systematically enhance the product, resulting in expedited development cycles and strengthened alignment with customer needs.

Collecting and analyzing user feedback to inform future iterations

Collecting and analyzing user feedback is a crucial step in the iterative development process. User feedback provides important insights into the user experience and identifies areas for improvement. Here are key steps to collect and analyze user feedback:

- **User feedback channels**: Establish channels, such as user surveys, feedback forms, or user interviews, to encourage users to provide their feedback. Utilize analytics tools to gain insights from user behavior.

- **Quantitative and qualitative analysis**: Collect both quantitative and qualitative data to understand user satisfaction, identify pain points, and discover opportunities for innovation. Analyze this data to extract meaningful patterns and insights.

- **Feedback prioritization**: Prioritize user feedback based on impact and feasibility. Focus on addressing critical usability issues and implementing changes that solve common pain points faced by users.

By continuously collecting and analyzing user feedback, businesses can gain a deep understanding of their users' needs and preferences. This enables them to make data-driven decisions and prioritize future iterations that will have the greatest impact on user satisfaction.

Balancing innovation and stability during the PDLC

Finding the right balance between innovation and stability is crucial to the success of the PDLC. While innovation drives competitive advantage, stability ensures a reliable and consistent user experience. Here are strategies to achieve this balance:

- **Innovation lab or R&D team**: Create a dedicated innovation lab or R&D team responsible for exploring and experimenting with new ideas. This allows for continuous innovation without disrupting the stability of the core product.

- **Feature gates or beta testing**: Implement feature gates or beta testing to introduce innovative features to a subset of users, allowing for validation and fine-tuning before a full-scale release. This mitigates risks associated with potential stability issues.

- **Continuous monitoring and maintenance**: Regularly monitor the product's performance and stability, and proactively address bugs, reliability issues, and performance bottlenecks. This ensures that the product remains stable and reliable over time.

By carefully managing innovation and stability, businesses can introduce new features and enhancements while maintaining a stable and reliable product experience for their users.

Iterative development and continuous improvement are critical for building successful products. By applying Agile development principles, collecting and analyzing user feedback, and balancing innovation and stability, businesses can create products that evolve with customer needs and preferences. Iterative development ensures that the product aligns with user expectations while allowing for frequent improvements. Continuous improvement enables businesses to constantly enhance their products, increasing user satisfaction and driving long-term success. By adopting these practices, businesses can create products that stay relevant, innovative, and valuable in an ever-changing market landscape.

Developing a product roadmap – PLM, product positioning, and pricing strategies

Successful product development in today's ever-changing business landscape relies on a well-structured and forward-thinking approach. A key component of this approach is creating a comprehensive product roadmap that forms the foundation for taking a product from a concept to market success. The product roadmap not only involves elements such as PLM, product positioning, pricing strategies, and understanding customer insights but also integrates customer feedback through robust testing of the GTM strategy. Businesses often utilize customer advisory boards or panels, engage with key customers, and leverage **Most Valued Professionals** (**MVPs**) within the user and partner community to showcase roadmap developments and gather early feedback before a broader public release. This iterative process ensures that the product roadmap aligns closely with customer needs and expectations.

In the previous section, we discussed the process of developing customer insights. By immersing ourselves in the perspectives of our target audience, we acquire invaluable knowledge that enables us to align our product offerings with genuine market demands.

Moving from customer insights to MVP and finalized products is a crucial phase in roadmap development. With a deep understanding of our customers, we can embark on the journey of designing a product that precisely caters to their needs. The MVP, an initial version of our envisioned product, allows us to gather real-world feedback and iterate, ensuring that our final offering is finely tuned.

Throughout this multifaceted journey of product development, the importance of PLM, product positioning, and pricing strategies becomes paramount. By embracing dynamic approaches to each of these elements, we can guide our product through various stages of its life—from conception to maturity and beyond. Furthermore, by strategically positioning our product in the market and devising competitive pricing strategies, we can create a compelling VP that resonates with our target audience.

In this section, we will delve deep into each of these components, exploring best practices, real-world examples, and innovative strategies that empower businesses to create robust product roadmaps that stand the test of time.

Effective PLM strategies

PLM is a methodical approach that enables businesses to manage each stage of a product's lifespan, from concept to discontinuation. By using specific methods catered to each stage, companies can maximize profitability, capitalize on opportunities, and prevent premature product failure. This section will explore the four stages of the **product life cycle** (**PLC**)—*introduction*, *growth*, *maturity*, and *decline*—and examine key PLM strategies for each:

1. **Introduction stage**: During this stage, businesses introduce new products to the market to meet demand or capitalize on emerging opportunities. Companies use two primary strategies for this stage: market research and the release of limited offerings—such as MVPs—to test customer interest.

2. **Growth stage**: Once products transition to the growth stage, increased demand leads to scalable production, brand building, and product improvements or extensions to stay competitive.

3. **Maturity stage**: During this stage, companies employ strategies such as price optimization, market diversification, and product differentiation to maintain the product's momentum.

4. **Decline stage**: This stage is marked by declining sales, causing businesses to use inventory management, product phase-out planning, and knowledge transfer strategies.

Apple and Tesla are two companies that have implemented effective PLM strategies, resulting in long-term product success. Apple updates its devices incrementally, while Tesla expands vehicles and battery technology. By implementing these effective PLM strategies, companies can keep their products relevant, competitive, and profitable in a constantly evolving market.

Strategic product positioning – crafting a compelling market presence

Strategic product positioning is a crucial aspect of achieving success in today's competitive business environment. It involves creating a favorable perception of a product in the minds of consumers by differentiating it from competitors and highlighting its unique benefits. To effectively position a product, businesses must understand its significance, conduct thorough market research, develop a **unique VP (UVP)**, and create a compelling positioning statement.

Product positioning aims to influence how consumers perceive a product compared to its competitors. It helps consumers understand why a particular product is superior and relevant. By establishing clear positions for different product tiers, businesses can create strong brand loyalty across customer segments, capture more market share, and avoid leaving gaps for competitors to attack.

For example, companies such as Apple produce multiple versions of a product such as the iPhone at different price points and feature sets—the iPhone SE for price-sensitive customers, the standard iPhone for mainstream users, and the Pro/Max editions for early adopters less sensitive to price. The sequencing of these product launches across the adoption curve, from early adopters to late adopters, allows Apple to compete effectively with itself while covering the spectrum of customer needs. This tiered approach to positioning and timed release of different versions helps build brand loyalty across customer segments and provides something for everyone while keeping competitors at bay.

Mastering multi-tiered product positioning strategies is essential for companies to create a strong market presence, drive sustainable growth, and cement customer loyalty across targeted segments in today's fiercely competitive global marketplace.

In a market with countless product choices, product positioning becomes even more crucial. It helps businesses cut through noise and capture the attention of their target audience, leading to increased brand recognition, customer loyalty, and higher sales.

To position a product effectively, businesses must conduct comprehensive market research to gain insights into their target customer segments and the competitive landscape. This research helps businesses tailor their positioning strategy to address specific customer needs and desires.

A compelling VP is at the core of effective product positioning. It articulates the unique benefits and value a product offers to customers. A strong VP aligns product features with customer needs and desires and becomes the foundation for successful positioning.

Crafting a clear and memorable positioning statement that communicates the product's unique positioning is essential. This statement guides all marketing efforts and ensures consistency across various channels.

Once the positioning statement is established, it should be integrated into all marketing materials to reinforce the product's position in the minds of consumers and build a cohesive brand identity.

By understanding the importance of product positioning, conducting market research, developing a UVP, and crafting a compelling positioning statement, businesses can create a strong market presence, build customer loyalty, and drive sustainable growth. Mastering the art of product positioning is essential for success in today's fiercely competitive global marketplace.

Innovative pricing strategies for product success

Beyond product positioning, the role of pricing in the marketing mix is also critical for the success of a product. An effective pricing strategy should go beyond setting a price. A deep understanding of customer behavior, market dynamics, and the product's life cycle is necessary. Let us look at various pricing strategies, such as cost-based, value-based, and competitive pricing, highlighting psychological pricing techniques and their impact on consumer behavior. Additionally, we will look at pricing models tailored for different stages of the PLC and strategic pricing approaches for new product launches and existing product repositioning.

There are three typical pricing strategies:

- **Cost-based** pricing is where the cost of production is added to a margin that ensures the product's selling price covers fixed and variable costs and provides a profit margin
- **Value-based** pricing focuses on the perceived value of products to customers rather than production costs
- **Competitive** pricing involves setting prices depending on competitors' pricing

Psychological pricing techniques are used to tap into consumers' subconscious and influence purchasing decisions. Charm pricing, prestige pricing, bundle pricing, and odd-even pricing are primary techniques.

Different pricing strategies should be employed depending on the PLC stage. For instance, skimming pricing in the introduction stage helps businesses capitalize on early adopters willing to pay a premium for the novelty. During the growth stage, maintaining or slightly adjusting prices is ideal. In the maturity stage, discount pricing or bundle offerings can help to maintain market share. In the decline stage, businesses may consider discontinuing the product or implementing clearance pricing.

Promotional pricing or freemium models can create buzz and encourage product trials during new product launches. In existing product repositioning, businesses may adopt premium prices to match the new positioning.

Creative pricing strategies are essential for a product's success. Value-based and competitive pricing models should be embraced instead of traditional cost-based pricing. Psychological pricing techniques influence consumers' decisions. Strategic pricing models serve different stages of the PLC. Strategic pricing for new product launches and repositioning efforts is crucial in today's competitive marketplace.

Balancing long-term vision and short-term goals in road mapping – navigating the path to product success

Another important thing growth product managers must consider when creating a successful product roadmap is to find a balance between long-term goals and short-term objectives. It is important to examine the key elements of a well-balanced product roadmap, including incorporating customer feedback and market trends, addressing the challenges of balancing immediate market demands with long-term vision, and adopting Agile product development methodologies.

A product roadmap should align with the company's vision, objectives, and long-term goals to contribute to sustainable growth and success.

To create a roadmap that resonates with customers and captures market opportunities, it is essential to gather and analyze feedback from all stakeholders, including end users, channel partners, value-added resellers, and integrators that build GTM solutions leveraging the products.

Soliciting input from channel partners and value-added resellers provides invaluable insights into product integration requirements, pain points in existing offerings, and desired features to meet customer needs. This feedback, combined with monitoring wider market trends, positions the product offerings to meet future customer expectations.

By regularly connecting with these stakeholder groups during roadmap development, product teams can deliver offerings that create value across the ecosystem, spur adoption through channels, and ultimately translate to higher customer satisfaction and commercial success.

Balancing short-term market demands with long-term vision is a challenge in roadmap development. Focusing solely on immediate gains can lead to a lack of strategic direction, while fixating on long-term vision may result in missed opportunities. A data-driven approach that considers customer feedback, market data, and competitive intelligence can help prioritize features that align with both short-term goals and long-term vision.

Traditional linear approaches to product development may be inflexible in today's dynamic business environment. Agile methodologies offer a more adaptable approach by emphasizing incremental progress and responsiveness to customer feedback and market shifts. Breaking the roadmap into smaller iterations allows for continuous value delivery and the ability to adjust priorities based on changing market conditions.

A well-crafted product roadmap aligned with the company's vision, incorporating customer feedback and market trends, and addressing the challenges of balancing short-term demands with long-term vision is key to success. Agile product development methodologies enhance adaptability and responsiveness. By striking a balance between long-term vision and short-term goals, businesses can deliver value, satisfaction, and sustainable growth in the ever-changing business landscape.

Fueling growth – mastering GTM planning for growth product managers

As a growth product manager, your responsibilities surpass the typical duties of a product manager. You are accountable for driving fast and sustainable growth for both the product and the business. This section aims to provide growth product managers with a GTM planning strategy that builds upon the groundwork laid in the product roadmap phase to help them succeed in their endeavors.

Launching a new product successfully requires careful planning and research to identify and understand the ideal target market. By analyzing customer demographics, behaviors, needs, and the competitive landscape, product managers can tailor strategies to resonate with the audience that will provide the greatest value and revenue potential. Beyond product positioning and pricing strategies, we will now examine other elements that are critical for growth product managers to master.

Market segmentation to provide focus

Rather than targeting a broad, heterogeneous market, segmentation enables focusing on the customer profiles that are the best fit for the product. Common segmentation criteria include the following:

- **Demographics**: Age, gender, income level, education, occupation, and so on help define observable attributes of target groups

- **Geographic**: Target customers locally, regionally, nationally, or globally based on where demand concentrates

- **Behavioral**: Purchase frequency, channel preferences, usage patterns, and brand loyalty inform marketing outreach

- **Psychographic**: Interests, priorities, values, and opinions shape messaging that aligns with their mindset

- **Firmographic**: Company size, industry, and technologies used are key for B2B products

The more precisely a market is defined, the better product positioning, pricing, and messaging can be tailored to maximize adoption and minimize wasted efforts.

Competitor analysis to provide perspective

Analyzing direct and indirect competitors equips product managers with an understanding of the competitive landscape to inform differentiation and positioning. Key insights include the following:

- **Product features and capabilities**: Assess UVP versus parity features
- **Pricing and business models**: Understand cost structures and pricing flexibility
- **Target customers**: Identify overlapping targets as well as white space opportunities
- **Marketing and promotion**: Evaluate the effectiveness of outreach channels and messaging
- **Market share and growth**: Estimate relative size and expansion potential
- **Strengths and weaknesses**: Highlight areas for improvement and leverage strengths

This analysis results in an actionable perspective on where the product aligns or diverges from incumbents and how to convey superior value.

Distribution paths to facilitate access

Evaluating distribution channels provides customers with access to the product across their preferred purchasing paths. Common direct and indirect channel options include the following:

- **Company website**: Self-service purchases, subscriptions, and support
- **Sales teams**: For high-touch enterprise sales
- **Retail**: Brick-and-mortar and online retail partners
- **Resellers/distributors**: Leverage partner relationships and infrastructure
- **App marketplaces**: Prominently feature SaaS apps and mobile apps

The optimal mix provides broad customer reach through their trusted channels, balanced with education and service quality control.

Marketing and promotions to drive awareness

Strategic marketing and promotions introduce the product, generate interest and enthusiasm, prompt trials or purchases, and convey ongoing value. Tactics may involve the following:

- **Social media**: Organic and paid campaigns tailored to platform users
- **Search engine marketing**: Targeted keywords and SEO maximize site visibility
- **Email marketing**: Segmented outreach personalized for different groups

- **Direct mail**: Reach users who are not active online and as an additional channel to reinforce awareness among those who are already online

- **Events**: Launch events, tradeshows, and webinars

- **Public relations (PR)**: Earned media exposure through press releases

- **Advertising**: Paid search, display, and video ads

- **Sales collateral**: Enable sales team success

- **Promotions**: Free trials, discounts, and giveaways reduce friction

An integrated, omnichannel approach expands the reach and frequency of engagement with the targeted audience.

In a later part of the book, we will cover some effective approaches for GTM strategies. The key is maintaining a customer-centric focus on delivering value and simplifying adoption for ideal buyers identified through rigorous segmentation and targeting. With thoughtful execution across these interconnected elements, product launches can maximize market fit, build awareness, and drive sustainable business growth.

Navigating the pitfalls of product planning

While a sound product strategy is essential for success, many challenges can derail effective planning and execution. By anticipating and proactively addressing these issues, product managers can increase the odds of launching and managing successful products. Let's examine some common product management challenges and some actions growth product managers can take to address them:

1. Acquiring sufficient customer insights

2. Unclear problem definition

3. Lack of prioritization

4. Weak cross-functional collaboration

5. Unrealistic timelines

6. Scope creep

7. Inadequate skill sets

8. Insufficient budget

9. Lack of buy-in

10. Weak product discovery

11. Ineffective launch planning

Acquiring sufficient customer insights

A deep understanding of target users is vital for product decisions. However, customer research is often inadequate or non-existent. Surveys may have low response rates or fail to capture meaningful insights. Stakeholder assumptions about customer needs may be inaccurate. Product teams should devote time to immersive, ongoing customer research through surveys, interviews, site visits, usability testing, and data analysis.

Unclear problem definition

Without clearly defining the core customer problem or need, products lack purpose. Symptoms may be treated over root causes. Cross-functional teams should align on specific dilemmas and pain points the product aims to solve.

Lack of prioritization

Trying to tackle too many initiatives at once leads to diluted focus and misallocated resources. Teams should collaboratively prioritize roadmap features based on criteria such as customer value, development effort, and strategic alignment. Saying "no" to lower-priority items maintains focus on executing what matters most.

Weak cross-functional collaboration

Siloed teams unable to align on vision and strategy result in disjointed, competing priorities. Improved cross-functional communication and transparency, combined with executive leadership reinforcing shared objectives, enhances coordination.

Unrealistic timelines

Aggressive schedules that underestimate required effort waste resources on rushed output. Product and engineering teams should collectively estimate reasonable timeframes, balancing urgency with sustainable pacing.

Scope creep

Letting feature scope expand unchecked blows out timelines, cost, and quality. Requirements should be clearly defined upfront, with a **change management** (**CM**) process for new requests. Stakeholders must understand trade-offs in adjusting scope.

Inadequate skill sets

Knowledge and skill gaps—whether in research, writing, analytics, technical domains, or leadership—lead to poor planning and execution. Assess team strengths, provide training, and augment capabilities through hiring or partnerships.

Insufficient budget

Trying to fund ambitious product initiatives without adequate financial resources strains teams and comprises delivery. Assess funding needs end to end, secure executive buy-in for budget requests, and consider phased rollout approaches.

Lack of buy-in

When stakeholders are not sufficiently convinced of product direction, pushback can derail progress. To gain alignment, product teams should make the business case, illustrate value to customers and the company, and incorporate feedback from focus groups or promotional releases. However, many of these stakeholder engagement elements carry monetary costs that can often be underestimated or overlooked by development teams. It is important to budget appropriately for expenses related to conveying the product roadmap effectively across the organization and end-user community. This upfront investment into buy-in helps pave the way for successful execution by ensuring all stakeholders are on board with the planned direction before costly development cycles commence. Budgeting for the softer aspects of product management translates to harder ROI through stakeholder alignment.

Weak product discovery

Underinvesting in the experimentation and learning required for new product development leads to ill-defined solutions or wasted effort on concepts without merit. Allocate resources to rapid prototyping, customer testing, and MVPs.

Ineffective launch planning

Insufficient launch planning around pricing, packaging, sales enablement, distribution partnerships, and marketing risks new products falling flat. Rigorously plan launches with cross-functional collaboration.

While certainly not exhaustive, anticipating these common pitfalls allows mitigation through adequate research, prioritization, collaboration, resourcing, and disciplined execution. Adopting product best practices while tailoring process to team strengths and context sets up initiatives for the highest probability of resonating in-market and achieving business success.

Real-world example

Microsoft tried to compete against Apple's exceedingly successful iPod when it launched the Zune digital media player in 2006. Unfortunately, critical missteps in product planning paved the way for Zune's ultimate failure and withdrawal from the market just a few years later.

In developing the Zune program, Microsoft did not conduct adequate consumer research to understand customer needs and preferences. It failed to clearly define the target demographic or which specific problems Zune would solve compared to the dominant iPod. Hundreds of features for Zune were proposed early on without any concept of an MVP or prioritizing by importance. The development process also suffered from siloed workstreams, without enough collaboration between industrial designers, software engineers, and marketing team members. In rushing Zune to market, Microsoft left insufficient time for **quality assurance (QA)** testing pre-launch as well.

After launch, Microsoft struggled with shifting direction and significant feature creep based on feedback from various internal stakeholders. The engineers assigned to the Zune program were highly specialized experts in firmware and hardware but lacked the broader user experience design skills that may have led to a more intuitive, engaging product. Attempting to directly compete with Apple's coveted iPod also ultimately proved more resource-intensive than Microsoft anticipated. Additionally, Microsoft failed to convince partners in the music and entertainment industries to fully buy into and promote the Zune ecosystem. There was also little genuine customer discovery research post-launch that could have guided ongoing improvement efforts.

By neglecting critical planning activities such as customer research, clear problem definition, cross-functional collaboration, realistic timelines, and discovery, Microsoft severely hampered Zune from the outset. Addressing these limitations in the planning process could have benefited the product and improved Microsoft's odds of gaining a foothold.

Summary

Product strategy and planning are crucial foundations for the growth of a product that can achieve market fit, adoption, and business value. This chapter offered a complete overview of core components throughout the life cycle of a product, including gathering customer insights, developing MVPs, crafting product roadmaps, executing GTM plans, and proactively addressing typical challenges.

Some of the key learnings include the importance of continuous customer research, embracing iterative design with rapid testing, prioritizing features based on customer value, and managing long-term strategic vision with near-term execution. Additionally, best practices were shared for positioning products, pricing strategies, distribution, marketing, and managing the PLC from introduction to decline.

By internalizing these elements, growth product managers can enhance their readiness to develop distinctive products that meet market needs, make informed decisions, secure stakeholder buy-in, coordinate cross-functional execution, and maximize adoption, satisfaction, and retention.

In today's rapidly changing business environment, having robust product strategy and planning capabilities is essential for sustainable innovation and outpacing competitors. Growth product managers can use the concepts covered in this chapter as a playbook to thrive in their expanded roles. By consistently applying the frameworks, processes, and practices outlined, they can confidently chart the course for product success and revenue growth both now and in the future.

In the next chapter, we will dive into details on how companies can set the stage for a thriving product-led business. We will examine the integral role leadership plays in establishing a clear product vision and rallying the organization around it.

Questions

1. What are some effective techniques for gathering customer insights to inform product development?
2. How can you determine the most important features to prioritize in product development?
3. What is an MVP and what are its benefits?
4. What should a product roadmap include?
5. What are some best practices for product launch planning?
6. How can you balance short-term execution and long-term product vision?
7. What risks should be mitigated in product planning?

Answers

1. Useful techniques include surveys, interviews, focus groups, site visits, usability testing, data analysis, and building user personas. The key is continuous immersion in the customer perspective.
2. Prioritization frameworks such as the value vs. effort matrix and the Kano Model categorize features based on customer value and development effort/cost. Focus on must-have versus nice-to-have capabilities.
3. An MVP is a minimal version of the product with just enough features to be usable and collect initial customer feedback. Benefits include faster TTM, reduced costs, and the ability to validate assumptions.
4. A product roadmap captures the strategic vision and near-term execution plan. It should include themes, initiatives, features, target release dates, and key results/metrics.
5. Rigorous launch planning includes positioning, pricing, packaging, sales enablement, distribution partnerships, marketing, customer onboarding, training, and post-launch assessment.
6. Agile development principles, continuous customer input, and separating innovation from core product stabilization enable focus on both horizon 1 and horizon 2+ priorities.
7. Key risks include unclear problem definition, lack of prioritization, unrealistic timelines, inadequate skills or funding, weak cross-functional collaboration, scope creep, and lack of stakeholder buy-in.

5

Setting the Stage for a Powerful Product-Led Enterprise

In today's highly competitive business landscape, adopting a product-led strategy is imperative for companies aiming to gain an edge and achieve hypergrowth. However, truly transforming into a product-led enterprise requires more than just developing great products—it necessitates creating an organization-wide culture and processes that revolve around the product experience and customer needs.

This chapter will provide an in-depth look at how **growth product managers (GPMs)** can spearhead and sustain this transition. We will examine the integral role GPMs play in establishing a clear product vision across the organization and rallying teams around it. The importance of fostering a customer-centric, experimentation-driven culture will be discussed, along with how to promote continuous improvement. Additionally, the essay will explore how processes such as agile development, customer feedback loops, and cross-functional teaming enable the success of a product-led approach.

By covering essential topics such as building a product-led culture, creating a compelling product vision, championing customer centricity, and implementing supporting processes, this chapter aims to thoroughly equip GPMs with the expertise required to catalyze and sustain product-led transformation initiatives in their organizations. Companies that master these core capabilities unlock the ability to leverage their products as the main vehicle for customer acquisition, retention, growth, and competitive differentiation.

The comprehensive insights provided will guide GPMs through each step of the journey to put the product experience and the customer at the very heart of everything their company does. We will specifically cover the following main topics:

- The importance of a product-led culture
- Creating a compelling product vision

- Fostering a customer-centric culture across the organization

- Implementing supporting processes and structures

By thoroughly equipping GPMs with this expansive set of expertise, this chapter aims to prepare readers to successfully spearhead and sustain product-led transformation initiatives, cementing product excellence and customer value as the cornerstones of organizational success. Let's get started!

The importance of a product-led culture

Growth is never easy. In an increasingly noisy and crowded marketplace, companies can no longer rely on traditional sales and marketing tactics to reliably gain and keep customers. A new approach is needed—one that centers on the product itself as the main vehicle for attracting, engaging, and delighting users. Companies that embrace a product-led culture to deliver compelling **user experiences** (**UXs**) are pulling ahead of the competition. By continuously optimizing their products to create organic adoption and retention, they are building the foundation for sustainable, scalable growth in the modern era.

Why product-led?

The days of driving growth through traditional sales, marketing, or competitive pricing alone are numbered. Relying heavily on these tactics is risky in today's landscape. Sales-led companies often struggle to acquire customers who don't immediately see their value. Marketing-led companies face ballooning costs trying to cut through noise. Competing primarily on price leads to an endless race to the bottom that slowly erodes margins. The winning strategy is to make the product itself the growth engine, to create something so inherently valuable that customers want to use and pay for it. This product-led approach creates growth that is organic, scalable, and sustainable over the long term.

In contrast, product-led companies such as Slack, Dropbox, and Canva find natural growth through satisfied users actively sharing, promoting, and evangelizing their products. Their growth stems from delivering an experience so compelling and essential that it sells itself.

By embracing a product-led culture that revolves around continuously optimizing the UX, companies can transform their products into a self-sustaining flywheel, propelling organic adoption and expansion. But this requires instilling an organization-wide commitment to and focus on product excellence and customer value above all else.

Defining a product-led culture

What exactly constitutes a product-led culture? There are several key attributes:

- **Customer centricity**: The customer is placed front and center, with their needs, pain points, and feedback directing product design and strategy. User research, ride-alongs, interviews, and advisory groups all aim to deeply understand user perspectives.

- **Data-driven**: Product decisions are driven by data and insights from metrics on adoption, engagement, churn, user behavior, market forces, and competitive offerings. Opinions and assumptions take a back seat.

- **Cross-functional collaboration**: Silos are dismantled, with tight collaboration across departments on shared product goals. Product, design, engineering, and support—all rally around the customer experience.

- **Continuous innovation**: Relentless focus on finding better ways. Empowered teams rapidly experiment, take risks, and implement customer-validated learning to continuously improve.

- **Customer engagement**: Proactive engagement turns users into product evangelists. Community building and peer sharing accelerate organic adoption. The product delivers so much value that it sells itself.

- **Product excellence**: An obsession with quality and solving real problems underpins everything. The bar for excellence is continually raised across UX (defined as the interaction and experience users have with a company's products and services), features, and performance.

Principles of a product-led culture

Becoming truly product-led requires more than just a shift in strategy—it necessitates adopting new philosophies and ways of working. At its core, a product-led culture revolves around constant optimization of the UX through practices such as customer obsession, design thinking, data-driven development, agile methodology, and democratized decision-making. Companies that embed these principles gain the foundation to rapidly understand users, build solutions that directly address their needs, frequently deliver value, and adapt based on feedback. This culture and mindset fuel the continuous improvement required to let the product propel its own viral growth. Some of the principles that characterize product-led thinking include the following:

- **Customer obsession**:

  - **Principle**: Keeping the customer at the forefront of every decision and action

  - **Example**: Amazon's relentless focus on customer experience, evident in its customer-centric approach to product recommendations and hassle-free returns, ensures it remains a leader in e-commerce

- **Design thinking**:

  - **Principle**: Applying design thinking methodologies and UX principles to create intuitive and user-friendly experiences

  - **Example**: Apple's design-driven approach is evident in its sleek, user-friendly products such as the iPhone, where every detail is meticulously crafted with the user's experience in mind

- **Data-driven development**:

  - **Principle**: Relying on data and user feedback to drive product improvements rather than relying solely on intuition or opinions

  - **Example**: Netflix uses viewer data to inform its content creation decisions, resulting in personalized recommendations and original content that resonates with its audience

- **Agile methodology**:

  - **Principle**: Embracing agile practices such as rapid iterations, continuous delivery, and incremental enhancements to respond quickly to changing user needs

  - **Example**: Spotify's frequent app updates and feature releases reflect its agile development approach, ensuring it adapts swiftly to user preferences and industry trends

- **Democratized decision-making**:

  - **Principle**: Decentralizing decision-making authority across autonomous teams to enable quick responses to customer feedback and market changes

  - **Example**: Atlassian encourages its teams to make decisions independently, fostering innovation and agility across the organization, as seen in products such as Jira and Confluence

- **Holistic collaboration**:

  - **Principle**: Involving cross-functional teams early in the product development process to ensure seamless execution of ideas

  - **Example**: Tesla's collaboration between engineers, designers, and manufacturing teams results in electric vehicles that seamlessly integrate innovative technology with sleek design

These principles collectively form the foundation of a product-led culture. When implemented cohesively, they enable organizations to do the following:

- **Understand users**: By constantly seeking user feedback and data, businesses gain deep insights into customer pain points, preferences, and behavior

- **Address user needs**: These insights drive the development of solutions that directly address user needs, resulting in products that customers truly value

- **Deliver value**: Agile development and continuous improvement ensure that products are continually updated to deliver ongoing value, keeping users engaged

- **Adapt and grow**: The ability to adapt quickly based on user feedback and market changes fuels viral growth and positions the product as a market leader

It is important to remember that a product-led culture isn't just about changing strategy; it's a holistic transformation that revolves around these principles. When embedded in an organization's DNA, they enable the creation of products that not only meet but exceed customer expectations, fostering growth and sustained success.

The values of a product-led culture

While principles provide the philosophical blueprint, instilling core values is key to bringing a product-led culture to life. Values such as innovation, risk-taking, transparency, autonomy, customer success, and data-informed decision-making enable the mindsets and behaviors essential for excellence. By encouraging constant improvement, embracing experimentation, empowering teams, building relationships, and letting data guide decisions, companies can embed product-led thinking into their cultural DNA. With these values permeating every layer of the organization and your product, customer needs become the true north guiding all strategy and operations. This collective commitment transforms products into thriving flywheels propelling sustainable growth. Key values that shape a product-led culture include the following:

- **Innovation**: A constant push for improvement
- **Risk-taking**: Embrace experimentation and a fail-fast mindset
- **Transparency**: Open communication and knowledge sharing
- **Autonomy**: Empower teams with ownership balanced by accountability
- **Customer success**: Build relationships beyond transactions
- **Data-informed**: Let insights guide decisions over assumptions

By embedding these principles and values throughout the fabric of their organizations, companies can ingrain product-led thinking into their cultural DNA.

Benefits of leading with products

Embracing a product-led culture pays dividends across the business. With the product experience as the North Star, companies can delight customers through superior UX and seamless onboarding, driving improved conversion, retention, and organic growth. Empowered, cross-functional teams rapidly innovate to stay ahead of the competition. Aligning everyone behind the shared mission of product excellence boosts focus and engagement. Agile processes accelerate **time to market** (TTM). The viral nature of great products becomes a growth flywheel. Customer satisfaction breeds loyalty and affinity. According to research, product-led companies grow 2.2x faster than other B2B firms. By putting product and user needs at the strategic core, sustainable expansion unconstrained by traditional tactics becomes possible. However, realizing this potential requires leadership in crafting a vision to guide teams. This brings us to the integral role of product leaders in steering direction. Adopting a product-led culture can confer these benefits:

- **Superior UX**: Continuously optimizing UX delights customers

- **Improved onboarding and retention**: Onboarding ease and stickiness reduce churn
- **Innovation edge**: Empowered teams rapidly experiment, unlocking new opportunities
- **Focus and alignment**: With the product as the North Star, teams rally around a shared mission
- **Engaged employees**: Autonomy, mastery, and purpose increase satisfaction
- **Faster TTM**: Agility and reduced bureaucracy accelerate release velocity
- **Competitive differentiation**: Great experience as a core differentiator
- **Growth flywheel**: Viral loops and **word of mouth** (**WOM**) fuel expansion
- **Brand affinity**: Exceeding user expectations grows admirers and loyalty

According to leading research, product-led companies grow on average 2.2x faster than other B2B firms. By putting product excellence and the customer at the very heart of operations, sustainable growth unconstrained by traditional models becomes achievable.

This cultural foundation establishes the environment for product-led success. However, realizing the potential requires leadership in crafting a strategic vision to steer product direction and provide the tools and incentives to motivate the execution of that vision. This takes us to our next section—the integral responsibilities of GPMs in shaping product vision.

Creating a compelling product vision

A strong product vision serves as a North Star guiding teams toward a desired future. It paints an ambitious yet grounded picture of the value and experience the product will deliver to users down the road. While executive leadership plays a key role, GPMs are crucial partners in researching needs, analyzing insights, and crystallizing this vision. The vision should outline the **unique value proposition** (**UVP**), underserved customer needs to be fulfilled, and how the product will improve users' lives. It tells an inspirational story that sparks excitement while providing loose guardrails for innovation. With a clearly defined vision, teams gain purpose and direction, rallying their efforts to bring this future state to life. This leads us to translate the vision into strategic priorities and roadmaps to make it actionable.

Defining vision

A compelling product vision serves as a guiding star—an ambitious yet actionable picture of the future product experience and the value it will deliver to customers. This vision guides teams by illuminating the true north—the purpose and goals underpinning day-to-day activities.

While executive leadership plays an integral role, GPMs are crucial partners in conducting research, analyzing insights, understanding needs, and crystallizing this vision.

The vision should outline what unique value will be delivered to users, which underserved customer needs will be fulfilled, and how the product will improve users' lives. It details problems that will be solved and frames the competitive playing field.

An inspiring vision tells a story that sparks excitement and belief in the future product. It provides guardrails without being overly prescriptive so that creativity and innovation can flourish.

With a clearly defined vision in place, teams have a shared sense of purpose and direction. Their efforts ladder up to bringing this future state to reality.

Translating vision into priorities

After defining the vision, GPMs play a key role in working with executives to translate it into tractable strategic priorities for the business.

GPMs collaborate closely with engineering leaders to map 2-3 years of product roadmaps and goals based on the vision. Which capabilities and features are required to realize this future? Which emerging technologies or UX paradigms should be leveraged?

Given limited resources and the inherent uncertainties of technology change, GPMs must guide teams to hone in on the vital few priorities with the biggest customer impact. Saying no to dilutive efforts maintains focus on the heart of the vision.

Equally important is guiding teams to define both quantitative and qualitative success metrics aligned with the vision. Vanity metrics should be eschewed for North-Star measures of customer value such as retention and **net promoter score** (**NPS**).

With strategic priorities defined and success metrics established, execution can commence with roles, incentives, and progress tracking all laddering up to the product vision.

Fostering aligned execution

With strategic priorities outlined, the next crucial step is fostering aligned execution across teams. GPMs play a vital role in promoting transparency, cross-functional collaboration, and accountability to bring the product vision to life. Here's how:

- GPMs should advocate for transparency through open Q&A forums, company wikis, and visibility into objectives

- Cross-functional collaboration is enabled through shared tools, informal knowledge sharing, and integrating workflows

- Accountability is reinforced by tracking progress metrics and celebrating wins that exemplify the vision

By connecting the dots between teams and clarifying how each function contributes to the broader vision, GPMs enhance execution through alignment.

Motivating and developing teams

Realizing an ambitious product vision demands dedicated, empowered teams working collaboratively. GPMs play a key part in motivation by conveying the "why" behind the vision—how achieving it will tangibly improve people's lives.

GPMs should connect features and technologies back to real customer needs to instill meaning and purpose. They should craft compelling narratives highlighting how employees' work makes an impact.

Recognition programs and monetary incentives that reinforce customer-centric behaviors also signal value alignment. Hackathons, design jams, and experiments provide interactive vision-building experiences.

Ongoing skills development enables teams to deliver excellence. GPMs should advocate for ample training resources, mentorship programs, and clear career progression opportunities.

Adapting and evolving

In dynamic markets, even the most compelling visions must evolve over time. GPMs play a critical role in enabling adaptation based on market feedback and technology progression. Encouraging rapid prototyping of new concepts provides validation through alpha and beta tests, and even internal testing programs. At Dell, teams ran **Manufacturing Test Builds (MTBs)** to trial actual device production. Microsoft had the famous "dogfooding" program for internal testing, asking teams if they were ready to "eat their own dogfood" and use their own products day-to-day. Overall, building mechanisms for ongoing concept iteration such as prototypes, limited market releases, and company-wide trials enables the vision to be realigned based on user feedback and market analyses. Conducting quarterly vision check-ins to retest assumptions is also vital for determining necessary pivots or adaptations. With so much change, products require structured pipelines for continuous evolution.

New and emerging technologies open unforeseen opportunities. GPMs should stay abreast of tech trends and explore use cases. This adaptability allows the vision to evolve while maintaining continuity of purpose. Teams feel empowered to innovate versus just implementing static specs.

In summary, while executives own the vision, GPMs are crucial partners in researching, formulating, communicating, and executing an inspiring product vision. With clarity and purpose, the vision serves as a North Star guiding sustainable growth powered by delivering unmatched value to customers.

An inspirational product vision provides the direction for teams to rally behind. But understanding user needs is what transforms vision into solutions loved by actual customers. We'll now explore how GPMs can champion deep customer centricity across their organizations to enable flawless execution.

Fostering a customer-centric culture across the organization

While leadership sets the vision, GPMs play a key role in instilling an obsessive focus on users across all layers of the organization. This means enabling the real **voice of the customer** (**VoC**) to directly inform every stage of ideation, development, and positioning. Rather than relying solely on segmentation, teams should have ongoing exposure to actual customer conversations, feedback, and insights. GPMs can advocate for increased user immersion through panels, advisory boards, co-creation sessions, and job shadowing. Early and frequent engagement builds empathy and understanding, sparking better innovation. Allowing siloed knowledge of users risks misalignment. By continuously translating insights into concrete requirements and stories, GPMs help embed the customer perspective into everyday work.

Embedding the customer perspective

While leadership defines the broad vision, GPMs play an integral part in fostering an obsessive focus on user needs across all levels of the organization. This means enabling the real VoC to directly inform each stage of ideation, development, and positioning.

Rather than solely relying on legacy segmentation approaches, teams should have ongoing exposure to actual conversations, feedback, and insights from real users. The customer prism should shape decision-making at all levels.

Active listening and co-creation are crucial. But just as important is translating insights into concrete requirements, stories, and specs that embed the user perspective into everyday work.

Advocating for user immersion

GPMs should push for increased direct exposure to real users across the organization by:

- Scheduling regular user panels, advisory boards, and co-creation sessions
- Requiring every team member to interact with users for a minimum number of hours per quarter
- Sending clips of user interviews for teams to listen to during sprints
- Organizing job shadowing and customer ride-alongs to build empathy

Early, frequent, and ongoing engagement sparks better understanding and innovation. Allowing siloed knowledge risks misalignment.

Co-creating with customers

GPMs should champion collaborative workshops, design jams, and hackathons focused on solving customer problems and co-developing solutions.

Identifying power users willing to engage in beta testing and early access programs provides invaluable insights. Customer advisory groups should be looped into ideation and planning.

Co-creation not only reveals needs but also forges brand advocates in the process, which creates brand loyalty.

Motivating teams through impact

Linking product initiatives directly to positive real-world impact is hugely motivating for teams. GPMs should craft compelling narratives of how the product improves users' lives and facilitates their goals.

Celebrating positive customer feedback, case studies, and reviews highlights the direct value generated. Recognizing teams that go above and beyond for users further reinforces customer-first values.

Help all employees across functions see how their work ladders up to user benefits. This focus fosters meaning and purpose day to day.

Instilling user perspective in workflows

Product managers can embed user perspective into team workflows using techniques such as the following:

- Requiring design specs to include persona profiles and stories
- Adding user quotes and photos to project boards
- Testing messaging and UX concepts with target users during sprints
- Creating quick reference guides on the latest pain points to inform development
- Asking "How would the user react?" during standups and planning

The goal is sustaining user focus at the forefront, not just occasionally. User perspective should permeate ongoing work.

Tearing down silos

GPMs should identify and dismantle silos that hinder user focus. Engineering and design may optimize for conflicting metrics. Sales might make claims that deviate from reality.

Promoting shared meetings, rotations, and critiquing across teams helps and appeals to shared values and goals. Remind teams that compartmentalized thinking hurts users and performance.

As stewards of the customer experience, GPMs must broker compromise and alignment focused on holistic optimization.

Operationalizing customer centricity

While mindsets matter, GPMs should advocate embedding customer centricity into formal systems and processes to sustain it.

Push for incorporating direct customer input into planning and prioritization. Advocate for customer experience metrics to factor into performance management and incentives.

Formalize mechanisms to gather feedback at each touchpoint. Create customer health scorecards and dashboards. The VoC should permeate decisions.

Structure product milestones to require customer validation before commitments are baked into processes so that customer centricity persists as personnel change.

Sustaining a learning culture

Customer needs continually evolve. GPMs should nurture a learning culture focused on proactive listening, not reacting after the fact.

Advocate for regular touchpoints through NPS surveys, interviews, win/loss analysis, and advisory groups. Monitor and review support tickets and community forums for emerging issues and address them proactively.

Journey mapping and usability audits at regular intervals reveal changing workflows and pain points. Leverage in-product engagements such as Appcues to uncover hidden frustrations.

Analyze feature usage and adoption metrics to identify underperforming capabilities. Holistically connecting quantitative and qualitative data provides a comprehensive view.

Great product cultures stay hungry to learn from users. GPMs should architect processes that embrace curiosity, external perspectives, and the drive for continuous improvement.

With a compelling vision defined and deep customer insight enabled, executing the vision requires modern processes and collaborative teaming models. Our next section explores how GPMs can implement agile, customer-focused processes to smoothly execute that vision.

Real-world example

At Autodesk Construction Solutions, the product team leveraged usage metrics and qualitative feedback to improve their product demo videos. They utilized a tool called Consensus to track viewing behavior, seeing which parts of videos prospects paused, rewound, or abandoned. The product managers then worked with technical marketers to revamp the videos, focusing on sections with high engagement and clarifying areas where viewers tended to drop off.

Additionally, Consensus notified sales engineers when a prospect watched a video multiple times or got stuck on a particular section. The sales reps could then proactively reach out to those prospects and have tailored conversations about their interests and pain points reflected through the video viewing patterns.

This showcases how connecting quantitative usage data with qualitative feedback provides a comprehensive view to uncover frustrations and improve the customer experience. The insights from Consensus enabled Autodesk to iterate on its demo videos to better align with customer needs.

Implementing supporting processes and structures

To enable key capabilities such as rapid iteration, **continuous delivery** (**CD**), and flexible response to customer feedback, product-led organizations rely on agile development practices. GPMs play a pivotal role in championing the transition from traditional sequential models to agile frameworks such as Scrum and Kanban. This involves reorienting engineers to work in short sprints focused on iterative enhancements rather than long-term roadmaps and specifications. Cross-functional teams self-organize to deliver features faster through rituals such as standups, retrospectives, and backlog grooming. Although the transition can pose hurdles, GPMs can coach teams through the agile learning curve to foster practices such as **continuous integration** (**CI**) that allow product-led organizations to learn faster, release faster, and meet dynamic customer needs.

Adopting agile development practices

Transitioning to agile development practices provides the foundation for key capabilities such as frequent iteration, CD, and flexible response to customer feedback that allow product-led organizations to thrive.

GPMs play a pivotal role in advocating for and facilitating the adoption of agile frameworks such as Scrum or Kanban to replace traditional sequential development models. This involves reorienting engineers away from long-term roadmaps toward working in short, defined sprints focused on iterative enhancements and development features.

Comprehensive documentation and specifications take a backseat to working software and rapid experimentation. The focus becomes regular inspection of progress and continuously adapting based on learnings rather than rigidly following prescriptive plans.

Cross-functional product teams are empowered to self-organize and collaborate closely across specialties to bring features to market quickly. GPMs help coach teams on agile rituals that enable transparency and continuous improvement such as daily standups, retrospectives, backlog grooming, and sprint planning.

Engineering practices such as pair programming, automated testing, and CI further enable higher-quality code at faster velocities.

This agile approach allows product-led organizations to learn faster, release faster, and meet dynamic customer needs better through flexible, adaptive processes versus linear waterfall development.

However, transitioning to agile can pose challenges. Engineers accustomed to detailed specifications may struggle without prescribed requirements. Conflicts can arise around priorities and scoping for sprints. Tight deadlines can lead to technical debt accumulation.

GPMs play a crucial role in overcoming these hurdles by coaching teams through the agile learning curve. They should start with a pilot team before scaling agile to foster capability building. Promoting open communication and constructive retrospectives allows improvement of processes. GPMs must also ensure technical debt is addressed by allocating resources accordingly.

With consistent facilitation and leadership, product managers can guide the successful adoption of agile practices that enable the rapid iteration essential for product-led organizations.

Instituting continuous customer feedback loops

To truly incorporate user perspectives into the **product life cycle** (**PLC**), GPMs must architect mechanisms to systematically gather, analyze, and act on continuous customer feedback.

This starts by identifying key points across the user journey to proactively request feedback, both qualitative and quantitative in nature. For example, in-app NPS surveys can gauge satisfaction while feedback buttons allow users to report specific issues.

Customer support conversations and app store reviews provide a rich source of qualitative insights that **sentiment analysis** (**SA**) and **natural language processing** (**NLP**) can help digest. VoC programs send periodic surveys to gain a representative sample.

To maximize response rates, GPMs should promote ease of providing feedback through simple interfaces and clear VPs. Keeping surveys focused and only requesting ratings where truly relevant optimizes participation.

Once collected, feedback must be classified by topic, urgency, severity, and other factors and then routed to the appropriate internal stakeholders for action. Bulk analysis can identify recurring themes and areas of concern.

By constantly listening to and analyzing the VoC and then sharing digestible insights across product, engineering, and support teams, GPMs enable the roadmap to flex based on real user needs.

However, some common challenges include survey fatigue, diminishing responses, unstructured feedback requiring manual analysis, reluctance from some teams to act on user feedback, and engineering arrogance where developers feel they know best—better than customers themselves. This complacency ignores that user wants are just as important as needs. There is often a fine line between useless features and delighters that truly excite. Keeping engineers humble, reminding them to not only hear but truly listen to customers, and conveying both needs and wants in compelling ways are all critical to avoiding a "we know better" mentality.

GPMs can overcome engagement issues by limiting survey frequency and clearly communicating how feedback is used to improve the product. Automation and **artificial intelligence (AI)** such as SA and NLP ease analysis at scale. Getting executives to endorse and participate in customer response initiatives creates buy-in.

Instituting seamless value-added feedback loops allows product-led organizations to incorporate user perspectives into every stage of development, facilitating customer-driven growth.

Fostering cross-functional team collaboration

Delivering great end-to-end customer experiences demands tight collaboration across functions such as product, engineering, design, support, sales, and marketing. However, organizational silos often inhibit this integrated approach.

GPMs play a pivotal role in tearing down walls between teams by promoting increased informal connections, providing tools such as Confluence wikis for transparency, and nurturing empathy across groups through job rotations and critiques.

They should advocate restructuring workflows to require cross-functional signoffs at key milestones versus handoffs. Implementing regular integrated business planning fosters alignment around shared goals.

Instituting shared performance metrics and objectives that cascade from vision down helps unite often disconnected groups. Celebrating group accomplishments builds collective identity versus individual focus.

However, deeply entrenched silos resist integration. GPMs may face reluctance from specialists protective of domain authority. Incentive structures rewarding local optimization undermine collaboration.

Product managers can overcome barriers by getting executives to build a collaborative culture and communicate the importance of cross-functional teaming. Rotations and critiques build an understanding of different viewpoints. Highlighting benefits such as faster throughput helps sell integration.

With concerted facilitation and leadership, GPMs can tear down silos and unify teams around shared missions and results to enable seamless execution. In a small start-up, everyone is well informed about each other's work, fostering an environment of organic, exciting, and innovative development. However, as organizations expand, the increase in connections, personnel, and interdependencies makes achieving this level of cohesion increasingly challenging. Therefore, it becomes imperative to introduce specialized tools and processes, with the pivotal role of GPMs emerging as the critical glue in facilitating this harmonious synergy.

Modern processes and structures complement the broader product vision and customer centricity by enabling smooth execution. GPMs play an integral role in architecting and championing systems and ways of working that allow product-led organizations to thrive and scale.

Today's hypercompetitive business landscape demands organizations continually deliver exceptional experiences that exceed customer expectations. These mandates of adopting a product-led approach should permeate the company culture, strategy, and execution.

By mastering the extensive set of capabilities covered in this guide, GPMs can successfully catalyze and sustain product-led transformations in their organizations.

Summary

By equipping GPMs with expertise across culture, vision, customer obsession, and modern processes, this guide aims to thoroughly prepare readers to spearhead successful product-led transformations in your organizations.

This chapter covers the key responsibilities and capabilities of GPMs. First, establish an insightful product vision based on research, then communicate it persuasively across the company. Translate the vision into strategic priorities and success metrics to focus teams and drive execution. Motivate teams by conveying the meaningful impact of their work and celebrating wins.

Foster cross-functional transparency, accountability, and collaboration around shared objectives. Promote adaptation by encouraging rapid experimentation and continuous learning based on user feedback. Champion customer centricity by facilitating immersive user research across the company and infusing user perspectives into all stages of development.

Tear down silos and unify teams around the customer experience. Broker compromises that optimize for user needs. Implement supporting processes such as agile, CD, and feedback loops that enable product-led success. Structure workflows, metrics, and incentives that reinforce product excellence and customer value.

By mastering this expansive set of leadership, cultural, and execution capabilities, GPMs can successfully transform their organizations into truly product-led enterprises fueled by delivering customer value and experience excellence. The future of business belongs to leaders who recognize this tremendous opportunity. With this comprehensive playbook in hand, that future is yours for the taking.

With a compelling vision set and cross-functional teams rallied behind executing that vision, the next crucial step is clearly defining and articulating the unique value your product delivers to customers. Doing so provides the foundation for resonating positioning and messaging that fuels adoption and growth. We will cover best practices for understanding target users, identifying differentiated benefits, crafting VP statements, and communicating product value effectively in the next chapter.

Questions

1. What are some key attributes of a product-led culture?

2. As a GPM, what are some ways you can help create a compelling product vision?

3. How can GPMs champion customer centricity across an organization?

4. What supporting processes allow a product-led culture to thrive?

5. What are some challenges when transitioning to a product-led culture and how can GPMs address them?

6. How can the concepts in this chapter help GPMs transform their organizations?

Answers

1. Several core attributes characterize a product-led culture:

    -   **Customer centricity**: Keeping the customer perspective at the forefront to ensure the product solves real user needs and pain points.

    -   **Data-driven**: Leveraging metrics and insights on user behavior to guide decisions rather than assumptions or opinions.

    -   **Cross-functional collaboration**: Tearing down silos to foster tight integration between teams such as product, engineering, and design on shared goals.

    -   **Continuous innovation**: Empowering teams to rapidly experiment, take risks, and implement learnings to constantly improve.

    -   **Customer engagement**: Turning users into product evangelists through community, content, and delivering so much value that the product sells itself.

    -   **Product excellence**: An unrelenting focus on quality, UX, and solving real problems that matter to customers.

2. As a GPM, I play a key role in working with leadership to craft an inspiring product vision. Specific ways I can help create a compelling vision include the following:

    -   Conducting extensive research into market trends, competitive offerings, and customer needs.

    -   Analyzing research insights to identify underserved user needs and areas where we can uniquely deliver value.

    -   Partnering with executives to crystallize a vision statement that outlines our future product's value and purpose.

    -   Translating the vision into a prioritized roadmap and key results to guide execution across teams.

- Defining quantitative success metrics such as engagement as well as qualitative metrics such as testimonials that align with the vision.

- Communicating the vision persuasively to teams through presentations, memos, Q&As, and tying work back to the vision.

- Adapting and evolving the vision over time based on market learnings while maintaining continuity.

3. GPMs have many avenues to champion customer obsession, including the following:

    - Requiring every team member to directly engage with customers for at least a quarter of an hour.

    - Organizing frequent qualitative research through user interviews, advisory groups, and job shadowing.

    - Sending video clips of customer interviews for teams to listen to during sprints.

    - Pushing for direct customer input during planning to inform decisions.

    - Motivating teams by crafting stories conveying the human impact of their work.

    - Adding user quotes, photos, and perspective statements to project boards.

    - Testing messaging concepts and UX with real users during development sprints.

    - Identifying and resolving silos causing misalignment of customer needs.

    - Incorporating customer experience metrics into performance management and incentives.

    - Sustaining a learning culture focused on continuously gathering and acting on user feedback.

4. Key supporting processes that enable product-led success include the following:

    - Adopting agile software development with short sprints, CD, and incremental enhancements to enable rapid iteration.

    - Implementing customer feedback loops across the user journey to gather insights at every touchpoint.

    - Fostering tight cross-functional collaboration through structures such as integrated business planning, shared KPIs, and collective rituals.

    - Facilitating transparency through open communication, visibility into objectives, and sharing wins.

    - Tracking product-led metrics such as NPS, customer satisfaction, adoption rates, and team velocity to guide improvement.

5.   Transitioning to product-led thinking poses challenges such as the following:

- **Organizational resistance**: GPMs can secure executive endorsement, highlight benefits, and start with small pilots.

- **Entrenched silos**: Rotations, critiques, restructured workflows, and shared KPIs break down barriers.

- **Lack of customer insight**: Architecting continuous feedback loops helps inform decisions.

- **Potential missteps**: Celebrating failures as learnings rather than punishments breeds a "test and learn" culture.

With consistent communication, **change management** (**CM**), and patience, GPMs can overcome obstacles through gradual, collaborative adoption.

6.   This chapter equips GPMs with an expansive set of capabilities to drive product-led transformation, including the following:

- Strategies for establishing an inspiring product vision and translating it into executable priorities.

- Techniques to foster customer obsession by facilitating immersive research and conveying real-world impact.

- Ways to implement modern processes such as agile and cross-functional teaming.

- Approaches for tearing down silos and unifying teams around the user.

- Solutions for common challenges such as resistance to change.

By mastering the concepts and practices introduced in this chapter, GPMs can successfully catalyze cultural, process, execution, and leadership changes needed to put product excellence and the customer at the center of operations. This future-proofs organizations by enabling innovation and growth driven by delivering unmatched user value.

6

Defining and Communicating Your Product Value Proposition

In the hypercompetitive world of business, products don't sell themselves on features alone. To drive sustainable growth in a product-led organization, teams must clearly articulate the unique value their offering delivers to customers better than any alternative.

This chapter will equip readers with a strategic approach to defining, crafting, and communicating differentiated value propositions that resonate with target users and propel product-led growth. We will specifically explore the following topics:

- The importance of defining and communicating the value of your product
- Defining your value proposition
- Crafting a compelling value proposition statement
- Communicating the value of your product – choosing the right channels to communicate your value proposition
- Partnering with marketing for success
- Pitfalls and challenges in defining and communicating the value of your product and how to overcome them

By the end, you'll have a comprehensive toolkit to shape value narratives that capture interest, spark desire, and ultimately create preference for your product over competitors. Let's get started!

The importance of defining and communicating value

Growth depends on effectively conveying why your product is worth paying attention to, trying, and purchasing over the alternatives. A strong value proposition answers the customer's question, *"Why is this right for me?"*

Articulating your competitive advantage and the tangible outcomes users gain builds interest and trust. On the other hand, unclear or unconvincing value messaging stifles adoption.

So, what exactly makes up a compelling value proposition? Let's break it down into its core components:

- The target customer
- Their underserved needs
- How you uniquely solve those needs
- The key benefits realized

Done right, a value proposition anchors all positioning and messaging with the customer perspective top of mind. With so much riding on clearly communicating differentiation, let's examine how to craft resonating value propositions.

Knowing your target customer and their needs

Customer understanding is the foundation of defining value. Teams that skip foundational research make erroneous assumptions about buyer needs and perspectives.

Immersive research not only reveals pain points but also nuances of worldview, decision-making processes, and the language that resonates. Here are proven approaches.

In-depth interviews

Directly engaging buyers through one-on-one interviews provides the richest insights into motivations, values, and thought processes. Open-ended questioning reveals surprising perspectives versus closed-ended surveys. Look for patterns across subjects as well as standout anecdotes that add color.

Develop proto-personas (a lightweight form of ad hoc personas created with no new research) to consolidate learning, then pressure test with additional interviews. Keep diving deeper into mental models.

User testing

Observing real users interact with your product is invaluable for uncovering usability issues and identifying sources of confusion. These user testing sessions, often referred to as "guinea pig sessions," help reveal gaps between perceived and actual user behaviors.

In addition to user testing, focus groups play a crucial role in gathering qualitative feedback on new concepts through guided discussions. Retrospective probing techniques delve into the "*why*" behind users' actions. Methods such as card sorting, tree testing, and first-click tests provide quick insights into users' mental models. For a deeper understanding of attention patterns, eye-tracking technology is employed.

Acknowledging the global reach of your product, it's essential to consider cultural nuances. In regions such as Asia, where communication styles and user behaviors may differ, incorporating non-interactive observed sessions can be particularly insightful. These sessions involve passive observation, allowing us to understand user interactions without direct engagement.

By tailoring our user testing methodologies to account for cultural diversity, we ensure that our insights are robust and applicable across various regions. This approach not only enhances the usability of our product but also contributes to a more inclusive and user-friendly experience for a global audience.

Empathy mapping

Empathy mapping workshops build an understanding of customer perspectives. Capturing what users *think, feel, say, and do* provides insights into their worldview.

Have cross-functional teams define proto-personas and then extensively map their thoughts, pain points, and emotions. Identifying disconnects between business assumptions and actual users' needs sparks creative solutions. Empathy begets value resonance.

Ongoing advisory engagement

Customer advisory councils and onboarding user groups provide sustained access to user perspectives long after initial research ends.

Early prototype access collects continuous feedback. Keep engaging power users who provide key insights. Maintain empathy along the journey. Regular check-in calls and periodic deep-dive interviews give ongoing qualitative data to inform strategy.

With deep customer empathy fueling your insights, we can transition to defining the differentiated value your product delivers.

Real-world example

The smart home security company Ring's core offering is a video doorbell and security cameras with motion alerts, live views, and smart integrations. Here are the steps they followed to shape value messaging:

1. Ring needed to intimately understand their target homeowner through research. They conducted in-depth interviews, asking open-ended questions about motivations, pain points, and decision-making. Key insights included increased package theft concerns, desire for visibility to entryways, and preference for DIY installation.

2. Next, Ring ran focus groups around new features such as facial recognition and anomaly detection. This revealed concerns about privacy violations. Users wanted visibility without compromising family members' rights. Empathy mapping workshops uncovered more nuances around emotional decision drivers.

Ongoing user panels provided longitudinal insights over time. For example, they learned new parents became more concerned about backyard safety for children. Ring could evolve messaging to match changing needs.

Armed with deep customer insights, Ring developed their core value proposition:

"Ring provides complete home visibility and real-time motion alerts so you always feel safe and in control."

This positioning speaks directly to the desire for entryway visibility and responsive motion detection. Specific benefit details address user needs surfaced through research.

To make it resonate, Ring brought the messaging to life with customer stories on their website:

"When Jamie got an alert that someone was at her front door, she could immediately see it was just her neighbor dropping off a package. She felt at ease knowing Ring was on guard."

Vivid examples such as this make the value tangible. When prospects imagine themselves benefiting, they are more compelled.

Ring also made their value proposition pillar of all marketing. Their website, ads, sales collateral, and demo scripts were aligned around visibility and control. At retail displays, messaging emphasized unique motion detection features.

This unified drumbeat ensured prospects only heard positioning reflecting real user needs. Ring's value proposition became ubiquitous across every touchpoint.

Defining and communicating values requires real customer empathy. Ring's deep research, informed messaging, and consistent reinforcement have helped them become a leading home security brand. Their value proposition resonates by putting the user's perspective first.

Defining your value proposition

With a deep understanding of target users' needs constructed, you can shift focus to sculpting a compelling value proposition by isolating the unique strengths of your product and the outcomes it delivers to customers. Key elements for conveying differentiated value include the following:

1. Key differentiators.
2. Core benefits.
3. Killer use cases.
4. Core messaging.

Key differentiators

Start by counting what tangible capabilities make your solution stand apart from competitors and alternatives. How does it improve upon the status quo? Key differentiators should do the following:

- Directly address frustrations and desires identified through customer research
- Offer tangible improvements over current solutions
- Align with target user priorities and decision-making considerations

- Provide competitive technical, creative, or servicing advantages
- Deliver innovative capabilities that competitors lack

By linking differentiated attributes directly back to customer needs, you craft powerful, relevant value messaging.

Core benefits

Next, translate differentiating features into clear benefit statements conveying actual outcomes users realize:

- Save time by ___.
- Increase sales by ___.
- Reduce costs by ___.
- Minimize frustration through ___.

Benefits should highlight both functional and emotional improvements users gain. They humanize sterile features and give buyers clear reasons to prefer your product.

Killer use cases

Illustrative use cases make abstract benefits tangible. For example, explaining how a restaurant owner uses Toast **point-of-sale** (**POS**) software to minimize food waste and lost revenue powerfully conveys value.

Identify standout customer success stories that epitomize your solution excelling for a specific need. Benchmark off best clients. Detail the before-and-after transforming results.

Use cases make benefits vividly real while providing social proof and relevance for prospects in analogous situations. They turn sterile features into compelling narratives.

Core messaging

With benefits defined, crystallize core messaging capturing your value prop for consistent reinforcement across touchpoints:

- Website and sales collateral headlines
- Positioning statements
- Email/ad taglines
- Social media captions
- Explainer video scripts

Repetition drives retention. Craft messages focused on communicating outcomes customers care about in relatable language.

With clear differentiation and benefits defined, we can now shift focus to crafting a compelling condensed statement encapsulating the value proposition.

Real-world example

Here is a real-world example of defining a value proposition, using the company Calendly:

Calendly provides automated appointment scheduling software that enables users to offer booking links through their website, email, or messaging platforms.

To define their *value proposition*, Calendly first identified key differentiators through customer research, including:

- Automated availability syncing with calendars

- Customizable booking links, questions, and options

- Integration across marketing platforms such as email and social

- User-friendly interface requiring no training

These capabilities directly addressed user frustrations around manual booking coordination that surfaced in surveys.

Next, Calendly translated *key differentiators* into *core benefit* statements such as:

- *"Streamline scheduling without the back-and-forth emails"*

- *"Reduce no-shows through automated reminders"*

- *"Delight customers with fast, flexible booking"*

The messaging focuses on convenience and customer satisfaction gains.

Illustrative use cases made benefits tangible. For example, Calendly highlighted a photographer who shares booking links on Instagram, enabling prospects to easily select session types and reserve times. This showcases the value of service businesses.

Core messaging headlines consistently reinforced value across their website, ads, and sales collateral:

- *"Scheduling Automated"*

- *"Bookings Made Easy"*

- *"Say Goodbye to Scheduling Chaos"*

Calendly's crisp value proposition statements derived from rigorous customer research now provide a clear direction guiding all communication. Defining differentiation and benefits provides clarity on how to best convey their value.

Crafting a compelling value proposition statement

After defining your value proposition through rigorous customer research and analysis of competitive differentiation, the next step is distilling everything into a concise, compelling statement that becomes your guiding light.

Exceptional value proposition statements eloquently encapsulate the following:

- Who your product is for
- The problem being solved
- Your unique solution
- The key benefit realized

Though compact, these statements pack a tremendous punch when executed skillfully. They provide a very clear reference that focuses messaging and positioning on what matters most to your ideal customers.

Consider how Mint.com, an online financial management tool, succinctly captured exactly who needs their product, the underlying frustration being addressed, their specific solution, and core benefit:

"Financial clarity for effortless budgeting. Intuitively track spending, set budgets, and control finances anytime through our web and mobile apps."

This example perfectly shows the key objectives for crafting a stellar value proposition statement. Let's explore best practices to emulate such excellence:

- **Target customers**: Start by explicitly stating who your product is tailored for. Resist vague references such as "consumers" or "professionals." Get ultra-specific in naming the persona, industry, company size, or niche so that it's abundantly clear who stands to benefit. This grounds the messaging in a concrete audience; for example, "For overscheduled HR managers at high-growth start-ups...". Such laser targeting focuses the rest of the messaging on customer-centric resonance.

- **Problem statement**: Next, call out the specific frustration, need, desire, or goal your defined customer segment experiences as uncovered during your research. Explain the "before" – what is the pain or challenge they face that warrants attention? Making it tangible clarifies why they should care about your solution; for example, "Who struggles with disjointed applicant tracking across platforms?...". Detail the annoying impediments and limitations of existing solutions to set up the "after" relief.

- **Solution**: Now, articulate how your product uniquely addresses the problem in a novel way competitors can't match. Explain your special sauce—your secret formula for excelling where others fall short; for example, "Unifies' AI-powered recruitment software suite automatically synchronizes candidate data across platforms...". Don't just state what you do but also how you do it better through proprietary innovations.

- **Benefit**: Close with the key result the user realizes from your solution. Focus on the most important emotional or functional outcome that really matters to the target persona; for example, "...so that you can efficiently scale hiring 5X faster." The benefit statement crystallizes the payoff for choosing your solution.

- **Cost of doing nothing**: To further illustrate the urgency of addressing the problem, articulate the negative consequences customers face by maintaining the status quo. Paint a vivid picture of tangible and intangible costs across operations, finances, reputation, and so on that inaction perpetuates; for example, "Manual tracking risks critical hiring delays and bottlenecks that undermine expansion goals and revenue." Quantify the time, money, and competitive disadvantage being tolerated.

- **Tie it together**: Weave the elements into a succinct user-focused narrative flowing from their need to your capabilities, to the end payoff.

Now, pressure test multiple draft options with target users to identify the optimal resonant language. Refine until you have meticulous clarity on who, what, how, and why the value proposition is tailored exactly to your ideal customer.

This value proposition statement then guides all other messaging as the definitive pinnacle articulation of your platform's purpose and differentiation.

With such an exceptional compass created, communicating the value across channels becomes easier. But how exactly should teams broadcast this vital message?

Integrating the statement across channels

Your statement provides raw material to inform content, campaigns, and positioning everywhere. For example, blog posts and ads would focus on the pains described in the problem statement. Case studies would highlight customers achieving the benefit.

Email newsletter copy may lead with the statement verbatim, while website pages elaborate on details. Sales collateral drives home your unique solution.

Product onboarding introduces capabilities highlighted in your statement. Support centers on achieving the promised benefit.

Executive narratives quote succinct wording as the thesis underpinning everything. Investor presentations encapsulate your purpose and differentiation.

As with a well-crafted brand slogan, repeating this mantra rhythmically reinforces retention and compounding identity. It becomes ubiquitous through a consistent integrated presence aligned with your positioning everywhere.

Evolving the statement over time

While core identity endures, situations evolve. As products grow and markets change, reassess whether value messaging requires realignment.

New capabilities demand inclusion. Competitive shifts may necessitate re-emphasis on different strengths. User needs morph over time.

Treat your statement as a living document to revisit periodically. But take care not to dilute its crispness through excessive wordiness or tangent focuses.

With vision, discipline, and continuous optimization, exceptional value proposition statements serve as lighthouses guiding organizations to intimately connect with customers through crystal clarity on who you serve, the frustrations you banish, and the meaning you provide.

Communicating your value across touchpoints

In today's crowded marketplaces, simply defining a compelling value proposition is not sufficient. Organizations must also master precisely communicating their differentiated value through targeted messaging and channels tailored to resonate with their ideal customer profile.

Rather than diluting impact through generic branding and broad claims, companies should pursue owned, earned, and paid tactics focused on conveying their unique value in a way that aligns with target users' preferences. Tactics to communicate value propositions effectively include the following:

- **Thought leadership content**: Educational, inspirational thought leadership content attracts and engages potential customers by delivering tangible value. Reports, e-books, blogs, commissioned research, customer stories, webinars, and whitepapers build rapport and credibility by providing helpful insights versus a sales pitch. Companies can nurture prospects by tailoring content across the buyer's journey from the early awareness stage through consideration and, ultimately, purchase. For example, an HR software provider could offer insights on remote work trends, diversity best practices, and automation to establish relevance with HR decision-makers.

- **Social media presence**: Strategic social media provides a way to engage modern buyers where they already spend significant time and attention. Compelling graphics, videos, and captions quickly convey value, while behind-the-scenes posts foster deeper relationships. Hashtag campaigns that demonstrate your solution helping customers excel in their industries provide social proof at scale. Partnering with relevant influencers expands reach into new niches. Humorous, entertaining content cuts through crowded feeds to connect. Paid adverts amplify your content by highlighting specific use cases and benefit-focused messaging targeted to ideal customer demographics. Retargeting nurtures previous visitors to return and convert.

- **Testimonials and reviews**: Credible validation from voices such as client advocates, industry influencers, and reputable publications fosters trust in your value proposition claims. These respected voices offer third-party proof points reinforcing your promised benefits. Customer testimonials that prospects can relate to make the benefits tangible. User reviews establish credibility through shared experiences with peers. Weaving such social validation throughout campaigns sustains confidence in your ability to deliver value.

- **Product experience and packaging**: Well-designed product experiences, packaging, branding, and aesthetics inherently communicate your value proposition. For example, Apple's renowned focus on simplicity, design, and user experience conveys core differentiation. Onboarding flows introduce capabilities addressing user pain points. Packaging highlights **unique selling propositions (USPs)** such as sustainability. While subtler, these touchpoints make powerful impressions.

- **Advertising and paid media**: Paid advertising provides a megaphone to target communicating your value proposition to specific demographics shown to be ideal customer profiles. Platforms such as Facebook, LinkedIn, Google Ads, Amazon Ads, and more enable precision outreach at scale matched to personas. For example, a pet supplement provider could highlight digestive benefits through Facebook ads targeted to health-conscious new pet owners. Programmatic display ads can retarget engaged visitors across sites. Paid ads enable amplifying your value far and wide.

- **Public and media relations**: Earned media exposure expands reach while providing credibility as an impartial earned endorsement. Positioning executives and founders as thought leaders on industry issues establishes relevance to target media outlets. For example, a construction tech start-up could offer contributed articles and media briefings positioning their CEO as a champion for safer job sites. This spotlights their modern solution to a shared problem.

- **Conference presence and events**: Industry conferences, trade shows, and local events provide opportunities to demonstrate value propositions first-hand through booths, speaking sessions, sponsorships, on-site activations, and networking. For example, an enterprise AI software provider could showcase ease of use and adoption through interactive demos at relevant tech conferences. Such real-world interactions bring messaging to life.

- **Website messaging**: A company's website home page is high-value real estate for immediately communicating its differentiation to visitors. A succinct tagline/headline communicates the core value proposition upfront. Supporting proof points such as testimonials and customer examples ground claims. Presenting the most important benefits prominently convinces visitors quickly. A sharp focus on showcasing differentiation outweighs vague positioning. Optimized navigation guides visitors seamlessly to resonance.

A compelling value proposition offers potent raw material; however, astute companies comprehend that achieving success demands precise outreach through various channels and customizing messages to align with customer priorities. This involves strategic dissemination of the value narrative through owned, earned, social, and paid touchpoints. By orchestrating an omnichannel approach, these value propositions metamorphose into exceptional customer experiences and establish a lasting competitive advantage.

While the core principles are straightforward, executing value proposition design well involves avoiding common pitfalls. Let's discuss the challenges teams face and how to overcome them.

Partnering with marketing for success

After detailing various owned, earned, and paid channels to communicate your product's value proposition, we must emphasize the importance of collaborating closely with marketing to maximize impact. While product teams focus on defining differentiation and crafting core messaging, marketing provides specialized expertise to resonate through polished branding, visual assets, and campaigns.

Aligning early with marketing

Effective product and marketing partnership begins early during the initial customer research stages. Marketing's specialization includes quant and qualitative market analysis through surveys, win/loss reviews, and customer panels identifying pain points. Collaboration here ensures product ideas are grounded in data-driven opportunity assessment before ideation.

Marketing also contributes branding principles, positioning guidance, and copywriting best practices when formulating your core value proposition messaging. Red flags can be raised regarding claims requiring substantiation or messaging risks. Consensus building early allows for mitigating issues.

Consistency between internal and external messaging

Close coordination between a product's internal positioning and marketing's external communications prevents confusing discrepancies. Misalignment risks product launches under-supported by collateral. Sync messaging across FAQs, one-pagers, presentations, lite papers, and sales enablement materials with value proposition focal points.

Marketing polishes messaging

While product managers focus on technical credibility and strategic messaging frameworks, marketing teams specialize in distilling concepts into compelling copy targeted to motivate behaviors. Their skills include drafting crisp taglines, striking visual assets, and intriguing content. Marketing can take raw product value messaging and refine it for maximum resonance.

Planning integrated campaign launches

Introducing new capabilities requires integrated campaigns across marketing, sales, and product teams to convey benefits aligned with user needs. Collaborative launch planning ensures messaging consistency, ample collateral, and coordinated initiatives across regions and **business units** (BUs). Steering committees help navigate complex efforts.

Channel expertise

Leveraging owned, paid, and earned communication channels requires marketing's specialized channel expertise. From configuring **customer data platforms** (**CDPs**) to perfecting pay-per-click bids, specialized tools and the latest tactical best practices exist with channel specialists. Provide key messages for conversion.

Website and advertising partnership

Your website remains a pivotal touchpoint for conveying differentiation. From home-page messaging to integration of value proposition elements across pages, a close marketing partnership ensures benefit-focused surfacing of unique strengths rather than generic claims. Marketing provides inputs on layout, **calls to action** (**CTAs**), and converting flows while the product informs substance.

Advertising creative development also demands collaboration to manifest messaging into compelling formats matched to channel capabilities, whether display ads, Facebook feeds, YouTube videos, or retargeting campaigns. View tag previews and provide feedback.

Ongoing optimization

Continuous optimization requires lockstep version testing, iterative messaging tweaks, campaign performance reviews, and lead qualification analysis to track resonance. Are prospects engaging with key content pieces? Does messaging require rebalancing to increase consideration rates? Marketing and product insights fuel rapid value proposition refinement.

Communicating a compelling yet credible product value proposition demands extensive marketing collaboration. Core differentiation claims require airtight alignment between internal positioning and external presentation. By working cross-functionally across the customer journey, seamless messaging can attract, engage, convert, and retain ideal users based on a shared understanding of their needs being fulfilled.

Avoiding pitfalls in value proposition design

While a strong value proposition provides a strategic foundation, executing resonant messaging can still be derailed by common pitfalls. Start-ups hoping to connect with customers must be vigilant in sidestepping these missteps.

Not actually solving a real customer need

Impactful positioning begins with products that address tangible pain points better than alternatives. Teams should avoid contriving solutions for nonexistent or superficial wants that lack a real market.

The cautionary tale of Juicero illuminates this pitfall. Juicero developed a beautifully engineered $400 juicing appliance capable of pressing wonderful fresh juice from proprietary produce packs. However, their solution failed commercially because it solved little real customer pain versus simply purchasing juice at a grocery store. Their messaging touted advanced tech capabilities rather than meaningful user benefits.

Extensive user research, prototyping, and concept testing help ensure you identify and build the right solutions before determining how to market them. Immerse yourself in your customers' world to observe actual frustrations and needs. Beware of internal biases projecting artificial wants onto users. Validation will reveal if the pain point is substantial enough to warrant a novel solution.

Putting features before benefits

Leading with technical capabilities or features often leaves buyers confused about why they should care. Customers think in terms of concrete outcomes and emotional benefits gained, not abstract features.

Early **electric vehicles** (EVs) frequently focused marketing on battery capacity, charging times, torque figures, and other technical specs. This angle failed to resonate with mainstream consumers. By instead emphasizing practical benefits such as environmental friendliness, fossil fuel savings, low maintenance, and accessible future-forward driving, EV marketing began connecting and driving adoption.

Shift messaging to focus on tangible improvements and emotional outcomes your offering enables over current solutions. Link features directly to real-world benefits with relevance to users' lives. For example, explain how your app's fast processing translates to users' ability to complete tasks in half the time.

Failing to differentiate from the crowd

Messaging that is vague, derivative of competitors' claims, or relies on unsubstantiated superlatives undermines credibility. Unsupported claims of being "the best" often provoke doubt rather than preference.

When Dropbox entered the cloud storage market, existing providers marketed around parity points such as selection size, reliability, and security. By instead emphasizing effortless automatic syncing and seamless remote collaboration, Dropbox carved out differentiation on unique benefits.

Ensure your messaging arises from true competitive advantages you can substantiate. Quantify **return on investment** (ROI) and bottom-line impact. Explain your special sauce that competitors lack. Support claims with credible evidence such as customer metrics and testimonials. Elucidate how your solution innovates where others fall short.

Not targeting specific buyer personas

Casting an excessively wide net with broad messaging often fails to deeply engage any specific group. Defined buyer personas exist for a reason—to allow tailored resonance.

Early iPhone marketing targeted a sweepingly wide swath of consumers without segmentation. By sharpening messaging to users who specifically valued mobile connectivity, apps, and modern design, Apple began honing in on more receptive niches.

Sharply define target customer segments beyond vague demographic data. Profile motivations, values, and pain points. Optimize language, case studies, and channels to intimately align with each persona. Customized resonance conquers generic "one-size-fits-all" appeals.

Inconsistency across touchpoints

Mixed messages confuse audiences and dilute potential impact. Disjointed messaging squanders opportunities to reinforce your platform at each touchpoint.

Salesforce maintains consistent messaging around workflow simplification and productivity gains across its website, ads, events, sales collateral, and product interfaces. This unified drumbeat drives retention and referrals.

Ensure coherency across all customer touchpoints, including your website, social channels, sales materials, product UI, email campaigns, and so on. Maintain messaging harmony centered on customer-focused themes rather than competing slogans.

Failing to evolve messaging

In dynamic markets, messaging requires continuous optimization as products and buyer expectations evolve. What resonated last year may not align with shifting user priorities.

GoPro's early marketing focused on extreme durability, versatility, and high-end specs catering to early tech adopter fans. But as their cameras gained mass market appeal, highlighting simplicity, accessibility, and content sharing became key to staying aligned with mainstream user needs.

Regularly revalidate positioning through market research, win/loss analysis, and customer advisory boards. Refresh case studies and testimonials to remain relevant. Plan periodic revamps to stay atop changing trends in consumer behavior, competitive forces, and industry landscapes.

Focusing excessively on brand image over benefits

While brand building for the long term is important, messaging still needs emphasis on tangible user benefits today. Flowery image-based messaging without grounding in real utility for customers can ring hollow.

Early messaging for satellite radio focused extensively on the novelty of national coverage, the number of stations, and buzzworthy celebrity content. By refocusing on crystal-clear reception, commercial-free music, and ubiquitous coast-to-coast access, providers such as SiriusXM connected with core motivations.

Ensure marketing campaigns balance aspirational brand building with specific benefit-driven claims. Flowery lifestyle imagery alone does not compel users. Intangible brand attributes need grounding in functional utility.

Relying too heavily on industry jargon

Highly technical messaging crammed with industry buzzwords and esoteric language risks confusing and alienating customers outside niche circles. Accessibility should be prioritized.

Early blockchain messaging was inundated with opaque references to decentralized ledgers, hashing algorithms, cryptographic proofs, and complex math. Mainstream audiences had little grasp of the benefits. Explaining security, transparency, and reduced fees in plain language proved more effective.

Avoid overusing specialized lingo. Translate capabilities into broadly relatable advantages using simpler constructs. While expertise should be conveyed, resist the temptation to get overly technical at the expense of clarity.

Even well-defined value propositions can flounder if teams neglect vigilant messaging discipline across all fronts. However, by avoiding the aforementioned common pitfalls, product managers can craft resonant narratives that deeply connect with markets. User-centricity must anchor all communication.

Summary

The chapter emphasized that clearly articulating the unique value a product delivers to customers is critical for driving adoption and growth. Without compelling messaging that resonates with target users, even the most innovative product will struggle to gain traction.

It outlined a strategic framework companies can follow to shape and disseminate a differentiated value proposition.

First, teams must dedicate significant effort to understanding their target customers and their needs through extensive research. This includes interviews, focus groups, user testing, and establishing ongoing advisory boards. Immersive techniques such as empathy mapping uncover nuances and worldviews. The goal is to gain deep insights into customer motivations, frustrations, and decision-making considerations.

With a firm handle on the user perspective, companies can define their value proposition by identifying key differentiators—capabilities that set their solution apart from competitors and status quo alternatives. Features should directly address user needs identified during research. Core benefits should highlight tangible improvements and emotional outcomes enabled. Teams can bring benefits to life through compelling use cases and customer success stories. This crystallizes consistent core messaging that captures the essence of the value proposition.

The next step is crafting a concise, memorable value proposition statement that distills the target customer, the problem being solved, the unique solution offered, and the key resulting benefit into a single compelling narrative. For example, `Mint.com` focused its statement on bringing financial clarity through intuitive tracking and control to simplify budgeting. Such crisp encapsulations become guiding North Stars.

With a value proposition defined, companies must still communicate it effectively through the right channels. This includes owned channels such as educational content, social media, and websites optimized to highlight differentiation. It also includes earned media such as PR, reviews, and testimonials that provide credible third-party validation. Paid advertising can target and scale tailored messaging to reach more ideal customer profiles. Touchpoints such as events, packaging, and product experiences also implicitly convey value. Each interaction is an opportunity to reinforce your platform's advantages.

Finally, the chapter highlighted pitfalls to avoid, such as focusing messaging on features versus benefits, failing to differentiate from competitors, using inconsistent messaging across channels, and not evolving messaging over time as user needs change. Teams that keep the user perspective at the center while relentlessly reinforcing coherent, benefit-driven messaging are best positioned for product-led growth.

This chapter provided start-ups with a strategic blueprint for defining, sharpening, and broadcasting their products' value propositions through rigorous customer understanding, differentiated messaging, and coordinated outreach across channels. The frameworks, examples, and best practices aim to equip teams to compellingly convey why their solution is the right choice over alternatives. The next chapter will provide you with a comprehensive playbook on how to systematically leverage experimentation through clear hypotheses, well-defined metrics, minimized biases, and analytics tools to rapidly iterate, test, and accelerate data-driven product optimizations for growth.

Questions

1. What are some key components of a strong value proposition?
2. Why is customer research so important for defining a value proposition?
3. How can companies bring their value proposition to life?
4. What are some best practices for crafting a value proposition statement?
5. Why is consistency across touchpoints important for communicating value?
6. How should companies evolve their value proposition over time?

Answers

1. A strong value proposition clearly articulates the target customer, their underserved needs, how your product uniquely solves those needs, and the key benefits realized. It conveys competitive differentiation and tangible outcomes users gain.

2. Customer understanding through research techniques such as interviews and testing is the foundation of defining value. It reveals pain points, motivations, and perspectives that inform credible, resonant messaging. Failing to do research risks erroneous assumptions about what users want.

3. Illustrative use cases and customer success stories make abstract benefits tangible. For example, explaining how a customer achieved a specific goal highlights real-world relevance. Vivid examples make the value prop vivid and relatable.

4. Exceptional statements concisely capture the target customer, their problem, your unique solution, and the key benefit realized. They distill the essence of your value prop into a crisp narrative flow from user need to end-result payoff.

5. Mixed messages dilute impact. A unified drumbeat focused on customer benefits across channels such as content, ads, website messaging, sales collateral, and product experience reinforces retention and credibility.

6. As products and user needs change, messaging should be reassessed and optimized regularly. However, core identity endures, so change with care to avoid dilution. Research and testing guide evolution.

Part 3:
A Successful
Product-Focused Strategy

Part 3 contains three chapters that delve into the operational aspects of implementing a customer-focused game plan. You'll learn validated methodologies concerning growth experiments, defining and tracking metrics, optimizing conversion flows, and boosting retention. The concluding section focuses on expansion revenue models and presents a vision for the future of the growth product manager role.

This part covers the following chapters:

- *Chapter 7, The Science of Growth Experiments and Testing for Product-Led Success*
- *Chapter 8, Define, Monitor, and Act on Your Performance Metrics*
- *Chapter 9, Guiding Your Clients to the Pot of Gold*

7

The Science of Growth Experimentation and Testing for Product-Led Success

Growth experimentation and testing have become a cornerstone of successful product-led growth in the fast-paced digital landscape. With consumers overwhelmed by a multitude of solutions, building a product alone is insufficient. To stand out, growth product managers must deeply understand users and iteratively optimize experiences through rigorous experimentation.

Growth testing provides the fuel for data-driven product refinements. By formulating hypotheses, running controlled experiments, and analyzing results, teams gain invaluable insights into user behavior. These learnings empower product managers to make informed decisions about improving funnels, evolving messaging, adding features, and more.

Without a focus on experimentation, product changes risk being guesses rather than informed bets. Teams that fail to systematically test and validate product-market fit will inevitably lose out to competitors who are optimizing experiences through research. In today's crowded field, relying on assumptions rather than data is a recipe for losing traction. There is also the risk of "groupthink" where team members end up agreeing with each other just to maintain social cohesion, rather than critically exploring products from an external user's perspective. It is important to continually gather outside feedback even after product release, as both user needs and competing offerings evolve rapidly. Failing to experiment and iterate based on real-world validation data means teams operate in a bubble, unaware of market shifts happening around them.

This chapter provides a comprehensive playbook on leveraging experimentation to accelerate product-led growth. We will cover core principles such as developing clear hypotheses, choosing proper success metrics, and creating structured testing processes. We will specifically explore the following topics:

- The importance of growth experimentation and testing in growth product management

- **Principles of growth experimentation**: Clear hypotheses, success metrics, and a structured testing process
- **Planning and executing effective growth experiments**: Selecting metrics, designing experiments, minimizing bias, and using analytics tools
- Analyzing experiment results and iterating on product features and marketing strategies
- **Types of growth experiments**: A/B testing, cohort analysis, funnel analysis, and more
- Empowering growth product managers for informed experimentation

By the end of this chapter, you will have acquired a comprehensive understanding of growth experimentation and testing as crucial drivers of product-led growth. Fundamental principles in growth experimentation will be covered, including the importance of defining clear hypotheses, establishing success metrics, and creating a structured testing process. You will also develop the ability to effectively plan and execute growth experiments, encompassing the selection of appropriate metrics and KPIs, the design of experiments that isolate specific variables, and strategies to minimize bias during experiment design and analysis.

Furthermore, you will gain insight into various common types of growth experiments, such as A/B testing, cohort analysis, and funnel analysis, and learn how to implement these techniques effectively. The chapter will also equip you with the necessary skills to leverage data and analytics in informing growth experimentation and testing, including setting up and utilizing analytics tools to track and measure experiment results. Finally, you will learn how to analyze experiment outcomes and apply iterative improvements to both product features and marketing strategies, facilitating continuous growth.

The significance of growth experimentation and user testing

In the high-stakes world of product-led growth, decisions can't be based on intuitive guesses or "gut feelings" alone. The path to success is paved with empirical insights derived from rigorous, controlled experimentation. When implemented systematically, experimentation serves as a powerful engine for innovation and a catalyst for exponential growth.

But what exactly makes disciplined experimentation so invaluable for product teams? What concrete strategic benefits does it confer? Let's explore the multifaceted value of embracing continuous controlled testing with a truly scientific mindset.

Reduced risk

Product innovation inherently carries risks. However, through small-scale experiments, teams can validate proposed changes and new features with a subset of users first before committing extensive development resources for a full-scale launch. This testing approach significantly mitigates risks of major quality issues slipping through or new capabilities not resonating as expected once released more widely. Experiments enable "testing the waters" to prevent big splashes.

For example, X (formerly Twitter) tested the waters with a small percentage of its user base when launching its Stories-like Fleets feature before rolling it out more broadly. This allowed them to gauge initial reception and work out issues on a smaller scale.

Accelerated learning

Experimentation offers the fastest path to learning. Rather than endlessly debating potential product changes qualitatively, teams can rapidly test creative ideas quantitatively with real users to gain empirical validation. Early user feedback testing helps steer products efficiently to meet emerging needs and desires. Disciplined experimentation enables compressing learning cycles from months to weeks.

For instance, Netflix routinely runs large-scale A/B tests with groups of subscribers to guide decisions on new content to produce and licensing deals to pursue based on empirical data.

Improved ROI

Testing also helps optimize **return on investment** (**ROI**) by identifying specific product modifications and positioning changes that will deliver outsized, needle-moving impact on key business metrics relative to the development effort required. Teams can double down on allocating resources to concepts that experiments prove users inherently want most, testing protects against squandered time by quantifying potential impact beforehand.

For example, Etsy used experimentation to determine that small visual changes to recommended products would lift revenues which guided decisions on where to allocate engineering time.

Increased agility

The smaller scale of controlled experiments enables much faster product iterations compared to prolonged development cycles. Testing provides an empirical basis for quickly pivoting when new concepts flop with users. This built-in feedback loop allows product teams to respond rapidly to dynamic, shifting user needs based on data versus gut feelings.

Fostered innovation

The freedom to quickly test creative but unproven ideas with target user groups fuels innovation. By avoiding punitive reactions to failure, teams are empowered to experiment rapidly with bold new innovations. Testing allows transforming potential failures into future successes through extracted learnings. Intelligent failure guides evolution.

For instance, Instagram wasn't deterred by the failure of the standalone Direct app. They extracted learnings about user messaging needs to integrate successful elements into Instagram itself.

Data-driven alignment

Testing provides objective data that rallies teams around hypotheses empirically validated by real user behavior instead of hunches or opinions. Controlled experiments give evidence to resolve internal debates and reinforce strategic priorities through facts discovered. Testing facilitates alignment on success metrics and focus.

Optimized user experiences

Testing also enables continuously honing products to remove usability friction points, optimize conversions, refine messaging tone and copy, and tailor experiences to maximize adoption, retention, and satisfaction rates. Every test provides an opportunity to learn how to improve engagement.

Sustained competitive advantage

Ultimately, a rigorous scientific testing mindset can foster a customer-centric organizational culture that learns faster and innovates ahead of rivals. Over time, mastering competency in experimentation creates barriers to competitors replicating success by embedding an organization-wide commitment to continuous learning and improvement.

Strategically leveraging experimentation means embracing a culture of questioning assumptions and proactively translating promising ideas and unknowns into testable hypotheses. Each hypothesis tested then uncovers valuable learning that feeds back into optimizing products, positioning, and marketing strategies based on empirical evidence versus hunches. But those learnings only happen through proper, meticulous execution. Next, we will dive into key principles that enable extracting clear, reliable insights from experiments.

Principles of growth experimentation

In the ever-evolving landscape of growth product management, success transcends mere chance; it demands the careful construction of experiments deeply rooted in rigorous methodology. This section aims to explore the fundamental aspects of crafting effective experiment design and its precise execution, all with the goal of unearthing transformative insights.

Designing and executing growth experiments with precision

Within the high-stakes realm of growth product management, success is not left to random fate; it emerges through the meticulous orchestration of experiments founded on a solid bedrock of rigorous methodology and execution. But what exactly defines effective experiment design and implementation? Throughout this comprehensive guide, we will unravel the intricacies of planning and executing controlled experiments that possess the potential to yield transformative insights.

Selecting strategic metrics

Every experiment seeks to reveal valuable insights about your product's performance or users' behavior. But those insights live within the metrics you choose to analyze. Not all metrics are created equal—the key is identifying ones aligned with your hypotheses and business objectives. Here's how to make the most of your metric selection:

- **Connect metrics to goals**: The first step is selecting metrics that directly map to the experiment's goals. If your aim is boosting user engagement, metrics such as session duration, **click-through rate (CTR)**, and retention become pivotal. But if you're testing ways to enhance revenue, conversion rate and average order value take priority.

- **Avoid analysis paralysis**: While more metrics give more perspectives, overloading experiments dilutes insights. Focus on a few KPIs that concisely illuminate the outcomes you care about most. Too many metrics confuse more than clarify.

> **Real-world example**
>
> A subscription service wants to improve retention, so they isolate key metrics such as user churn rate, subscription renewal rate, and time between renewals. These metrics provide clear signals on the experiment's impact on retention.

Crafting controlled experiments

Quality experiment design hinges on meticulously controlling variables to extract accurate, statistically significant insights. Techniques such as A/B testing shine by enabling apple-to-apple comparisons. Here's how to craft controlled experiments that yield genuine, scientifically valid insights:

- **The power of A/B testing**: A/B testing, also known as **split testing**, is a technique comparing two versions of a product or messaging. By keeping all variables constant except the one being tested, you can isolate the impact of that specific change on user behavior.

> **Real-world example**
>
> An e-commerce site wants to reduce cart abandonment. They test their current checkout flow against a simplified redesign by splitting visitors between the two experiences. By tracking conversion rates, they see which version better minimizes abandonments.

- **Reducing biases through randomization**: Randomly assigning users to control and test groups counters bias by evenly distributing variables across samples. This allows for a fair assessment of the change itself, not other human factors.

- **Blinding mitigates perception biases**: Blinding helps combat biases stemming from expectation. In a double-blind study, neither subjects nor researchers know group assignments. This yields untainted behaviors.

Leveraging controlled variables, representative randomness, and blinding ensures experiments produce genuine, scientifically valid insights.

Planning and executing effective growth experiments

1. **Create an experimentation roadmap**: Maintain a roadmap of upcoming tests documenting hypotheses, test leads, timing, scale, and expected impact. This provides visibility into experiment priorities and coordination.

2. **Secure adequate resources**: Verify your team has the data, engineering, and analysis bandwidth to support planned testing velocity and scale. Underpowered experiments waste effort.

3. **Write targeted hypotheses**: Sharpen hypotheses by focusing on specific, quantitatively measurable outcomes from high-impact changes tied to business goals. Vague hypotheses lead to muddled insights.

4. **Determine sample demographics**: Leverage statistical tools and power calculators to define the minimum sample size needed for statistical confidence in results. Overpowered tests limit launched features.

5. **Consider external factors**: Account for technological, regulatory, seasonal, or other external factors that may sway results for targeted user segments or markets. Pragmatic considerations strengthen experiment integrity.

As part of planning and executing growth experiments, once success metrics have been established as the North Star, there are additional critical elements to consider, including creating experiment roadmaps to coordinate tests and priorities; securing the necessary data, engineering, and analytics bandwidth; formulating targeted, measurable hypotheses; determining appropriate sample sizes; and accounting for external factors that may influence results. We will explore structured frameworks around each of those shortly. Before running any tests, it is also vital to discuss techniques for designing well-controlled experiments themselves, as the quality of experiment design hugely impacts the integrity of insights extracted. Core tenets of controlled design such as A/B testing, randomization, blinding, and leveraging analytics tools will be covered in the following subsections.

Designing controlled experiments

The quality of your experiment design plays a pivotal role in extracting accurate and statistically significant insights. Two essential techniques, A/B testing and randomization, are at the heart of designing controlled experiments.

Reducing biases through randomization

Randomly assigning users to control and test groups is essential to counteract bias by evenly distributing variables across samples. This approach allows for a fair assessment of the change itself, rather than the influence of other human factors.

Blinding mitigates perception biases

Blinding is a crucial technique for combating biases stemming from expectations. In a double-blind study, neither the subjects nor the researchers know the group assignments. This ensures that the observed behaviors are untainted by knowledge of which group they belong to, leading to more accurate results.

Leveraging analytics tools

Analytics tools are indispensable for collecting, analyzing, and interpreting data generated by growth experiments. Here are some key considerations when leveraging these tools:

- **Choose the right analytics platform**: Select an analytics platform that aligns with your experiment's objectives and allows for accurate data tracking. Popular choices include Google Analytics, Mixpanel, and Optimizely, each offering unique features and capabilities.

- **Implement proper tracking**: Ensure that you have robust tracking in place to collect data accurately. This may involve implementing event tracking, setting up conversion goals, and integrating with other data sources to obtain a holistic view of user behavior.

- **Continuous monitoring and analysis**: Monitor the data generated by your experiments in real time. Look for patterns, anomalies, and statistically significant differences between groups. Analytics tools can help automate this process and provide insights into which variants are performing better.

- **Iterate and optimize**: Use the insights gained from analytics tools to inform your next steps. If an experiment produces positive results, consider scaling the changes across your product or service. Conversely, if an experiment doesn't yield the desired outcomes, use the data to refine your approach and conduct further iterations.

Minimizing bias throughout the experiment

Beyond design, meticulous planning enables smooth experiment execution and reliable results. Here are key practices to consider:

- **Creating an experimentation roadmap**: Maintain a roadmap of upcoming tests documenting hypotheses, test leads, timing, scale, and expected impact. This provides visibility into experiment priorities and coordination.

- **Securing adequate resources**: Verify your team has the data, engineering, and analysis bandwidth to support planned testing velocity and scale. Underpowered experiments waste effort.

- **Writing targeted hypotheses**: Sharpen hypotheses by focusing on specific, quantitatively measurable outcomes from high-impact changes tied to business goals. Vague hypotheses lead to muddled insights.

- **Determining sample sizes**: Leverage statistical tools and power calculators to define the minimum sample size needed for statistical confidence in results. Overpowered tests limit launched features.

- **Considering external factors**: Account for technological, regulatory, seasonal, or other external factors that may sway results for targeted user segments or markets. Pragmatic considerations strengthen experiment integrity.

By investing in meticulous planning and support structures, teams enable continuous optimization through trusted experiment results. Now, let's see these practices come together through a real-world example.

Optimization in action – testing to boost app retention

Let's consider that a fitness app wants to improve user retention. They start with a measurable hypothesis:

"Sending onboarding emails will increase 30-day retention by 10%"

They design an A/B test with 100,000 new users randomly split between a control group receiving no emails and a test group receiving onboarding emails. The product team remains blinded to the groups to avoid bias.

The key metric measured is the day 30 retention rate. After the 30-day experiment period, the test group retained users at a 9.2% higher rate, confirming the positive impact of onboarding emails.

This example demonstrates how disciplined methodology transforms assumptions into insights to guide optimization. Next, we'll cover statistical techniques to support reliable analysis.

Analyzing experiment results and iterating on product features and marketing strategies

The true measure of an experiment's impact lies in what happens after the data is collected. A thorough analysis of results provides pivotal insights into the efficacy of changes tested, illuminating what resonated with users and what fell flat. Armed with these learnings, teams can determine the next steps around iterating, pivoting, or scaling successful changes.

Let's explore best practices for extracting actionable insights from experiment analysis to fuel ongoing optimization:

- **Compare control and test groups**: The crux of result analysis involves juxtaposing the performance of control and test groups against your defined success metrics. Did the test group exhibit a lift in conversion rates, engagement, or other KPIs compared to the control? Statistical significance testing quantifies the likelihood that results were due to chance.

  For example, an e-commerce site might find their redesigned product page led to a 2.3% increase in add-to-cart rate compared to the old page. However, significance testing reveals the results are not statistically significant, meaning the uplift could be random noise. No change is warranted.

- **Analyze qualitative feedback**: Quantitative metrics alone don't tell the whole story. Surveys, social media monitoring, and customer support interactions can provide qualitative insights into why certain changes succeeded or failed. This human context enables interpreting ambiguous quantitative results.

  For instance, a drop in engagement metrics might be explained by user complaints about intrusive notifications. The root cause is illuminated by qualitative data even when quantitative data is unclear.

- **Assess results' alignment with hypothesis**: Revisiting your original hypothesis and considering results provides perspective on whether the experiment confirmed or invalidated your assumptions. Don't ignore unexpected findings that emerge. Rigorously questioning assumptions in an unbiased way leads to the most powerful learnings.

- **Determine next steps**: With a full picture of what the data says, determine appropriate next steps. Successful changes showing strong statistical significance may warrant scaling the features or messaging across your entire user base. However, smaller wins might require additional validation through repeat testing. Non-significant results call for refinement and retesting or moving on.

Real-world example – optimizing app onboarding

A fitness app wanted to improve user retention, so they hypothesized that adding onboarding videos would increase 30-day retention by 5%.

They tested two versions of the app, one with just their standard onboarding flow and one with onboarding videos added. After analyzing results, the video version retained users at a 7% higher rate, confirming their hypothesis.

However, further analysis showed lower video completion rates than expected. Reviewing user feedback uncovered onboarding was still too complex. Videos helped but didn't address core issues.

This led the team to fully redesign the onboarding flow for greater simplicity before investing further in video content. The qualitative insights were key to determining the right optimization path despite the positive quantitative metrics. To further empower your approach to experimentation and product optimization, consider the following key principles.

Embracing a growth mindset

When experiment results are underwhelming, avoid seeing it as a failure. A growth mindset views every test as an opportunity to learn and refine. Negative results provide lessons to create better hypotheses and features in future tests.

For example, Instagram placing less emphasis on chronological feeds after initial user backlash taught important lessons about balancing algorithmic relevance with user expectations. This informed how they evolved feed algorithms moving forward.

Continuous optimization fuels growth

No single test provides all the answers. Optimizing products and positioning is a continuous journey of experimentation, analysis, and iteration. But with a rigorous focus on extracting insights from past tests to inform future innovation, teams can accelerate product-market fit.

Analysis and iteration transform superficial data points into actionable strategic insights that ultimately elevate user experiences. By maintaining a growth mindset and focusing on continuous improvement, teams leverage experimentation to sustainably propel product-led success.

Thoughtful analysis converts ambiguous experiment data into clear actions. Best practices include the following:

- **Checking statistical significance**: Calculate p-values to determine the probability results occurred by chance. P-values under 0.05 give high confidence group differences were statistically significant, not random.

- **Accounting for confounding factors**: Consider external factors such as seasonality and technical issues when analyzing results. Causation doesn't always equal correlation. Critically examine multiple possible explanations.

- **Avoiding cherry-picking data**: Don't just spotlight metrics showing positive outcomes. Analyze the full picture—conflicting data often provides the most powerful learnings.

- **Adding qualitative insights**: Supplement quantitative metrics with qualitative data from surveys, interviews, and support tickets to understand the human "why" behind the "what."

- **Reproducing results**: Verify reproducibility by rerunning experiments across audience segments before scaling changes. Consistency confirms reliability.

- **Synthesizing learnings**: Compile experiment highlights, recommendations, implications, and next steps into shareable reports distributed to stakeholders. Facilitate organization-wide learning.

Growth experiments wield their full potential only when backed by rigorous methodology, planning, execution, and analysis. By embracing these best practices, product teams can translate promising ideas into validated insights that propel product-led success. The future belongs to organizations that harness testing as a core competitive advantage. With this comprehensive guidebook, you now hold the key to uncovering your product's full potential through evidence-based experimentation. Ready to start unlocking growth? Let us dive into different types of growth experiments in the next section.

Types of growth experiments

In the labyrinthine world of growth product management, informed decisions are currency, and data is the goldmine from which it's extracted. As a growth product manager, your toolkit is incomplete without a trio of potent analytical techniques: A/B testing, cohort analysis, and funnel analysis. These techniques aren't just tools; they're compasses that navigate you through the complexities of user behavior, helping you refine strategies, optimize user experiences, and ignite the flames of sustained growth. Let's delve into each of these techniques and explore how they can revolutionize your growth strategy.

A/B testing – crafting the perfect blend of impact and innovation

At the heart of growth experimentation lies A/B testing—a method that epitomizes the essence of controlled exploration. This technique is particularly effective for scrutinizing changes in design, copy, and user experience.

> **Real-world example**
>
> Imagine an e-commerce platform contemplating a redesign of its home page. The product team develops two versions—the current design (*A*) and a new, sleeker version (*B*). By conducting an A/B test, the team randomly assigns users to either version *A* or *B* and measures metrics such as CTR, conversion rates, and time spent on the page. The result? Insights into which design resonates better with users, enabling the team to optimize the home page and enhance user engagement.

Valuable insight

When executing A/B tests, remember the significance of statistical significance. Ensure that the sample size is large enough to make valid conclusions. Additionally, isolate variables to attribute changes accurately, and be cautious of "novelty" effects—users might initially prefer a new design simply because it's fresh, but that might not be a lasting preference.

Cohort analysis – understanding the evolution of user groups

While A/B testing peers into the nuances of individual changes, cohort analysis dives into the broader spectrum of user behavior. Cohort analysis involves grouping users based on specific characteristics, such as sign-up date, and then tracking their behavior over time. This technique helps you uncover how different user groups interact with the product and identify trends and patterns.

> **Real-world example**
>
> Picture a mobile gaming app that releases new levels every week. Through cohort analysis, the product team categorizes users based on the week they started playing. By tracking retention rates, engagement levels, and in-app purchases over subsequent weeks for each cohort, the team gains insights into how different user groups engage with the new content and whether retention strategies need adjustments. Microsoft also leveraged cohort analysis to assess which day of the week to release Windows security updates. By tracking stability metrics and support call volumes for groups who received updates on different weekdays, they ultimately landed on releasing on Tuesdays—now known industry-wide as Patch Tuesday. This cohort-driven approach provided data to guide the update timing decision.

Valuable insight

When conducting cohort analysis, focus on the right metrics for each cohort. Cohorts might exhibit varying behavior, so tailor your analysis accordingly. Also, bear in mind that not all cohort differences are significant; some might be due to seasonality or other external factors. Contextual understanding is key.

Funnel analysis – paving the path of conversion

Growth doesn't unfold like a single event; it's a journey through stages of conversion. Funnel analysis illuminates this journey by tracking user interactions across different stages—such as sign-up, activation, and purchase—and identifying drop-offs at each stage. This technique is your GPS through the landscape of user engagement, helping you pinpoint areas that need optimization.

> **Real-world example**
>
> Consider a subscription-based service aiming to enhance its conversion rates. By analyzing the funnel—starting from user sign-up to activation and ultimately to subscription—product managers can identify bottlenecks. If a significant number of users drop off after signing up but before activating, the team knows where to direct its optimization efforts.

Valuable insight

Funnel analysis doesn't just unveil the where; it also sheds light on the why. Utilize user feedback, surveys, and qualitative insights to understand why users drop off at specific stages. Remember that funnels are iterative; even minor changes in the user journey can yield substantial improvements.

In the realm of growth product management, success is the offspring of insights, and insights are born from data. A/B testing, cohort analysis, and funnel analysis aren't just tools; they're your allies in your quest for data-driven growth. A/B testing empowers you to sculpt experiences, cohort analysis unveils behavior trends, and funnel analysis guides users along the path of conversion.

As you harness these techniques, remember that data is not static; it's a river that flows with user interactions, preferences, and choices. As a growth product manager, your role is to navigate this river, steering your product toward the shores of innovation and user-centricity. Armed with the knowledge of A/B testing, cohort analysis, and funnel analysis, you're poised to orchestrate growth strategies that transcend speculation and embrace the precision of insights.

Empowering growth product managers for informed experimentation

In the dynamic landscape of growth product management, intuition and instinct have paved the way for data-driven strategies. As a growth product manager, your decisions aren't merely fueled by gut feelings—they're steered by the insights that data and analytics provide. In this section, we delve into the pivotal role of data and analytics in driving informed experimentation, optimizing user experiences, and orchestrating growth strategies that transcend speculation.

Analytics tools setup – crafting the infrastructure of insights

Picture data as the raw material from which insights are forged, and analytics tools as the furnaces that transform this raw material into invaluable insights. The setup of robust analytics tools is the foundation upon which your data-driven growth experiments stand.

The first step is selecting the right analytics tools. Platforms such as Google Analytics, Mixpanel, and Amplitude are treasure troves of information, providing real-time data on user interactions, behaviors, and preferences. These tools offer insights into the journeys users embark upon within your product, illuminating the paths they take, the challenges they face, and the opportunities they encounter.

Implementing tracking mechanisms within your product allows these tools to capture every interaction, from clicks and scrolls to feature usage and conversions. These mechanisms serve as your eyes and ears, collecting data that paints a vivid picture of user behavior and engagement.

> **Real-world example**
>
> Consider an e-commerce platform implementing Google Analytics. By tracking user behavior, the product team can identify which products are frequently viewed but not purchased, indicating potential issues in the conversion process. This insight prompts the team to optimize the checkout process, resulting in higher conversion rates.

Data-informed decision-making – the art of insightful direction

Data is more than numbers on a screen; it's a symphony of user stories, behaviors, and preferences. The true power of data lies in its ability to guide decisions, shaping strategies that resonate with users and drive growth.

Data-driven decision-making involves both quantitative and qualitative data. Quantitative data, such as CTR and conversion rates, offers numerical insights. Qualitative data, derived from user feedback, surveys, and interviews, adds depth and context to the numbers, helping you understand the "why" behind the "what."

Through data analysis, growth product managers can identify pain points that users encounter within your product. High bounce rates on a specific page might indicate a confusing layout, while low engagement on a feature might point to its lack of utility. Armed with these insights, you can prioritize enhancements that directly address user challenges.

In the realm of strategic decision-making, however, the concept of being *data-informed* emerges as a nuanced and balanced approach. While data and its analysis play a pivotal role, it is equally crucial to harmonize this quantitative perspective with human intuition and creativity. The fixation on data alone, often rooted in past patterns, can inadvertently stifle innovation and limit the potential for forward-thinking strategies. The essence of a *data-informed* approach lies in leveraging data as a valuable guide rather than an absolute determinant. Let's understand the two approaches further and how the balanced approach could yield superior results for growth product managers.

Data-informed approach versus data-driven approach

The following are the major differences between a data-informed approach and a data-driven approach:

- **Data-informed approach**:
  - **Definition**: A data-informed approach integrates data as a significant input but not the exclusive driver of decisions. It combines quantitative and qualitative insights with human expertise and intuition.
  - **Characteristics**: Decision-makers consider data alongside industry knowledge, experience, and intuition, fostering a flexible and adaptive approach that allows for creativity and innovation.
  - **Flexibility**: Openness to adjusting strategies based on a combination of data findings and contextual understanding.
  - **Human element**: Acknowledges the importance of human judgment and creativity in interpreting and acting upon data.

- **Data-driven approach**:
  - **Definition**: A data-driven approach heavily relies on data analysis to inform decisions. Decisions are predominantly made based on statistical patterns, trends, and quantitative insights.
  - **Characteristics**: Decision-makers depend heavily on data, sometimes rigidly adhering to historical patterns without considering external factors or intuitive insights.
  - **Rigidity**: Tendency to stick strictly to data findings without considering external factors or intuitive insights.

- **Past-focused**: Often leans on historical data, which may not be forward-looking or adaptive to changing circumstances.

Benefits of a data-informed approach

In navigating the complex landscape of decision-making, embracing a data-informed approach offers a dynamic synthesis of quantitative insights and human intuition, fostering a decision-making environment that transcends the constraints of rigid data-driven methodologies. Some of the benefits of a data-informed approach include the following:

- **Balanced decision-making**: Integrating data with intuition facilitates a balanced decision-making process, preventing overreliance on historical patterns and encouraging adaptability to changing circumstances

- **Fosters innovation:** By avoiding a fixation solely on past data, a data-informed approach provides room for creative thinking and innovative solutions that might not be apparent in historical trends

- **Contextual understanding**: Recognizes that data is most valuable when interpreted in context, and human judgment plays a crucial role in understanding the nuances

- **Agility in decision-making**: Enables quicker responses to emerging trends or unexpected challenges, as decisions are not bound by historical data alone

Real-world example

Imagine a tech company launching a new software feature based on **user behavior analytics (UBA)**. While data may reveal patterns in feature usage, a data-informed decision involves considering qualitative feedback and the broader market context. If user engagement drops after an update, qualitative data might uncover user dissatisfaction due to a change in the user interface. A data-informed response would then involve not just reverting to the previous version based on data but also incorporating user feedback to enhance the user experience further. This holistic approach ensures decisions are not solely dictated by data but are enriched by human insights, leading to more effective and user-centric outcomes.

Another example can be found during the COVID-19 pandemic. The CEO of a hotel booking platform faced a critical challenge. An immediate, data-driven response to the crisis – plummeting hotel bookings and financial uncertainty – would typically lead to downsizing or pausing operations. However, with the strategic guidance of Tim Cakir, a growth consultant, the CEO adopted a data-informed approach. Recognizing the opportunity in the crisis, Tim advised leveraging the downtime to upgrade the hotels' digital infrastructure. Despite the daunting data, they offered to revamp the technology systems of these hotels for free, preparing them for a post-pandemic recovery. This forward-thinking strategy, blending data insights with visionary thinking, resulted in a significant payoff. As travel resumed, the platform emerged as a market leader, equipped with a stronger, more loyal customer base.

In a world increasingly driven by data, it's crucial to remember that numbers alone don't hold all the answers. Balancing a data-driven mindset with a data-informed approach is key to innovative and empathetic decision-making. While data-driven methods rely on past and present metrics to guide decisions, a data-informed perspective integrates these insights with human intuition, creativity, and foresight. This balance allows us to not only respond to the current trends but to anticipate and shape future ones. It's about using data not as a rigid rulebook, but as a compass, guiding us through the complexities of human behavior and market dynamics. (*Tim Cakir, Growth Consultant and AI Addict*)

Experimentation is the lifeblood of growth, often commencing with assumptions that serve as stepping stones toward innovation. However, it is the discerning lens of data that acts as the ultimate arbiter of truth in this journey. By meticulously analyzing user behaviors, one can either validate or debunk these assumptions, anchoring growth strategies in the tangible reality of user interactions rather than speculative notions.

Yet, the journey from raw data to actionable insights is not a direct path. Raw data requires meticulous processing, and normalization techniques become the architects of clarity. Metrics, when subjected to the scrutiny of mean, median, and mode averages, not only account for but also minimize the impact of outlier data points, creating a more refined perspective. Further refinement comes from triangulating normalized data from diverse sources, providing a comprehensive foundation for accurate trend analysis. This process transforms experiments from speculative hypotheses into concrete learnings, propelling continual optimization.

Growth product managers, tasked with navigating this intricate landscape, must heed the call for a balanced approach. Their ability to unearth new revenue opportunities hinges not just on intuition but on the judicious use of data to validate hypotheses. The journey from assumptions to insights is a dynamic interplay of creativity and analytical rigor. It is the integration of these elements that sustains a growth product manager's capacity for continuous improvement, ensuring they stay attuned to the ever-evolving marketplace and dynamic competition.

While data analysis anchors decisions in tangible insights, it is the symbiosis of intuition and analytics – that is, the data-informed approach – that empowers growth product managers to not only uncover opportunities but also to perpetually refine and elevate their strategies.

The symphony of growth

In the realm of growth product management, data and analytics aren't just tools—they're the orchestra that orchestrates your growth symphony. The harmonious blend of quantitative insights and qualitative context crafts a narrative that guides your experiments, enriches your user experiences, and propels your product toward sustained growth.

As you embark on your journey of data-driven experimentation, remember that the insights you unearth are the bridges that connect your product to the hearts and minds of your users. It's a journey of evolution, adaptation, and refinement—a journey where data isn't just a passive observer; it's your co-pilot, your compass, and your catalyst for innovation. Armed with the insights of analytics tools and the wisdom of data-driven decision-making, you're equipped to navigate the intricate currents of growth with confidence and precision.

Decoding experiment analysis and iteration for ongoing growth

In the realm of growth product management, every experiment is a voyage—a voyage from hypothesis to insight, from data to decision. Yet, the journey doesn't culminate with data collection; it transcends into the realm of analysis and iteration. As a growth product manager, your role extends beyond experimentation; it's about harnessing the power of analysis to pave the path for ongoing growth. In this section, we delve into the intricacies of analyzing experiment results, embracing an invaluable growth mindset, and the art of iteration that keeps your product on the trajectory of evolution.

Analyzing experiment results – the pillars of informed decision-making

When the curtains fall on an experiment, a new phase of enlightenment begins. This phase hinges upon the thorough analysis of experiment results—a process that provides insights into the efficacy of the changes, the resonance of user interactions, and the impact on the chosen success metrics.

The crux of result analysis lies in comparing the performance of the control and experimental groups. By juxtaposing these two groups against the chosen success metrics, you unveil the narrative of impact. Did the changes lead to improved conversion rates, higher engagement, or increased revenue?

Experiment results lay the foundation for strategic decisions. Depending on the outcomes, you have several avenues to explore. If the experimental group outperforms the control group, implementing changes across the product might be the next step. If the results are inconclusive or subpar, it's time to reassess the changes, iterate, or even discard the feature altogether.

> **Real-world example**
>
> Imagine a fitness app testing a gamified rewards system to boost user engagement. After analysis, it was revealed that the experimental group demonstrated a notable increase in daily app usage and interaction. Armed with this insight, the product team decided to implement the rewards system across the entire user base.

Embracing a growth mindset – embracing failure as an ally

In the arena of growth experimentation, the dichotomy of success and failure is reframed. Failure isn't a culmination; it's a catalyst for innovation. Embracing a growth mindset is paramount as you navigate the landscape of experiment analysis and decision-making.

Not every experiment yields a resounding success, and that's perfectly fine. Each experiment, whether it results in desired outcomes or not, carries with it a treasure trove of insights. "Failures" are opportunities to learn, refine strategies, and unearth hidden nuances that might lead to more impactful experiments in the future.

A growth mindset compels you to iterate and adapt based on experiment results. If the outcomes are underwhelming, don't see it as a setback. View it as a stepping stone toward an enhanced strategy. Iterate on the changes, tweak variables, and experiment anew. The journey of growth is paved with continuous iteration.

> **Real-world insight**
>
> A mobile app introducing a new feature to enhance social interactions experiences a lukewarm response in the initial experiment. Instead of discarding the idea, the product team analyzes feedback and usage patterns. They discover that users find value in the concept but are deterred by a convoluted user interface. Armed with this insight, they iterate on the design, simplifying the interface, and conduct a new experiment with promising results.

The symphony of evolution

In the grand orchestra of growth product management, experiment analysis and iteration are the harmonies that elevate your product to new heights. It's not about singular experiments; it's about the collective symphony of insights and adaptations that fuel ongoing growth.

As you stand at the crossroads of experiment analysis and decision-making, remember that your role isn't just about interpreting numbers—it's about shaping the trajectory of your product. Embrace a growth mindset, where every experiment, whether a triumph or a learning experience, propels you toward innovation and progress. Armed with the wisdom of analysis and the courage of iteration, you're poised to orchestrate a symphony of evolution—one where growth isn't an endpoint but a perpetual journey of discovery and refinement.

Summary

In this chapter, I have provided a comprehensive guide for leveraging experimentation to drive product-led growth. It emphasized how testing and validating ideas with real user data enables continuously improving products and experiences in a sustainable way.

We first covered the immense value proposition of experimentation, including reduced risk, accelerated learning, improved ROI, increased agility, fostered innovation, data-driven alignment, and optimized user experiences. This establishes an imperative for rigorously testing assumptions.

Key principles for effective growth testing were then explored in detail. This included formulating clear, measurable hypotheses connected to business goals. Choosing appropriate success metrics aligned with objectives was highlighted while avoiding analysis paralysis through too many vanity metrics.

Proper controlled experiment design was also covered extensively, including A/B testing techniques, randomness, and blinding to isolate variables. The chapter also stressed detailed planning for tests and securing adequate resources. Writing targeted hypotheses, determining minimum sample sizes, and accounting for external factors were also discussed as crucial for reliable, impactful experiments.

Various experiment types were then detailed, including funnel analysis for finding conversion bottlenecks, cohort analysis for longitudinal user insights, and multivariate testing for complex variable optimization. The pivotal role of analytics tools in gathering qualitative and quantitative data was also discussed in depth.

Finally, I covered in this chapter best practices for sound analysis, such as examining statistical significance, reviewing qualitative insights, and assessing alignment with hypotheses. A growth mindset that treats setbacks as opportunities for refinement was encouraged. Continuously iterating experiments based on insights was positioned as critical for evolution.

By internalizing these disciplines around controlled tests, analytics, a growth mindset, and continuous iteration, product managers can systematically optimize customer experiences, accelerate product-market fit, and ultimately drive sustainable business growth. In this next chapter, we will equip you with the knowledge and strategies needed to harness the power of performance metrics for informed decision-making and sustainable growth within your product-led organization.

Questions

1.   What are some key principles of effective growth experimentation?

2.   What are some common types of growth experiments?

3.   How can teams design rigorous experiments?

4.   Why is a growth mindset important for experimentation?

5.   How are analytics tools used in experimentation?

6.   What does sound analysis of experiment results involve?

Answers

1. Key principles include developing clear hypotheses, choosing proper success metrics, following a structured testing process, minimizing biases, and leveraging analytics tools to gather data.

2. Common experiments include A/B testing, funnel analysis, cohort analysis, multivariate testing, and using analytics tools. Each provides unique insights.

3. Use techniques such as A/B testing, blinding, and randomness to isolate variables and reduce bias. Determine appropriate sample sizes for statistical significance.

4. A growth mindset views setbacks as opportunities to refine hypotheses and ideas. It encourages iteration rather than giving up when results underwhelm.

5. Analytics tools collect quantitative and qualitative data on user behaviors and product performance to extract insights from experiments.

6. Sound analysis examines statistical significance, looks for qualitative insights, checks alignment with hypotheses, reproduces results, and synthesizes learnings for stakeholders.

8

Define, Monitor, and Act on Your Performance Metrics

Effective product management hinges on having a precise understanding of how your existing products are performing as well as accurately projecting and measuring the potential impact of new or unreleased products. Defining the right performance metrics provides the clarity needed to make data-driven decisions that optimize the customer experience, convert users into loyal customers, and fuel business growth.

This chapter will provide a strategic framework for identifying, monitoring, analyzing, and acting on performance metrics to maximize your product's success. Specifically, we will cover the following topics:

- The importance of performance metrics
- Defining the right performance metrics to align with business objectives and product strategy
- Monitoring and analyzing performance metrics
- Using performance metrics to drive growth
- Analyzing experiment results and iterating on product features and marketing strategies
- Establishing a performance-driven culture

You will learn how to define, monitor, analyze, and act on the right metrics to optimize the customer journey, inform smart product investments, rally teams around shared objectives, and propel sustainable business growth.

Equipped with these capabilities, you can leverage metrics as a core competitive advantage to deliver tremendous customer value, outpace rivals, and accomplish business goals with precision.

Now, let's explore how to harness metrics to unlock growth.

The strategic importance of performance metrics

Performance metrics are the oxygen for growth. In today's digital landscape, leveraging the right metrics and optimizing them is essential for product teams to drive impact and achieve success. However, many teams struggle to identify and fully harness the metrics that matter most.

Precise performance metrics serve as the compass guiding products to accomplish key outcomes. By quantifying product health across areas such as acquisition, activation, engagement, retention, and revenue, metrics provide empirical insights to assess where things stand and inform data-driven improvement efforts.

For example, a SaaS company may track new free trial signups over time and find that new registrations have been declining quarter-over-quarter. This highlights an opportunity to diagnose issues in the acquisition funnel and refine strategies to regain momentum. Additionally, monitoring the retention rate could reveal increasing churn among long-term paid users. This signals potential problems with delivering ongoing value that warrant investigation. Let's explore the core strategic reasons why performance metrics are vital for modern digital products across these dimensions:

- To quantify product health and performance
- To mitigate risk
- To focus innovation on validated user needs
- To increase team alignment
- To speed up iteration and adaptation
- To optimize user journeys end-to-end
- To fuel data-driven decision-making

Metrics provide empirical insights into all aspects of product performance including user acquisition, activation, engagement, renewal, and revenue growth. Quantifying these areas enables data-driven assessments of product health and guides improvement efforts.

For example, monitoring new user signup trends over time quickly reveals whether acquisition efforts are gaining or losing momentum. Tracking retention rate metrics highlights potential issues with the user experience or value proposition.

Mitigate risk

Continuous monitoring of metrics provides an early warning system to proactively identify risks and prevent downstream failures. Metrics such as technical errors, customer complaints, and churn can flag issues at their onset before they snowball into larger problems. Proactive mitigation minimizes blind spots.

As an example, a sudden spike in loading errors for a mobile app can signify emerging infrastructure problems. Catching this early allows rapid fixes before it severely degrades the user experience. In fact, research done by Google shows that mobile users have very little patience for slow-loading apps, with some statistics showing that up to 57% of users will abandon an app that takes longer than three seconds to load. This demonstrates the importance of performance and load times in mobile app experience and retention.

Focus innovation on validated user needs

Metrics provide invaluable visibility into customer pain points and feature needs. This focuses product development and innovation on delivering solutions with empirically validated market demand rather than on guessing what users might want.

For instance, gradual declines in time spent per session could indicate waning engagement that points to opportunities to enhance core features and value. Validated needs drive priorities.

Increase team alignment

Defining shared metrics across functions such as product, engineering, marketing, and support fosters alignment on common objectives and outcomes. This breaks down functional silos in favor of unified data-driven execution.

Marketing may focus on visitor and trial signup metrics while the product team looks at engagement. Shared metrics get them collaborating to drive end-to-end funnel optimization.

Speed up iteration and adaptation

Access to real-time metrics enables rapid testing of new ideas with users, learning from feedback, and adapting products to build customer-centric experiences faster. A tighter iteration loop powered by data delivers greater agility.

For example, experimenting with tweaks to onboarding flows based on user drop-off data points to optimization opportunities much faster than prolonged qualitative research alone.

Optimize user journeys end-to-end

Metrics identify friction points and drop-offs within user journeys to focus optimization efforts on crafting tailored, seamless experiences. This enables smoothing flows, refining messaging, and enhancing features to maximize adoption and satisfaction.

Funnel analysis often reveals a high fall-off at signup. This metric's insight informs tailored messaging and streamlined flows to reduce barriers to entry.

Fuel data-driven decision-making

Comprehensive performance metrics enable justifying strategic investments and trade-offs backed by data rather than hunches or gut feelings alone. Metrics ground decisions in customer reality rather than speculation, sharpening capital allocation.

For example, metrics may show that a new feature drove a 15% increase in retention rate. This data-driven insight clearly validates further investment in expanding that feature.

As growth product managers, we can pitch story ideas and frameworks to respected publishers such as the **Harvard Business Review** (**HBR**) to provide more evidence-based guidance to buyers and practitioners through their articles.

For instance, growth topics such as retargeting and lead scoring have a huge business impact but limited empirical analysis. We can suggest that HBR write rigorously researched, data-driven articles on topics such as the following:

- Optimizing retargeting spend and nurture streams to increase ROI on marketing investments and accelerate growth
- Applying evidence-based analysis to address common myths around lead scoring methodologies and home in on approaches that truly improve lead quality
- Guiding marketers on effectively leveraging new technologies such as AI and big data to experiment and optimize programs powered by empirical insights
- Providing continuous learning frameworks and emerging research to help marketers upskill amid rapidly changing digital environments
- Improving performance across revenue teams by addressing flawed assumptions in lead management that create downstream sales effects
- Leveraging HBR's neutral, trusted perspective to bring consensus across industries on best practices in areas with currently conflicting views such as account-based marketing

Evidence-based perspectives tuned to the practical realities that marketers face would provide immense value. The HBR has an opportunity to fill a major gap through compelling and rigorous analysis of topics central to modern marketing success.

To see these benefits in action, let's look at an example.

> **Real-world example: FabFitFun's metrics-driven activation improvement**
>
> FabFitFun offers a subscription box service shipping customized kits of full-sized wellness, beauty, and lifestyle products to members. By leveraging metrics, it uncovered an activation issue: many new subscribers were not engaging beyond the initial signup. Analyzing onboarding funnel metrics revealed a high drop-off at the content personalization step. Further qualitative research highlighted **user experience** (**UX**) friction. In response, FabFitFun optimized the signup flow to be more intuitive and seamless. This drove higher activation rates, increasing retention and revenue.

With the right metrics foundation powering data-driven optimization, product teams can maximize their chances of crafting customer-centric experiences that convert and delight.

Defining the right performance metrics

The strategic importance of performance metrics is clear. However, metrics are only valuable when they provide meaningful insights tied to business goals. This requires thoughtful selection of the right metrics and hands-on leveraging to unlock their full potential.

Defining the right metrics aligned to business goals provides a crucial foundation. But metrics only unlock their full potential when leveraged through robust monitoring and analysis to extract meaningful insights that drive strategy and optimization. Let's start by exploring some of the critical success factors when defining your performance metrics.

Connecting metrics to business objectives

Always ground metrics in business objectives and strategies. What outcomes define success? Common goals include the following:

- **Acquisition**: Visitors, signups, demos
- **Engagement**: DAU (daily active users)/MAU (monthly active users), session length, feature adoption
- **Revenue**: ARR (annual recurring revenue), churn, CAC (customer acquisition cost) payback period
- **Satisfaction**: NPS (net promoter score), CSAT (customer satisfaction score), reviews

When identifying the right performance metrics, it is crucial to tightly connect them to overarching business goals and desired outcomes. However, we must also consider other critical factors such as avoiding vanity metrics, keeping the quantity focused, iterating metrics over time, and leveraging analytics platforms:

- **Avoid vanity metrics**: Vanity metrics seem positive but don't demonstrate progress toward goals. For example, the number of app downloads doesn't necessarily indicate engaged, retained users.

- **Keep metric quantity focused**: While more metrics provide more perspectives, an overload obscures priority. Seek the smallest viable set that gives you a high signal on the customer journey and business health.

- **Iterate metrics over time**: As products and strategies evolve, revisit metrics to ensure continued relevance. Certain metrics become important over time.

  For example, early-stage startups may focus more on acquisition and activation metrics. More mature companies shift emphasis to retention, referrals, and lifetime value.

- **Leverage analytics platforms**: Platforms such as Amplitude, Mixpanel, and Looker make gathering metrics easier. Tap capabilities such as funnels, cohorts, and retention to uncover insights.

  But don't just report metrics—closely analyze them to understand customer journeys and experiences. Metrics only serve their purpose when translated into insights that guide actions.

By thoughtfully selecting metrics tied to goals, avoiding vanity metrics, and revisiting them over time, you can maintain focus on the outcomes that truly matter for product success.

Monitoring and analyzing performance metrics

Once the right metrics are defined, diligent monitoring and analysis unlock their power to inform product strategy:

- **Automate dashboards and reporting**: Automating dashboards provides real-time visibility into metric performance and trends. Configure alerts on thresholds to enable agile responses. Leading analytics tools such as Amplitude and Mixpanel enable easy dashboarding. Set these up to monitor key metrics daily. Use Slack or email alerts for priority metrics such as system errors. Consider integrating these dashboards with your organization's CRM system to provide cross-functional visibility into metrics tied to customer experience and satisfaction. Having this single source of truth empowers teams across the organization to analyze performance data, identify issues, and collaborate on solutions.

- **Segment across relevant dimensions**: Break down metrics across dimensions such as user types, cohorts, marketing channels, geos, and usage tiers. Differences can reveal improvement areas for tailored optimization.

  For example, an e-commerce site may find conversion rates vary across traffic sources. This analysis could inform tailored onboarding flows optimized for each channel.

- **Identify trends and outliers**: Look beyond isolated data points to uncover trends, correlations, and anomalies. Changing dynamics or unusual patterns often signal opportunities or issues.

  A sudden drop in new trials may indicate problems with acquisition channels. These trends inform investigation and intervention to mitigate risks.

- **Connect to user outcomes**: Tie analysis back to actual user outcomes. How do metrics reflect the ability to meet user goals? Ground data in human experiences and needs.

Feature usage metrics mean little without being tied back to user jobs-to-be-done. Identify gaps between metrics and ideal jobs-being-done to guide strategy.

- **Leverage segmentation**: Break down metrics by relevant segments such as user cohorts, marketing channels, and demographics. Differing outcomes can guide tailored optimization.

  For example, a media site sees lower retention for users referred through social channels. This difference highlights opportunities to refine targeting and messaging.

- **Run cohort analysis**: Analyze metric patterns over time across user cohorts. This reveals how behavior evolves and provides early signals on issues impacting certain cohorts.

  For instance, examining weekly retention cohorts helps identify potential retention dipping with recent cohorts that warrant intervention.

- **Monitor growth and decline rates**: Trends and ratios matter more than absolute numbers. A growth rate dropping from 5% to 3% quarter-over-quarter reveals declining momentum despite overall growth.

- **Review user research and feedback**: Connect quantitative metrics to qualitative insights from user research and feedback. The human context informs the metric-driven, quantitative "what" with the qualitative "why."

  For example, an increase in churn coupled with feedback about confusing app navigation points clearly to simplification opportunities.

As part of diligent metrics monitoring, it is critical to watch for early signals of negative changes or trends across key performance indicators. Rapid course correction enabled by metrics can mitigate declines before they spiral. However, when responding to metric changes, we must thoughtfully distinguish temporary, short-term fluctuations in metrics from more sustained changes that indicate systemic issues warranting intervention. Short-term changes may reflect normal ebbs and flows or seasonal impacts that will self-correct, while long-term downward trends often reflect product or market factors necessitating action. These sustained negative changes deserve a rapid response, whether it involves fixes to the product experience, optimizations across the conversion funnel, or realignment of business strategy to market realities. Insightful metrics analysis provides the vision to know when to stay the course amid temporary bumps versus changing tack. Last but not least, it is important to emphasize that while rigorously crunching numbers is crucial, deriving meaning to guide decisions is where the magic lies. Metrics must illuminate the "why" behind outcomes.

Using performance metrics to drive growth

Defining the right metrics provides the foundation. But translating metrics into growth requires rigorously monitoring and analyzing data to inform strategy and optimizations. This leads us to the critical question—how can we actively harness metrics insights to fuel sustainable, product-led growth?

The true measure of metrics lies in how they guide actions that accelerate growth. Analyzed thoughtfully, metrics become powerful catalysts to do the following:

- **Illuminate successful areas to build on**: Analyze areas of strong performance and identify the factors driving success. Double down on amplifying these growth drivers.

  For example, if your activation rate metric shows a positive spike after an onboarding redesign, investigate further to understand exactly what resonated. Refine and extend those effective elements to sustain momentum.

- **Prioritize solutions to key user issues**: Surface pain points and blockers hindering users by analyzing poor-performing metrics. Guide engineering efforts toward solving these high-impact problems first.

  Low ratings for a core feature reveal that it isn't delivering the expected value. Before building new features, invest in better understanding pain points through user research and rapidly iterating to improve them.

- **Inform roadmap prioritization**: Let metrics guide the sequencing of the product roadmap. For instance, if activation is lagging, prioritize onboarding improvements over building new advanced features.

- **Optimize user journeys end-to-end**: Continuously optimize messaging, flows, and experiences at each touchpoint in the user journey based on metrics data. Small tweaks can yield big gains over time.

  For example, if trials from social channels have lower conversion rates, customize onboarding for those channels to address differences in expectations versus those of other channels.

- **Support strategic business decisions**: Leverage metrics insights to inform budgeting trade-offs across growth investments in engineering, marketing, support, and more.

  Metrics could show the ROI on enhancing in-app support is two times greater than when increasing the advertising spend. This validates shifting the budget to improving support.

- **Rally teams around shared objectives**: Use shared metrics to align cross-functional teams toward unified outcomes. Shared goals foster collaboration as opposed to disjointed efforts across silos.

  Unite tech, product, and marketing teams to coordinate driving movement on key conversion funnel metrics tied to revenue targets. This builds joint ownership of outcomes.

  The following are some of the leading brands that have tapped metrics to guide growth:

  - **Amazon optimizes experience at scale**: Amazon obsessively monitors operational metrics such as shipping times, content accuracy, and review rates to enable swift issue resolution and experience optimization as it scales globally. This has been crucial to its continued domination.

- **Netflix leverages metrics to inform content strategy**: By relentlessly analyzing viewing metrics, Netflix gleans insights into user content preferences that inform what new shows and movies to produce. This data-driven content strategy has been key to its meteoric rise.

- **Starbucks informs store locations with data**: Starbucks heavily leverages geo-based metrics on current store performance, user demographics, and mobile app activity to inform optimal locations for new stores. This metrics-driven expansion underlies its staggering growth.

Thus, savvy product teams continuously harness metrics to illuminate growth paths, prioritize solutions, and inform experience optimization. Metrics enable perpetual evolution guided by customer needs. But optimizing metrics requires building capabilities across teams:

- **Cultivate shared ownership of metrics**: Break down silos by facilitating collaboration across functions to drive metric improvements. Marketing, product, and engineering teams must share accountability.

- **Communicate compelling stories with metrics**: Metrics alone aren't inspiring without powerful narratives. Connect metrics to user outcomes to craft compelling stories that motivate teams.

- **Target quick wins to build momentum**: Pursue some early, quick wins on lagging metrics to build team momentum as opposed to only chasing long-term optimization initiatives.

- **Upskill teams on leveraging metrics**: Conduct workshops and training to expand data fluency across teams. Empower every function to leverage insights.

While many metrics focus targets growth, sustained success requires promptly responding when data indicates declines. Rapid course correction enabled by metrics mitigates downward trends before they spiral. We must act decisively upon sustained negative metric changes while allowing short-term fluctuations to self-correct. Experimentation can guide course corrections by testing potential remedies to reverse concerning trends across engagement, retention, or revenue metrics. Timely intervention demonstrates the agility that metrics-empowered teams possess in contending with market dynamics. Growth is not linear, but by harnessing metrics to guide both opportunities and course corrections, product teams augment their chances of long-term success.

By combining metrics-driven focus with cross-team coordination, products can achieve sustained optimization and innovation, guided perpetually by user data and market realities. This future vision relies on building strong metrics competencies and culture.

Analyzing experiment results and iterating on product features and marketing strategies

One of the key pillars of effective product management is the capacity to analyze experiment results and use them to inform the iteration of product features and marketing strategies. In this section, we delve into the intricacies of this process, exploring how data-driven insights can drive product improvement and customer satisfaction.

The power of experimentation

Before we dive into analyzing experiment results, it's essential to underscore the significance of experimentation in modern product management. In a dynamic and competitive marketplace, relying solely on intuition or gut feeling is a risky proposition. This is where experimentation steps in as a crucial tool.

Experiments provide invaluable controlled environments to trial potential course corrections when metrics point to underperformance. We can test remedy hypotheses by rolling out variations of product experiences, pricing models, promotional offers, and more to subsets of users. By assessing the impact of reversing negative trends, experiments enable data-backed validation of appropriate interventions to improve outcomes, whether across activation, retention, sales, or other key areas. However, when analyzing results, we must thoughtfully distinguish temporary fluctuations from sustained changes in metrics to avoid overcorrection. Experiments help teams determine appropriate responses to short-term ebbs versus long-term shifts warranting meaningful course adjustment.

Setting the stage for experiments

To embark on a successful experimentation journey, it's essential to lay a strong foundation. This includes defining clear objectives, forming hypotheses, and selecting appropriate metrics for measurement. Let's take a closer look at these key components:

- Defining clear objectives
- Forming hypotheses
- Selecting appropriate metrics

Defining clear objectives

Every experiment should start with a well-defined objective. What specific aspect of your product or marketing strategy are you seeking to improve? Are you trying to boost user engagement, increase conversion rates, or reduce churn? By articulating your objectives clearly, you set a precise direction for your experimentation efforts.

Forming hypotheses

Hypotheses are the guiding principles of experimentation. They articulate what you expect to happen when you make a particular change. For instance, you might hypothesize that simplifying the user registration process will lead to a higher signup rate. Crafting robust hypotheses ensures that your experiments have a purpose and are aligned with your overall goals.

Selecting appropriate metrics

Metrics are the lifeblood of experimentation. They provide the means to quantify the impact of your changes. When selecting metrics, it's crucial to choose those that directly relate to your objectives.

For example, if your goal is to improve user engagement, metrics such as DAU or time spent in-app are highly relevant.

Conducting experiments

Once you've laid the groundwork, it's time to execute your experiments. A/B testing is a common method employed in the digital realm. It involves randomly dividing your user base into two groups: one group experiences the control (the existing version of your product), while the other encounters the treatment (the version with the proposed changes).

For instance, if you're experimenting with a new homepage layout, half of your users will see the current layout, while the other half will see the updated version. By comparing the performance metrics of these two groups, you can gauge the impact of your changes.

The importance of rigorous analysis

After conducting your experiments, you're left with a wealth of data. However, data alone doesn't yield insights; it requires careful analysis. Here are the key steps in analyzing experiment results:

- Checking statistical significance
- Accounting for confounding factors
- Avoiding cherry-picking data
- Adding qualitative insights
- Reproducing results

Checking statistical significance

Statistical significance is crucial to determine whether the observed differences in performance metrics are meaningful or merely due to chance. Typically, a p-value of less than 0.05 is considered statistically significant, indicating that the results are likely not random.

Accounting for confounding factors

Real-world experiments are often influenced by external factors, such as seasonality or technical issues. It's essential to account for these factors when interpreting results. Causation doesn't always equal correlation, so it's vital to critically examine multiple possible explanations for your findings.

Avoiding cherry-picking data

When analyzing experiment results, resist the temptation to focus solely on metrics that show positive outcomes. Comprehensive analysis involves looking at the full spectrum of data. Sometimes, conflicting data can provide the most profound insights into user behavior and preferences.

Adding qualitative insights

Quantitative metrics tell you what's happening, but they don't always explain why it's happening. Supplement your analysis with qualitative data gathered from surveys, interviews, and support tickets. Understanding the "why" behind the "what" can uncover user motivations and pain points that quantitative data alone might miss.

Reproducing results

To ensure the reliability of your findings, consider reproducing experiments across different audience segments before implementing widespread changes. Consistency in results across various groups confirms the reliability of your insights.

Iterating and implementing changes

With a solid understanding of your experiment results, it's time to iterate on your product features and marketing strategies. Here's how you can effectively implement changes:

- Synthesizing learnings
- Prioritizing changes
- Setting targets and goals
- Continuous improvement

Synthesizing learnings

Compile the highlights, recommendations, implications, and next steps from your experiment results into shareable reports. These reports facilitate organization-wide learning and ensure that insights are disseminated to key stakeholders.

Prioritizing changes

Not all insights from experiments are created equal. Some may have a more substantial impact on your objectives than others. Prioritize changes based on their potential to drive growth or improve user experience.

Setting targets and goals

Once you've decided on the changes to implement, set clear targets and goals. These should be **specific, measurable, achievable, relevant, and time-bound (SMART)**. Tracking progress against these targets will help you measure the success of your iterations.

Continuous improvement

Iteration is not a one-time event but an ongoing process. Continuously monitor the impact of your changes and be prepared to adjust if they don't yield the desired results. Remember that customer preferences and market dynamics evolve, so your product must evolve with them.

Analyzing experiment results and iterating on product features and marketing strategies is a dynamic and cyclical process. It requires a commitment to data-driven decision-making, a willingness to learn from both successes and failures, and a culture of continuous improvement.

By following a structured approach to experimentation, analysis, and iteration, product teams can harness the power of data to create products that not only meet user needs but also drive sustainable growth. In the next section, we'll explore how to establish a performance-driven culture that encourages data-driven decision-making across the entire organization, from leadership to frontline employees.

Establishing a performance-driven culture

Amid an increasingly hypercompetitive digital landscape, relying solely on intuition and gut instinct is no longer enough—leveraging data to guide decisions has become imperative. But adopting isolated metrics tools alone won't suffice. To truly unlock the sustained power of metrics, organizations must focus on building an enduring metrics-driven culture. This requires addressing four key questions:

- Why does a metrics culture matter?
- What does an ideal metrics culture look like?
- How can organizations instill metrics-driven thinking?
- What pitfalls should be avoided?

Let's explore these topics in detail.

Why does a metrics culture matter?

A robust metrics culture fuels data-driven decision-making, alignment, and continuous optimization—capabilities that enable sustainable growth in dynamic markets. A strong metrics-driven culture empowers teams with the vision to know when to stay the course versus when to change direction. Easy access to dashboard data gives product and marketing teams enhanced perceptivity to detect when short-term metric fluctuations warrant patience versus when sustained downward changes necessitate a rapid response. This data-backed visibility facilitates informed decisions on interventions. A culture obsessed with metrics optimization develops organizational muscle memory for swiftly intervening to course correct when data reveals the imperative.

Speeding up data-driven decisions

By grounding discussions and debates in metrics rather than opinions, teams can rapidly align on actions backed by customer data. This results in faster, higher-quality decisions unencumbered by politics or egos.

For example, Amazon requires executives to bring detailed data representation to strategy meetings. Opinions carry less weight without supporting metrics.

Breaking down silos

Shared metrics get different functions rowing in the same direction. This focus on unified goals transcends organizational silos that often derail execution.

HubSpot designed office spaces around big-screen dashboards to reinforce cross-functional metrics focus.

Promoting continuous improvement

A culture obsessively focused on metrics optimization nurtures perpetual refinement of customer experiences and offerings as markets evolve. The hunger for improvement never ceases.

Nordstrom heavily emphasizes metrics such as NPS across the organization to maintain customer-centricity, even amid massive growth.

Fueling innovation

The curiosity to constantly test and experiment in search of better metrics opens the door to innovative ideas and offerings that may better delight customers.

Building competitive advantage

An enduring metrics-driven culture that permeates decision-making and unites teams is difficult for rivals to replicate. This unique culture becomes a differentiator.

Thus, a metrics culture accelerates data-driven execution, breaks down silos, optimizes customer experiences, spurs innovation, and ultimately drives competitive advantage. But what does this ideal culture look like?

What does an ideal performance culture look like?

A robust metrics culture is characterized by several key attributes:

- **Metrics-driven dialogue**: Conversations center around metrics and trends instead of opinions. Constructive data-driven debate is the norm.
- **Metrics tied to goals**: Individual and team goals align tightly to metrics that reflect wider organizational objectives.

- **Universal metrics literacy**: All employees possess data fluency skills to analyze trends and derive insights from metrics.

- **Shared metrics ownership**: Metric accountability spans cross-functional teams with shared goals, not just siloed departments.

- **Customer-centric metrics perspective**: Metrics are viewed as reflections of customer experiences to foster human connections.

- **Growth-enabling metrics analysis**: Analysis focuses on learning and improvement versus strictly monitoring or reporting of metrics.

- **Celebration of metrics wins**: Wins driven by metrics improvements are highlighted and celebrated across the company.

Combined, these cultural attributes enable organizations to sustain metrics-driven thinking and decision-making for continual optimization. But how can teams instill these qualities?

How can organizations instill a metrics culture?

The responsibility of growth product managers extends beyond simply leveraging metrics—we must spearhead building an enduring metrics-driven culture within our organization. This instills the mindsets, habits, and incentives across teams that enable metrics to become a sustained competitive advantage.

But transforming culture requires thoughtful change management. We must get buy-in across the organization and implement changes that stick. Here are some effective ways that growth product managers can instill metrics-driven thinking:

- **Guide dialogue with data**: Require metrics-backed analysis in meetings and discussions rather than pure opinions. Facilitate constructive debate around trends.

- **Incentivize outcomes based on metrics**: Tie individual and team-based rewards and recognition to metrics gains. Prevent the perception that activity equals results.

- **Invest in data literacy training**: Conduct ongoing training to develop organization-wide fluency in extracting insights from metrics.

- **Democratize metric visibility**: Ensure metrics dashboards and performance data are readily accessible to all employees to empower decision-making.

- **Foster cross-team metrics collaboration**: Encourage and reward cross-functional teams coordinating to achieve shared metric objectives.

- **Communicate compelling metrics stories**: Bring metrics data to life by connecting trends back to human needs and emotions. Spark intrinsic motivation.

- **Celebrate metrics heroes**: Publicly highlight teams and individuals who move the metrics needle in positive ways. Recognize data-driven contributions.

- **Continually refine and iterate**: Solicit feedback and revisit approaches to instill metrics-driven thinking and improve data-oriented decision-making over time.

Instilling an enduring metrics-driven culture is key to unlocking the strategic power of data. But culture change does not happen overnight. As growth product managers, we need thoughtful strategies to drive the adoption of data-oriented mindsets and behaviors across an organization.

Getting teams to buy into leveraging metrics requires addressing common challenges head-on. We must get past notions that metrics are just extra work or primarily serve leadership. Instead, we need to demonstrate how metrics tangibly empower all employees and departments.

The responsibility extends beyond just analyzing metrics ourselves—we must actively build metrics fluency and data-driven thinking across the organization. This involves change management finesse. Progress will take patience, persistence, and addressing missteps along the way.

Now that we've covered approaches to instill a metrics-driven culture, let's discuss common pitfalls to avoid on this journey. With proactive mitigation of risks and pitfalls, we can realize the immense potential of metrics to guide products from data to decisions to positive outcomes.

Avoiding common pitfalls

While a metrics-driven culture can yield immense benefits, leaders must also be aware of potential pitfalls that can derail progress. A diligent focus on metrics can also go astray without thoughtful management.

As growth product managers championing culture change, we must safeguard against these hazards:

- **Metrics theater**: This occurs when metrics are presented for optics but not actually used to drive decisions and outcomes. Leaders reference metrics in speeches or reports for signaling, but when it comes to reality, decisions are still based on gut feelings and politics. This "metrics washing" erodes trust in data.

- **Conflicting metrics**: When departments have competing or misaligned metrics, it fosters confusion and unhealthy internal competition as opposed to collaboration on shared goals. This risks overall organizational objectives being lost in the shuffle. Marketing caring only about leads while sales focuses on bookings is a common example.

- **Analysis paralysis**: An overzealous focus on analysis can lead to decision inertia where teams get stuck gathering data without ever acting decisively. Too much analysis breeds inaction. Teams must balance analysis with agility and continuous progress.

- **Metrics myopia**: Pursuing metrics gains can sometimes cause teams to lose sight of the bigger picture and overall company health. Short-term metric lifts can paper over cultural dysfunction or talent exodus. Guard against myopic metrics tunnel vision.

- **Incentivizing bad behaviors**: Incentives tied to metrics can also drive unintended behaviors, such as sacrificing customer experience for short-term metric gains. Leaders must proactively identify and address potential incentive gaming.

Avoiding these pitfalls requires carefully scoping metrics programs, auditing existing processes, and vigilantly monitoring for risks as part of the change management process. But done right, organizations can tap into metrics while steering clear of hazards.

As growth product managers, we must remain cognizant of these risks and advocate for responsible, ethical data practices. With diligence and care, we can amplify the upside of metrics while circumventing dangers. Our leadership is pivotal in harnessing metrics as a sustainable competitive advantage.

Real-world examples of metrics-driven cultures done right

Cultivating a performance-driven culture is not just about collecting data but also integrating it into the very fabric of an organization's DNA. To illustrate this concept in action, we turn to some of the world's most renowned companies that have seamlessly integrated metrics into their daily operations. These real-world examples showcase how metrics have become the lifeblood of their decision-making processes, from refining customer experiences to empowering frontline employees, shaping physical work environments, and cascading objectives throughout their organizations. These lessons from Netflix, Starbucks, Shopify, and Google highlight the diverse ways in which metrics can drive success when woven into an organization's culture.

Netflix

Netflix perpetually A/B tests and optimizes its consumer experience based on monitoring intense amounts of metrics on streaming, recommendations, browsing, discoveries, and more. This obsession with metrics optimization has been core to its meteoric rise.

Key takeaway: Metrics are embedded in daily decisions across the company, not just analytics teams.

Starbucks

Starbucks leverages real-time metrics on customer ordering patterns and store throughput down to 15-minute intervals to mobilize baristas to adjust store operations and staffing dynamically.

Key takeaway: Democratizing metrics access empowers frontline workers.

Shopify

Shopify designs public office spaces with metrics displays to reinforce cross-functional, data-driven thinking. Its "obsession chamber" highlights real-time metrics.

Key takeaway: Physical environments can embed a metrics-driven culture.

Google

OKRs (**objectives and key results**) aligned to metrics cascade from the executive level down across Google. Achieving objectives is tied to performance management and rewards.

Key takeaway: Cascading metrics-based OKRs unify large organizations.

Building an enduring metrics-driven culture

As growth product managers, spearheading an enduring metrics-driven culture is pivotal to both organizational success and our own career growth. When metrics become deeply embedded across teams and processes, they unlock immense potential.

But transforming culture requires long-term commitment, investment, and persistence. It does not happen overnight. Here are some ways we can drive this change as leaders:

- **Secure executive buy-in**: Get early top-down support for a metrics focus. This gives initiatives credibility and the resources needed to thrive. Demonstrate the competitive benefits of a metrics culture.

- **Create a strategic data roadmap**: Define a multi-quarter roadmap articulating the vision, key milestones, and metrics for the culture change initiative. This provides structure and focus.

- **Evangelize a metrics mindset**: Continually communicate with teams on how metrics focus benefits them and adds value for customers. Highlight quick, early wins to build momentum. Inspire with the vision.

- **Democratize data access**: Break down data silos by ensuring all teams have access to dashboards and self-service analytics tools. Knowledge is power—empower through data.

- **Address resistance head-on**: Change inevitably faces resistance. Identify pockets of resistance early and address concerns through training, support, and empathy.

- **Coach metrics fluency**: Conduct ongoing metrics literacy programs to develop organization-wide skills in analyzing data and extracting insights. Fluency underpins adoption.

- **Incentivize aligned behaviors**: Tie individual OKRs and incentives to metrics that reflect wider business objectives. This drives accountability to shared goals.

- **Sustain momentum for the long haul**: Persistently communicate results, celebrate wins, and iterate on the program. Culture change is a marathon, not a sprint.

- **Lead by example**: We must model metrics-driven leadership in our own work before expecting teams to adopt this mindset. Walk the talk.

Instilling an enduring metrics culture takes time but pays dividends for years to come in the form of organizational agility, customer focus, and growth. As growth product managers, we have a unique opportunity to spearhead this transformation through strategic roadmaps, executive advocacy, change management, and leading by example.

With commitment and focus, we can build metrics-driven organizations primed to continually learn, optimize, and out-innovate rivals. An organization grounded in data is positioned to flourish amid dynamic market landscapes. The future belongs to teams who become metrics masters.

Now we understand how to effectively define, report, and build performance metrics for your organization, we will need to delve into the intricacies of customer success and its pivotal role in nurturing product-led growth, which we will cover in the next chapter. We'll explore the stages of the customer journey, metrics for measuring success, leveraging feedback, and structuring effective customer success teams to drive sustainable growth and maximize the potential of your product.

Real-world example of a product-led organization with a strong metrics-driven culture

Slack is widely recognized as a product-led company that has instilled data-driven thinking into its culture. Some ways Slack leverages metrics across the organization are as follows:

- Engineers monitor platform metrics to quickly identify and fix reliability issues before they escalate. This reduces disruptions to the user experience.

- Product managers analyze usage trends and feedback to guide roadmap prioritization based on what will best serve customer needs.

- Marketing tracks funnel conversion rates to optimize campaigns and highlight opportunities to improve acquisition.

- Customer support uses metrics such as reply times and satisfaction scores to enhance the user experience.

- Executives tie company-wide OKRs to metrics such as engagement, retention, and growth to align all employees.

- Teams hold data-informed reviews of trends, insights, and opportunities to collaborate across departments.

- Data literacy training and metrics tools empower people in non-technical roles to leverage data.

- Public messaging celebrates metrics achievements as collective wins for the company.

This comprehensive use of metrics flows from Slack's customer-centric culture. Data provides insights into user needs and guides decisions at all levels to best serve them. This metrics focus has been key to Slack's rapid product-led growth.

> **Impacts on performance**
>
> Slack's product-led growth has been fueled by a strong metrics-driven culture that has translated to impressive business results. Some examples of the financial impact are as follows:
>
> 1. By continuously monitoring platform metrics, Slack engineers minimize disruptions and maintain industry-leading uptime of 99.9%+. This consistent reliability drives greater user retention and conversion.
>
> 2. Optimizing adoption and engagement based on usage metrics has helped Slack surpass 10 million daily active users and grow recurring revenue to over $630 million annually.
>
> 3. Marketing's data-driven optimization of acquisition funnel efficiency has reduced Slack's customer acquisition costs by 50% over five years.
>
> 4. Support's laser focus on satisfaction metrics has resulted in Slack achieving industry-leading **net promoter scores** (**NPS**) of over 70. This drives increased referrals and word-of-mouth adoption.
>
> 5. Tight alignment on growth metrics has powered the increase in Slack's enterprise customer base from just 100 in 2015 to over 85,000 as of 2019.
>
> Overall, Slack's ability to translate metrics insights into outstanding user experiences and growth has yielded incredible business results. After launching in 2014, Slack achieved a market valuation of over $20 billion in just five years. Its metrics-driven culture focused on customer needs has clearly fueled tremendous financial success.

Summary

This chapter provides a strategic framework for defining, monitoring, analyzing, and acting on performance metrics to maximize product success. It emphasizes the immense value of metrics for enabling data-driven product management.

We cover the strategic importance of performance metrics in areas such as quantifying product health, mitigating risks, focusing innovation on validated needs, increasing team alignment, speeding up iteration, optimizing user journeys, and fueling data-driven decisions. Best practices for defining the right metrics are then explored, including connecting metrics to business objectives, avoiding vanity metrics, keeping the quantity focused, and leveraging analytics platforms.

Effective monitoring and analysis techniques are discussed, such as automating dashboards, segmenting users, identifying trends and outliers, running cohort analysis, and connecting data to user outcomes. The chapter explains how to actively use metrics insights to build on successes, prioritize solutions, inform roadmaps, optimize journeys, support decisions, and rally teams.

Establishing a metrics-driven culture is covered by securing executive buy-in, creating a data roadmap, evangelizing a metrics mindset, democratizing data access, addressing resistance, coaching fluency, incentivizing aligned behaviors, sustaining momentum, and leading by example. Real-world examples of metrics-driven cultures are provided.

The chapter emphasizes that as growth product managers, we play a pivotal role in spearheading cultural transformation through metrics initiatives. It argues that an enduring metrics culture fuels agility, customer focus, and growth, providing a competitive advantage. The chapter highlights the immense strategic value of metrics and how product managers can harness data to unlock sustainable growth.

The future will belong to product managers who harness metrics as their greatest asset to deliver tremendous value. Are you ready to unlock the power of metrics to propel product-led growth? The epic journey awaits you.

Questions

1. Why are performance metrics essential to modern product management?

2. What are some best practices for choosing the right metrics to focus on?

3. How can product teams approach continuous monitoring and analysis of metrics to drive insights?

4. In what ways can metric insights actively inform both product and business strategies and decisions?

5. How can organizations build cultures focused on metrics and data-driven thinking?

Answers

1. Performance metrics are essential to modern product management because they provide empirical, quantitative insights into all aspects of a product's health and performance. Metrics enable data-driven assessment of what's working well and opportunities for improvement across dimensions such as user acquisition, activation, engagement, retention, and revenue growth. This allows product teams to optimize experiences, mitigate risks, align on goals, speed up iteration, and fuel strategic decisions with validated customer data as opposed to guesses.

2. Best practices for choosing effective metrics include tightly aligning to business goals and desired outcomes, avoiding vanity metrics that don't provide meaningful insights, keeping the total metrics lean and focused, balancing quantitative and qualitative data, and revisiting metrics as business objectives evolve. Thoughtfully selected metrics tuned to outcomes provide the compass for data-driven product optimization.

3. To continuously monitor and analyze metrics, product teams should automate metric reporting through tools such as dashboards, uncover trends and outlier events, conduct segmentation analysis to identify issues specific to key user groups, and relate metrics back to actual user experiences through techniques such as user interviews and usability testing. Deriving meaning from the data is key—not just gathering metrics for metrics' sake.

4. Metric insights should actively inform both product and overall business strategies and decisions. This includes sharpening product roadmap prioritization based on usage and value data, guiding refinements to optimize user experiences, justifying investment trade-offs with revenue and growth metrics, and unifying teams across the organization around core objectives measured through shared metrics and KPIs.

5.   Organizations can build cultures focused on metrics and data-driven thinking through actions such as facilitating meetings and discussions grounded in data-backed dialogue, tying incentives and rewards to metrics gains, conducting data literacy training, democratizing metric visibility, fostering cross-functional collaboration on metrics, communicating compelling stories from data, celebrating metrics heroes, and continuously refining approaches over time based on feedback.

9

Guiding Your Clients
to the Pot of Gold

In today's competitive business environment, achieving sustainable growth isn't just about acquiring customers; it's about guiding them to unlock the full potential of your product—a journey we often liken to discovering a hidden treasure trove.

The era of product-led growth has ushered in a profound shift in how companies approach customer **retention, acquisition, and development (RAD)**. No longer is it enough to merely acquire customers; instead, the goal is to guide them toward realizing the full potential of your product—a metaphorical *pot of gold* that awaits both your customers and your business.

In this chapter, we will embark on a journey that places customer success at the forefront of your growth strategy. We'll explore the essential role of customer success in the context of product-led growth and delve into the strategies, techniques, and skills necessary to lead your customers to that proverbial pot of gold. As growth product managers, the skills you acquire from this chapter will prove invaluable in driving sustainable business growth, fostering enduring customer relationships, and, ultimately, achieving your growth objectives. We will explore the following key topics:

- The importance of customer success in product-led growth

- The customer journey—onboarding, adoption, and retention

- Leveraging customer feedback and success stories

- Scaling customer success teams—hiring and training

- Building strong customer relationships—engaging with customers, delivering value-added services, and driving upsell and cross-sell

- Establishing a performance-driven culture—the keystone of long-term customer success

By the end of this chapter, you will have acquired a diverse skill set essential for any growth product manager looking to excel in the realm of product-led growth. These skills encompass understanding the paramount importance of customer success in guiding customers through the entire journey, measuring success using metrics and **key performance indicators** (**KPIs**) while leveraging customer feedback and success stories for product improvement and growth, mastering the art of scaling customer success teams, and cultivating strong, lasting customer relationships. These skills collectively serve as your compass, guiding you through the complexities of product-led growth and enabling you to lead your customers toward success and uncover the treasure trove of opportunities that lie ahead.

As we journey through these topics, you'll acquire the knowledge and skills needed to lead your customers toward the pot of gold—a future where both your customers and your business flourish. Let's embark on this exciting exploration of customer success in the realm of product-led growth.

The importance of customer success in product-led growth

In the dynamic world of growth product management, where your role revolves around driving product-led growth, understanding the pivotal role of customer success is paramount. This chapter aims to shed light on the concept of customer success within the scope of growth product management. We will emphasize why it is not just beneficial but critical for achieving sustainable growth, and how you can strategically align customer success with your broader growth strategy. Additionally, we'll explore the nuances of guiding customers toward maximizing the value they derive from your product, ultimately leading them to unlock its full potential.

Defining customer success in a growth product management context

Before we delve deeper into the significance of customer success in growth product management, it's crucial to establish what we mean by *customer success* in this specific context. **Customer success**, in a growth product management context, encompasses more than just ensuring customers achieve their desired outcomes when using your product. It involves actively guiding customers to realize the maximum potential value your product can offer.

In this approach, your product takes center stage. Customers are encouraged to independently discover, adopt, and utilize the product's features and functionalities. However, the journey doesn't conclude with the initial sale or sign-up; it extends throughout the entire **customer life cycle** (**CLC**).

A real-world example that exemplifies this definition is Airbnb.

Airbnb, the global accommodation marketplace, disrupted the traditional hospitality industry by allowing individuals to list their homes and travelers to find unique, cost-effective lodging options. But what truly set Airbnb apart was its commitment to customer success.

When a host lists their property on Airbnb, the success of that listing depends on various factors: attractive photos, clear descriptions, competitive pricing, and, most importantly, positive guest experiences. Airbnb recognized that for hosts to succeed, they needed to ensure that guests enjoyed their stays.

To achieve this, Airbnb implemented several customer success initiatives, as follows:

- **Education**: Airbnb provided hosts with educational resources, including guides on creating appealing listings, setting competitive prices, and delivering exceptional hospitality. This not only helped hosts but also contributed to guests' positive experiences.

- **Reviews and ratings**: The platform introduced a robust review and rating system. This encouraged hosts to maintain high-quality listings and provided guests with valuable insights when choosing accommodations.

- **Customer support**: Airbnb invested in responsive customer support teams to address any issues promptly. This helped resolve conflicts, mitigate problems, and ultimately enhanced both host and guest satisfaction.

- **Continuous improvement**: Airbnb continuously improved its platform based on user feedback. Features such as instant booking, enhanced search filters, and secure payment options were introduced to make the user experience smoother and more secure.

Airbnb's dedication to customer success, seen through the lens of both hosts and guests, played a pivotal role in its explosive growth. Hosts felt supported and empowered, while guests found the platform trustworthy and enjoyable. This alignment of customer success with the growth strategy led Airbnb to become a household name and a prime example of how customer-centric approaches can drive success in growth product management.

As Brian Chesky, Airbnb's co-founder and CEO, aptly put it:

> *"What we're trying to do is create a world where you can belong anywhere. We want to make sure that people feel like they can belong in the homes they stay in and feel like they can belong anywhere in the world."*

This commitment to creating a sense of belonging and success for both hosts and guests underscores the essence of customer success in the growth product management context.

Customer success in growth product management goes beyond traditional customer support. It involves proactively assisting customers in navigating their journey, ensuring they experience the full spectrum of benefits your product provides, and driving them toward long-term engagement and satisfaction.

Why customer success is essential for sustainable growth

Customer success isn't merely a buzzword in growth product management; it is the linchpin for achieving sustainable growth. Here are several compelling reasons why customer success is essential for growth product managers:

- **Retention and loyalty**: In your role, retaining customers is as crucial as acquiring new ones. Customer success efforts directly influence customer retention rates. Satisfied and engaged customers are more likely to renew subscriptions, continue using your product, and become vocal advocates.

- **Word of mouth (WOM) and referrals**: Happy customers tend to share their positive experiences with peers, leading to WOM referrals. In today's digital age, positive customer sentiment can significantly impact your product's reputation and attract new users.

- **Reduced churn**: Churn, or the rate at which customers stop using your product, can impede growth. Effective customer success strategies can mitigate churn by addressing customer issues, enhancing user experiences, and ensuring continuous value delivery.

- **Increased lifetime value (LV)**: Satisfied customers are more inclined to expand their product usage and invest in additional services or upgrades, contributing to increased **customer LV (CLV)** and revenue growth.

- **Competitive edge**: Exceptional customer success can differentiate your product in a crowded marketplace. In your role, how you support and guide customers can be a key distinguishing factor.

- **Data-informed decision-making**: Your customer success efforts generate valuable data and insights. Analyzing customer behavior, feedback, and usage patterns can inform product improvements, feature development, and marketing strategies, aligning with your role's data-driven nature.

- **Iterative product development**: Growth product managers thrive on iterative product development. Customer success teams play a vital role in gathering user feedback and collaborating with product teams to refine and enhance the product based on real user needs and preferences.

A real-world example – the Salesforce story

One of the few companies that exemplify the power of customer success is Salesforce, the global leader in **customer relationship management (CRM)** software. Here's why:

- **Retention and loyalty**: Salesforce's success narrative isn't solely founded on acquiring new customers; it's rooted in retaining and nurturing them. As one of the pioneers, Salesforce introduced the role of **customer success managers (CSMs)**. Recognizing that customer retention is as pivotal as acquisition, Salesforce has consistently delivered value and supported customers throughout their CRM journey. This unwavering commitment has fostered a loyal customer base that eagerly renews subscriptions, extends product usage, and evolves into fervent advocates.

- **WOM and referrals**: Salesforce's customer-centric approach has transformed satisfied clients into enthusiastic advocates. Happy customers share their positive experiences with peers and colleagues, unleashing the power of WOM referrals. These referrals, driven by authentic user satisfaction, have magnified Salesforce's reputation and magnetized a stream of new users.

- **Reduced churn**: Salesforce's mastery of customer success strategies has allowed it to adeptly mitigate churn. By addressing customer concerns swiftly, continuously refining user experiences through product enhancements, and ensuring the seamless delivery of value, Salesforce has effectively curtailed churn rates.

- **Increased LV**: Salesforce's satisfied customers don't merely remain users; they become integral partners in growth. This partnership often leads to expanded product usage and investments in additional services or feature upgrades. Consequently, CLV has soared, becoming a substantial driver of revenue growth.

- **Competitive edge**: In a fiercely competitive CRM software market, Salesforce's exceptional commitment to customer success has become a defining competitive advantage. Its unwavering support and guidance to customers have set it apart in a crowded marketplace, positioning it as the preferred choice for businesses seeking CRM solutions.

- **Data-informed decision-making**: Salesforce's commitment to customer success generates a wealth of data and insights. It meticulously analyzes customer behavior, solicits feedback, and closely monitors usage patterns. This data-driven approach informs product enhancements, fuels feature development, and shapes targeted marketing strategies. It aligns seamlessly with its role's data-driven nature.

- **Iterative product development**: Growth product managers at Salesforce thrive on iterative product development, which is a process in which a company continuously makes improvements to its product based on ongoing feedback and testing, rather than releasing a fully complete version all at once. The customer success teams at Salesforce serve as the linchpin in this process, gathering real-time user feedback and collaborating seamlessly with product teams to refine and enhance the CRM platform. This user-centric approach has been instrumental in Salesforce's ability to remain at the forefront of an ever-evolving industry. As Salesforce's user base grew over time, so did the ecosystem of skills surrounding the platform. More Salesforce users led to greater demand for Salesforce-related skills in the market, which became desirable for Salesforce customers looking to maximize their CRM investment. This also created well-paid career opportunities for those with Salesforce skills. In turn, having a robust ecosystem of skilled talent focused on Salesforce provided further competitive advantage as Salesforce solidified its status as the predominant CRM platform.

In essence, the Salesforce journey is a compelling testament to how a steadfast commitment to customer success translates not only into growth but sustainable and enduring growth. By retaining and nurturing customers, harnessing the power of referrals, reducing churn, and continuously enhancing its product through user-driven insights, Salesforce has secured a prominent and lasting position in the CRM market. Its success story underscores the profound impact of customer success on achieving sustainable growth in the field of growth product management.

Aligning customer success with your growth strategy

To harness the full potential of customer success in your role as a growth product manager, it is important to align customer success efforts with your broader growth strategy. This alignment ensures that customer success becomes an integral part of your company's growth DNA. Here's how you can achieve this alignment:

- **Shared objectives**: Ensure that your objectives and those of your customer success team are in harmony with your organization's overall growth objectives. This synergy fosters collaboration and bolsters your efforts.

- **Data integration**: Establish seamless data-sharing mechanisms between your customer success, product development, and marketing teams. This data exchange ensures that customer feedback informs product enhancements and that marketing strategies resonate with customer preferences.

- **Cross-functional collaboration**: Encourage cross-functional collaboration among teams. For instance, as a growth product manager, collaborating closely with sales and marketing ensures consistent messaging and customer experiences.

- **Feedback loops**: Implement feedback loops to facilitate the integration of customer insights into product development. Regular meetings or channels for sharing feedback ensure that the **voice of the customer** (**VoC**) is a central driver of product improvements.

- **Customer-centric culture**: Cultivate a customer-centric culture across your organization. Make certain that every team member comprehends the value of customer success and how it contributes to the company's growth goals.

Understanding the importance of customer success is fundamental for growth product managers. It involves guiding customers through their journey, helping them unlock the full potential of your product, and ensuring their long-term satisfaction and loyalty. By aligning customer success efforts with your growth strategy, you can leverage its power to drive sustainable growth and maintain a competitive edge in your role as a growth product manager.

The customer journey – onboarding, adoption, and retention

Now we understand what customer success means and why it's critical for growth product managers to also focus on this beyond customer acquisition activities, let's explore the pivotal stages of the customer journey: onboarding, adoption, and retention, offering practical strategies and real-world examples to guide you through each phase. Furthermore, we will delve into the significant role of leveraging customer feedback and success stories in enhancing your product and driving growth.

Strategies for seamless onboarding

Effective **onboarding** is the gateway to a positive customer journey. It serves as the initial handshake between your product and the customer. Let's explore strategies for a seamless onboarding experience, accompanied by real-world examples:

- **Personalized onboarding**: Tailoring the onboarding experience to individual customer needs is paramount. Take Netflix, for example, which uses sophisticated algorithms to recommend personalized content to new users based on their viewing history and preferences.

- **User-friendly onboarding**: Simplicity is key. Dropbox, with its intuitive file-sharing interface, offers a hassle-free onboarding process that ensures users quickly grasp its core functionalities.

- **Educational resources**: HubSpot provides an extensive library of resources, including webinars, e-books, and templates, which guide users through their marketing and sales platform's onboarding process.

- **Progress tracking**: Duolingo gamifies language learning by tracking users' progress, awarding badges, and setting daily goals, motivating learners to complete their onboarding journey.

- **Feedback loops**: Slack encourages users to provide feedback during onboarding to fine-tune its platform continually, enhancing the user experience.

With a strong foundation laid during onboarding, the next challenge is nurturing adoption and engagement throughout the customer journey.

Nurturing adoption and engagement

After a successful onboarding, the focus needs to be on maintaining **customer engagement**. Here are strategies and examples to ensure active user participation:

- **Regular communication**: Airbnb sends personalized travel recommendations and host updates to keep users engaged and informed about potential trips, fostering a sense of community.

- **Customer support**: Zendesk offers comprehensive customer support through various channels, ensuring users always have a lifeline when they encounter issues or need assistance. These channels include email, live chat, phone support, an online knowledge base, community forums, social media, and a formal ticketing system.

- **User communities**: WordPress's vast user community allows users to share experiences, seek advice, and collaborate on projects, keeping them engaged and invested in the platform.

- **Personalized content**: Spotify's algorithmic playlists and **Discover Weekly** feature provide users with a constant stream of personalized music recommendations, making them more likely to continue using the service.

- **Feedback channels**: Amazon's **Was this review helpful?** feature not only encourages user feedback but also helps other customers make informed decisions, fostering engagement and trust.

Moving forward, let's explore techniques that ensure long-term retention and value for your customers.

Techniques for long-term retention and value

Long-term **customer retention** is indeed crucial for the sustained success of a business. It involves strategies and practices that go beyond merely acquiring new customers and focus on keeping existing customers satisfied and loyal. Here, we'll elaborate on some of these techniques and provide more insights into customer retention:

- **Continuous improvement**: Apple's approach to continuous improvement extends beyond product enhancements to the entire user experience. Regular iOS updates not only fix bugs but also introduce new features, performance improvements, and security enhancements. This keeps customers engaged and loyal, as they anticipate and appreciate these updates. The key takeaway here is that businesses should invest in refining their products or services over time to meet evolving customer needs and expectations and stay ahead of the competition.

- **Customer education**: Adobe's provision of learning resources such as tutorials and guides is a smart way to empower users and help them make the most of the software. By facilitating skill development and mastery, Adobe enhances the value proposition of its Creative Cloud suite. To implement this, businesses can create educational content, training materials, or knowledge bases to guide customers in using their products effectively, resulting in higher customer satisfaction.

- **Subscription models**: Microsoft's Office 365 utilizes a subscription-based pricing model that offers ongoing value to customers. Subscribers receive not only the latest software updates but also cloud-based collaboration tools, such as Microsoft Teams and OneDrive. Companies can follow a similar model by offering subscription plans that provide continuous value, such as access to premium features, updates, and customer support. This can create a sense of ongoing engagement and justify the subscription cost.

- **Cross-selling and upselling**: Amazon's **Customers who bought this also bought** feature is a prime example of cross-selling. It encourages customers to add related or complementary products to their purchases, increasing the average transaction value. To apply this strategy, businesses can identify complementary products or services within their portfolio and suggest them to customers during the buying process. This not only boosts sales but also enhances the overall customer experience.

- **Data-informed insights**: Netflix's use of advanced analytics to recommend content is a testament to the power of data-driven insights. By understanding user preferences and behaviors, Netflix can tailor content recommendations, thus increasing user engagement and retention. Companies should collect and analyze customer data to provide personalized recommendations, offers, and content, fostering a sense of customization and relevance.

Incorporating these techniques into your customer retention strategy can help ensure long-term customer loyalty. Businesses should also consider the importance of leveraging customer feedback and success stories, as these can be invaluable for driving product growth. Customer feedback provides insights into areas that need improvement, while success stories serve as powerful testimonials to attract new customers and reinforce the trust of existing ones. By continuously refining your offerings, educating your customers, and using data-driven insights, you can build strong, lasting relationships with your customer base. We will cover other effective customer retention techniques in *Chapter 10*.

Leveraging customer feedback and success stories

In addition to continuous improvement, customer education, subscription models, cross-selling, and data-driven insights, another vital component in the quest for lasting customer loyalty is the effective utilization of customer feedback and success stories. These two elements can be powerful tools in driving product growth and ensuring that your business not only retains its customer base but also continues to thrive. Let's now delve into the strategies and benefits of leveraging customer feedback and success stories in your customer retention efforts.

The insights gained from customer feedback and success stories are invaluable for product improvement and growth. Here are some strategies growth product managers can use to harness these insights effectively:

1. **Gathering customer feedback**: Customer feedback is the foundation of any customer-centric strategy. It provides valuable insights into what customers like and dislike and what improvements they would appreciate. Gathering feedback can be done through surveys, interviews, social media, or direct communication.

    Real-world example: Amazon, the e-commerce giant, places a significant emphasis on customer feedback. It encourages customers to write reviews for products they've purchased. These reviews not only help potential buyers make informed decisions but also provide Amazon with valuable data about the quality and popularity of products. Amazon uses this feedback to constantly improve its product recommendations, **inventory management** (IM), and customer service.

2. **Using feedback for continuous improvement**: Once you've collected customer feedback, it's essential to put it to good use. Act on the feedback by making relevant changes to your products, services, or processes to address customer concerns or desires.

    Real-world example: Tesla, the electric car manufacturer, uses customer feedback to improve its vehicles. Tesla frequently releases **over-the-air** (OTA) updates that not only fix bugs but also introduce new features, some of which are suggested by customers. This approach showcases Tesla's commitment to meeting customer demands and keeping them loyal to the brand.

3. **Personalized communication**: Tailoring communication and interactions to each customer's preferences and needs can significantly boost retention. Customers appreciate feeling understood and valued as individuals.

    Real-world example: Spotify, the music streaming service, uses data-driven insights to personalize user experiences. Spotify's playlists, such as **Discover Weekly** and **Release Radar**, are created based on a user's listening history. These personalized playlists not only keep users engaged but also make them feel that Spotify understands their musical tastes, fostering customer loyalty.

4. **Implementing loyalty programs**: Loyalty programs reward customers for their repeat business. This can take the form of discounts, exclusive access, or rewards points, which encourage customers to keep coming back.

    Real-world example: Starbucks' loyalty program, Starbucks Rewards, offers customers points for each purchase, which can be redeemed for free drinks or food. This program not only increases customer retention but also encourages higher spending, as customers strive to earn more rewards.

5. **Showcasing success stories**: Success stories or case studies that highlight how customers have benefited from your products or services can be incredibly persuasive in retaining and attracting new customers.

    Real-world example: Salesforce, a CRM platform, features a variety of customer success stories on its website. These stories describe how businesses across different industries have used Salesforce to improve their operations, boost sales, and provide better customer service. Such stories demonstrate proof of the real-world value of Salesforce's product, increasing customer trust and retention.

6. **Encouraging user-generated content**: Encouraging customers to create content about their experiences with your product or service can serve as powerful testimonials. This can include reviews, social media posts, or even user-generated videos.

    Real-world example: GoPro, a maker of action cameras, actively encourages customers to share their action-packed experiences captured with GoPro cameras. The GoPro Awards program rewards users for sharing their content on GoPro's website and social media. This user-generated content not only serves as authentic testimonials but also inspires others to purchase and use GoPro products.

7. **Responding to customer complaints**: How you handle customer complaints and issues can significantly impact customer retention. Prompt and effective resolution of problems can turn dissatisfied customers into loyal advocates.

    Real-world example: Zappos, an online shoe and clothing retailer, is known for its exceptional customer service. It empowers its customer service representatives to go to great lengths to resolve customer issues, including sending flowers or even arranging a pizza delivery. This extraordinary level of customer care has helped build a strong, loyal customer base.

8. **Social proof and testimonials**: Leverage social proof through customer testimonials, case studies, and endorsements to build trust and credibility.

    Real-world example: Walt Disney World Resort is known for its customer testimonials and the *planDisney* panel (formerly known as *Disney Parks Moms Panel*). This platform features real guests who answer questions and provide advice to potential visitors. These unbiased opinions and personal experiences help build trust and encourage more people to visit the park, thereby boosting customer retention.

9. **Referral programs**: Encourage existing customers to refer friends and family to your business. This not only attracts new customers but also strengthens the bond between existing customers and your brand.

    Real-world example: Dropbox, a cloud storage service, successfully used a referral program. Users were rewarded with additional storage space when they referred others to sign up for Dropbox. This approach helped Dropbox grow rapidly and retain customers who referred others, as they had a vested interest in the service.

10. **Social media engagement**: Actively engage with your customers on social media platforms. Respond to comments, answer questions, and join conversations relevant to your industry or product.

    Real-world example: Oreo, the cookie company, is known for its engaging social media presence. It often responds to trending topics with clever, on-brand content. This not only keeps its existing customers engaged but also attracts new ones through the viral nature of social media.

Incorporating these strategies into your customer retention efforts can lead to more satisfied and loyal customers. Remember—customer feedback and success stories are not only valuable for retaining existing customers but also for attracting new ones. By demonstrating your commitment to improvement and customer satisfaction, you can create a virtuous cycle of growth and loyalty in your business.

The customer journey is a dynamic process that requires continuous adaptation and attention. By implementing strategies for seamless onboarding, nurturing adoption and engagement, ensuring long-term retention and value, and leveraging customer feedback and success stories, businesses can create a customer-centric approach that not only retains existing customers but also drives sustainable growth. Understanding and optimizing each phase of the customer journey is the key to long-term success in today's competitive marketplace.

Scaling customer success teams – hiring and training

In one of the previous sections, we discussed the crucial aspects of onboarding, adoption, and retention strategies to enhance customer success. These strategies play a pivotal role in establishing a strong foundation for the growth of your customer base. Now, let's shift our focus toward scaling customer success teams through hiring and training. This phase is equally vital for your company's growth, as it involves expanding your customer success team strategically to meet the increasing demands of your customer base. In this section, we will guide growth product managers on the best practices for hiring and training customer success teams, with real-world examples to illustrate these strategies in action.

Scaling your customer success teams is an essential step in ensuring your company's continued growth and success. As your customer base expands, so does the need for a dedicated and efficient customer success team. Hiring and training the right individuals is not just about increasing headcount; it's about finding the right people who can effectively engage, support, and retain your customers. Here are some key strategies to consider:

1. **Defining roles and responsibilities**: Before you start hiring, it's crucial to define clear roles and responsibilities within your customer success team. Each role should have specific objectives, whether it's customer onboarding, account management, or support.

    Real-world example: Salesforce, which is a leading CRM provider, has distinct roles within its customer success team. It has customer success managers, who focus on strategic account management, and customer support teams that handle technical inquiries. This clear division of labor ensures that each customer interaction is efficient and tailored to the customer's needs.

2. **Identifying the right skill set**: When hiring, look for candidates who possess the skills and qualities necessary for customer success. These may include empathy, strong communication skills, problem-solving abilities, and a deep understanding of your product or service.

    Real-world example: HubSpot, a marketing and sales software company, values candidates who exhibit empathy and a passion for helping customers. Its support team is trained to not only resolve issues but also provide value through every interaction, strengthening customer relationships.

3. **Leveraging data and metrics**: Data-informed decision-making is crucial when scaling your customer success team. Analyze customer data to determine when and where you need additional support. Use metrics such as customer satisfaction scores, **net promoter score** (**NPS**), and churn rates to identify trends and opportunities for improvement.

    Real-world example: Zendesk, a customer service software company, uses its own tools to track customer support metrics. It analyzes ticket data to identify peak support hours and patterns, allowing it to allocate resources effectively.

4. **Streamlining onboarding and training**: Efficient onboarding and training processes are vital to getting new team members up to speed quickly. Develop a structured training program that includes product knowledge, customer interaction best practices, and role-specific training modules.

    Real-world example: Amazon has an intensive onboarding process for its customer service representatives, focusing on in-depth product knowledge and soft skills development. They are trained to empathize with customers and provide solutions effectively.

5. **Promoting continuous learning**: The learning process doesn't stop after the initial training. Encourage ongoing learning and development for your customer success team. Offer opportunities for skill enhancement, cross-training, and exposure to new challenges.

Real-world example: LinkedIn's customer success team is encouraged to keep learning through various resources, including access to LinkedIn Learning courses. This continuous learning helps them stay up to date with industry trends and better support their customers.

6. **Fostering a collaborative culture**: Create a culture that promotes collaboration within your customer success team and with other departments such as sales, marketing, and product development. This collaboration ensures a seamless experience for the customer and allows for the sharing of insights and best practices.

   Real-world example: Slack, a collaboration software company, emphasizes cross-functional collaboration between its customer success and product teams. This synergy enables it to address customer needs and feedback effectively, resulting in improved product features and customer satisfaction.

7. **Automating routine tasks**: To scale effectively, consider automating routine and repetitive tasks, allowing your customer success team to focus on higher-value activities. Automation can help with customer communication, data analysis, and support ticket routing.

   Real-world example: Airbnb uses automation to handle routine booking and payment processes, allowing its customer support team to concentrate on complex customer inquiries and critical issues. This approach increases efficiency and enhances the overall customer experience.

8. **Monitoring and adjusting**: Regularly monitor the performance of your customer success team and adjust your strategies as needed. Pay attention to customer feedback and make continuous improvements based on the insights you gather.

   Real-world example: Spotify's customer success team relies on customer feedback to make platform enhancements. They actively seek input from users and incorporate it into their product roadmap, fostering a strong customer-centric approach.

Scaling customer success teams through strategic hiring and training is a vital component of achieving long-term growth and success for your company. By defining roles and responsibilities, identifying the right skill set, leveraging data, streamlining onboarding and training, promoting continuous learning, fostering collaboration, automating routine tasks, and consistently monitoring and adjusting, you can build a strong and effective customer success team.

Real-world examples from industry leaders such as Salesforce, HubSpot, Zendesk, Amazon, LinkedIn, Slack, Airbnb, and Spotify illustrate the diverse approaches that successful companies employ to scale their customer success teams. Growth product managers should take these lessons to heart and implement them with a strategic mindset to ensure that their customer success teams are not just growing in numbers but are also contributing significantly to the overall success of the organization.

By adhering to these best practices and learning from the experiences of industry leaders, growth product managers can develop a comprehensive strategy for scaling customer success teams, which will result in higher customer satisfaction, increased customer retention, and ultimately, sustained business growth.

Building strong customer relationships – engaging with customers, delivering value-added services, and driving upsell and cross-sell

In the previous section, we discussed critical aspects of scaling customer success teams through strategic hiring and training, which lays the foundation for accommodating the growth of your customer base. Expanding your customer success team is an essential part of the equation. Now, let's shift our focus to building strong customer relationships by engaging with customers, delivering value-added services, and driving upsell and cross-sell.

This phase is all about utilizing your skilled and trained customer success team to cultivate lasting relationships with your customers while creating additional value and opportunities for growth. By focusing on building strong customer relationships, we not only aim to enhance customer retention but also explore ways to increase the share of wallet from existing customers through upsell and cross-sell strategies. In this section, we will guide growth product managers on the best practices for building strong customer relationships with real-world examples to illustrate these strategies in action.

Examples of upsell and cross-sell strategies include the following:

- **Usage-based upsell**: Analyze product usage data to identify power users and opportunities to upsell them to higher tiers or premium add-ons based on their heavy usage. For example, Dropbox upsells additional storage.

- **Value-added bundled offerings**: Bundle additional complementary products/services and position them as a premium tier. Highlight the additional value, convenience, and discounts. For example, Amazon Prime bundles faster shipping with media content.

- **CLC offers**: As customers use your product longer, their needs advance, and their appetite for premium capabilities increases over time. Target them with exclusive offers for advanced functionality at anniversary milestones.

- **Referral pass credit**: Provide loyal promoters referral reward credits applicable toward premium upgrades to incentivize organic WOM and upsell adoption.

- **Cross-sell based on integrated usage**: If you offer a suite of integrated products, analyze usage metrics to identify complementary products existing users may benefit from but haven't tried. Then, target them.

- **Post-onboarding nurture offers**: After customers complete the onboarding journey, they better understand product capabilities and how you create value. Use these insights to make tailored upsell offers.

- **In-app upsell messaging**: Identify natural integration points in your application workflows to seamlessly message users with relevant upsell offers while they already have your product top of mind.

Strategies for engagement, value-added services, upsell, and cross-sell opportunities

Building and nurturing strong customer relationships is at the heart of sustainable business growth. Engaging with customers, delivering value-added services, and strategically driving upsells and cross-sells are key elements of this process. Let's delve into customer-centric strategies that are instrumental in achieving sustainable business growth with a focus on customer expansion. It's important to note that some of these strategies, while critical for customer retention, are equally effective in driving **customer expansion**. These multifaceted approaches center on building strong relationships with your customers, ultimately resulting in not only retaining them but also growing your share of their wallet:

1. **Personalized engagement**: Engaging with customers on a personal level is a cornerstone of sustainable business growth. Tailoring your communication and support to each customer's unique needs and preferences is not only effective for customer retention but also opens doors to cross-sell and upsell opportunities.

    Real-world example: Netflix's recommendation engine is a prime example of personalized engagement. By analyzing user behavior and preferences, it recommends content that not only keeps customers engaged but also leads to cross-sell opportunities, as users discover and subscribe to new services or content.

2. **Proactive support**: Proactive support involves identifying potential issues before they become major problems. Anticipating customer needs is crucial for both retention and expansion efforts, as it allows you to address issues before they lead to churn and opens opportunities for cross-selling value-added services.

    Real-world example: Apple's automated diagnostics system is effective in proactively addressing potential issues. Offering solutions before customers face disruptions not only enhances customer retention but also creates openings for cross-selling additional services or accessories.

3. **Value-added services**: Providing services that go beyond the core product or service offering is a vital component of both customer retention and expansion. These services not only enhance the customer experience but also create opportunities for upsell and cross-sell.

    Real-world example: Amazon Prime's suite of value-added services, including free 2-day shipping, exclusive streaming content, and discounts, is a prime example. These services drive customer loyalty and increase spending on the platform, contributing to both retention and expansion goals.

4. **Educate and inform**: Educating your customers about your product or service, as well as industry-related topics, is a trust-building approach that benefits customer retention and creates opportunities for cross-selling additional features or services.

    Real-world example: HubSpot's educational content not only helps customers better understand inbound marketing and sales but also positions the company as an expert in the field. This facilitates upsell opportunities for premium products and services.

5. **Feedback and collaboration**: Actively seeking feedback and input from your customers is a practice that fosters trust, supports product improvements, and offers opportunities for both customer retention and expansion.

   Real-world example: Microsoft Azure's engagement with enterprise customers to gather feedback and insights is an approach that leads to product enhancements, increased loyalty, and expansion opportunities through tailored solutions.

6. **Data-informed upselling and cross-selling**: Utilizing data and insights gathered from customer interactions is a powerful technique for identifying upsell and cross-sell opportunities. Tailoring your offerings based on the customer's behavior and preferences contributes to both customer retention and expansion.

   Real-world example: Amazon's recommendation algorithm, based on customer purchase history and behavior analysis, drives both upsell and cross-sell by suggesting related products, thereby enhancing customer loyalty and increasing share of wallet.

7. **Loyalty programs**: Implementing customer loyalty programs is an effective approach for not only retaining your most valuable customers but also increasing your share of their spending. These programs can include exclusive discounts, early access to new features, and other incentives, fostering customer loyalty and expansion opportunities.

   Real-world example: Starbucks' loyalty program encourages repeat business through rewards, offering benefits that not only drive customer engagement but also create opportunities for cross-selling additional products and services.

8. **Timely communication**: Maintaining open and timely communication with your customers keeps your brand top of mind. This approach is critical for customer retention and aids in creating cross-sell and upsell opportunities.

   Real-world example: WhatsApp Business enables real-time communication, which not only offers a convenient channel for customer support but also fosters timely engagement that can lead to cross-sell opportunities.

By understanding that the aforementioned customer-centric strategies, though often associated with retention, are equally effective in achieving customer expansion, growth product managers can implement a holistic approach to CRM. This approach results in not only retaining customers but also increasing the share of wallet from existing customers, ultimately contributing to sustainable business growth.

Establishing a performance-driven culture – the keystone of long-term customer success

Throughout this chapter, we've explored the intricacies of customer success, focusing on strategies that are not only effective for retaining existing customers but also for expanding your share of their wallets. However, achieving these dual goals cannot be realized without a fundamental component—establishing a **performance-driven culture**. This culture, which operates at both the team and individual levels, underpins the successful execution of the strategies discussed, ensuring that the customer remains at the heart of your organization's mission.

Why a performance-driven culture matters

The strategies we've discussed for retaining and expanding your customer base are reliant on a culture that values and prioritizes customer success. Without this cultural foundation, it's challenging to consistently deliver on the promises of personalized engagement, proactive support, value-added services, and targeted upsell and cross-sell efforts.

Here's why a performance-driven culture matters:

1. **Consistency**: A performance-driven culture ensures that customer-centric practices are consistently applied across the organization. It sets the tone for everyone to deliver excellent service and value consistently.

2. **Accountability**: Individual and team accountability for customer success and expansion is a cornerstone of a performance-driven culture. It ensures that responsibilities are clear and that results are monitored and improved upon.

3. **Continuous improvement**: Such a culture fosters a commitment to ongoing learning and innovation. Teams are encouraged to seek better ways of serving and expanding their customer base.

4. **Customer centricity**: It places the customer at the center of every decision and action. When the entire organization is aligned around the goal of customer success, it's easier to identify and act on opportunities for retention and expansion.

Establishing a performance-driven culture is no small task, but there are common practices that can help guide your organization in this direction:

1. **Clear communication**: Clearly communicate the organization's mission, values, and expectations regarding customer success and expansion. Ensure every team member understands their role in achieving these objectives.

2. **Setting performance metrics**: Define and measure KPIs that are aligned with customer success and expansion goals. Make these metrics visible to all team members and hold regular reviews to track progress.

3. **Training and development**: Invest in training and development programs that equip your teams with the skills and knowledge they need to excel in customer-centric roles. This includes product knowledge, communication skills, and understanding customer needs.

4. **Recognition and rewards**: Implement a system of recognition and rewards for outstanding performance in customer success and expansion efforts. This can be in the form of bonuses, promotions, or simply acknowledging exceptional work.

5. **Data-informed decision-making**: Foster a culture where decisions are based on data and insights gathered from customer interactions. Encourage teams to utilize data to identify opportunities for improving customer success and expansion efforts.

6. **Regular feedback**: Create a feedback loop where team members can provide input on strategies and processes. Encourage them to share their experiences with customers, both positive and negative, to drive continuous improvement.

7. **Cross-functional collaboration**: Encourage cross-functional collaboration and knowledge sharing. Ensure that different departments work together to deliver seamless customer experiences and identify expansion opportunities.

8. **Customer-centric rituals**: Establish rituals that keep the customer in focus. For example, kick off meetings with customer success stories, and regularly share customer feedback and success metrics with the entire organization.

It is important to emphasize that the strategies for retaining and expanding your customer base are underpinned by the establishment of a performance-driven culture. This culture aligns the entire organization with the central mission of customer success. It encourages accountability, continuous improvement, and customer centricity, all of which are essential for achieving long-term customer success. By implementing the common practices mentioned, you can create an environment that not only retains and expands your customer base but also propels your organization toward sustained growth and prosperity.

Summary

In the ever-evolving landscape of business, customer success has become the pot of gold at the end of the rainbow. In this comprehensive chapter, we've explored various strategies and practices that can guide organizations toward achieving customer success and sustaining long-term growth. The underlying premise is clear: keeping your existing customers satisfied and engaged and expanding their engagement with your products and services is the key to unlocking sustained product growth.

The chapter began by emphasizing the importance of a solid foundation. By laying the groundwork with strategies for effective onboarding, adoption, and retention, organizations can ensure that the customer journey starts on the right foot. These early stages set the tone for the entire relationship, ensuring that customers feel valued and supported from day one. We highlighted real-world examples, such as Zendesk, Salesforce, and Slack, to illustrate how leading companies excel in these foundational aspects.

Once the foundation is in place, it's essential to scale your customer success teams strategically. This section emphasized the significance of defining roles and responsibilities, identifying the right skill set, and fostering a collaborative culture. Real-world examples from companies such as Amazon, LinkedIn, and Airbnb demonstrate the importance of efficient onboarding, continuous learning, and cross-functional collaboration for effective scaling.

The subsequent segment focused on the critical art of building strong customer relationships. Engaging with customers, delivering value-added services, and driving upsells and cross-sells are highlighted as key elements of this process. While some of these strategies are traditionally associated with customer retention, we emphasized that they are equally effective in customer expansion. Real-world examples from Netflix, Apple, Amazon, and Starbucks illustrate how personalized engagement, proactive support, value-added services, and tailored communication are integral to both retention and expansion.

The final section underscored the pivotal role of a performance-driven culture in customer success. We explained why such a culture is essential and outlined common practices for fostering it. Clear communication, setting performance metrics, training and development, recognition and rewards, data-informed decision-making, regular feedback, cross-functional collaboration, and customer-centric rituals are some key elements that contribute to the establishment of such a culture.

In essence, this chapter painted a comprehensive picture of the journey toward customer success, emphasizing that it's not just about acquiring customers but ensuring they remain engaged, satisfied, and open to further opportunities. By following these strategies and establishing a performance-driven culture, organizations can not only retain their existing customers but also maximize their share of the wallet, driving sustainable growth and prosperity. The pot of gold, in the form of loyal, engaged customers, is attainable for those willing to invest in their customer success journey.

Questions

1. What are foundational strategies for effective customer success, and why are they important?

2. How can organizations strategically scale their customer success teams to meet increasing demands?

3. Why are personalized engagement and value-added services essential for customer relationships, and how do they contribute to both retention and expansion?

4. What is the role of feedback and collaboration in customer success, and how can these practices benefit both retention and expansion?

5. How can a data-informed approach contribute to upselling and cross-selling, and why is it important for customer expansion?

6. Why is establishing a performance-driven culture crucial for long-term customer success, and what are common practices for achieving this culture?

Answers

1. Foundational strategies for customer success include onboarding, adoption, and retention. These strategies are crucial because they establish a strong customer relationship from the start, ensuring that customers feel valued and supported throughout their journey with your product or service. Examples such as Salesforce and Zendesk demonstrate how these strategies lead to customer satisfaction and loyalty.

2. To scale customer success teams effectively, organizations should define clear roles and responsibilities, identify the right skill set, leverage data and metrics, streamline onboarding and training, promote continuous learning, foster a collaborative culture, automate routine tasks, and monitor and adjust their strategies. Leading companies such as Amazon and Slack show the significance of these approaches in efficient team scaling.

3. Personalized engagement and value-added services are essential because they create a strong customer-centric focus. They enhance customer satisfaction and loyalty, which are critical for retention, while also creating opportunities for cross-selling and upselling. Netflix and Amazon Prime exemplify how these approaches foster engagement, satisfaction, and increased spending.

4. Feedback and collaboration involve actively seeking input from customers and internal teams. These practices support product improvements and enhance customer relationships, benefiting retention. Additionally, they lead to custom-tailored solutions and create upsell opportunities for expansion. Microsoft Azure and Spotify demonstrate the power of this collaborative approach.

5. Data-informed decision-making enables organizations to identify upsell and cross-sell opportunities based on customer behavior and preferences. This approach is crucial for customer expansion as it tailors its offerings to individual needs and preferences. Amazon's recommendation algorithm showcases how data can drive both upselling and cross-selling.

6. A performance-driven culture is essential as it ensures consistency, accountability, continuous improvement, and customer centricity throughout the organization. Common practices for achieving this culture include clear communication, setting performance metrics, training and development, recognition and rewards, data-driven decision-making, regular feedback, cross-functional collaboration, and customer-centric rituals. These practices create a holistic environment for both customer retention and expansion, as demonstrated in the examples of organizations such as Starbucks and Amazon.

Part 4:
Winning the Battle and the War

Part 4 contains three chapters that discuss "winning the battle and the war," putting a spotlight on growth product managers, evolving from using reactive retention tactics to using proactive customer-centric growth strategies that cement enduring loyalty and expand wallet share responsibly.

This part covers the following chapters:

- *Chapter 10, Maintaining High Customer Retention Rates*
- *Chapter 11, Unlocking Wallet Share through Expansion Revenue*
- *Chapter 12, The Future of a Growth Product Manager*

10

Maintaining High Customer Retention Rates

You have probably heard of the saying "*Acquiring a new customer can cost five times more than retaining an existing customer.*" As we venture further into the world of growth product management, we find ourselves in *Chapter 10*, a chapter that unveils the art of *Maintaining High Customer Retention Rates*.

In the ever-evolving marketplace, where innovation and competition are constant, customer retention stands as the linchpin of sustainable growth. It is not merely an option but a necessity in this landscape. Customer churn—the silent enemy—can deplete profits and stifle progress. This is where growth product managers step into the spotlight. They must embrace the significance of customer retention—not just to save customers but as a defense against the costly repercussions of churn.

In this chapter, we will explore the critical skills that growth product managers must cultivate to thrive in this arena:

- The importance of customer retention in product growth
- Strategies for improving customer retention
- The role of customer feedback in improving retention—collecting and acting on customer feedback to improve retention
- Measuring and tracking customer retention
- Customer-centric retention—focusing on customer needs and expectations to build long-term relationships

These skills, which are weaved throughout this chapter, are your keys to unlocking the potential of *customers for life*. They will provide you with the knowledge, insights, and practices needed to rise above the competition and guide your organization toward enduring success.

The importance of customer retention in product-led growth

Imagine this: a growth strategy where your product becomes the driving force behind customer acquisition, conversion, and, most importantly, retention. This is the essence of **product-led growth** (**PLG**), a transformative approach that has emerged as the compass for businesses navigating the dynamic currents of today's ever-evolving market. Customer retention within the realm of PLG is not just beneficial; it's a fundamental necessity.

Fundamentally, PLG relies on the notion that if your product is valuable and user-friendly, customers will not only sign up but stick around. Therefore, retention becomes a central component of PLG as it directly influences the sustainable growth trajectory. By retaining existing customers and ensuring they continue to derive value from the product, organizations can build a solid foundation for consistent PLG.

Defining customer retention in PLG

In the context of PLG, customer retention goes beyond the simple act of retaining customers. It involves nurturing and deepening the relationship between the user and the product. To define customer retention within PLG, it's crucial to consider the following elements:

- **Continual engagement**: Customer retention is not about passive users; it's about keeping them actively engaged. In a PLG model, users should consistently find value in the product, which encourages them to stay and explore further.

- **User-centric approach**: Retaining customers in PLG is achieved by focusing on the customer experience for both end users and economic buyers. It's about understanding the customer journey for all stakeholders, addressing their pain points, and consistently delivering a product that meets their evolving needs. This means not only making sure the end users see value in using the product but also ensuring the economic buyers (such as executives who approve purchases) realize tangible ROI and benefits from the products being bought.

- **Subscriptions, upgrades, and renewals**: In many PLG models, the revenue model revolves around subscriptions, renewals, and upgrades. Therefore, customer retention involves keeping users on these revenue-generating paths, not only retaining them but also increasing their lifetime value. This means getting customers to renew their subscriptions on an ongoing basis, as well as upselling them to more advanced tiers and features.

The role of retention in sustainable growth

Sustainable growth is the holy grail of business success. It's not merely about short-term spikes in user numbers or revenue but about building a strong, resilient, and adaptable enterprise. In the context of PLG, the role of retention in achieving sustainable growth is paramount. Let's dive into some of the critical roles it plays.

Stability in the user base

In the world of PLG, the stability of your user base is a linchpin in the pursuit of sustainable growth. High customer churn can lead to erratic growth patterns, making it challenging to plan for the future. Imagine a scenario where a **Software-as-a-Service** (**SaaS**) company offers a user-friendly project management tool and a significant portion of their user base is made up of freelancers and small businesses. If customer retention is not prioritized, freelancers and businesses may migrate to competitors' tools due to a lack of support or evolving needs. This churn can result in unpredictable drops in user numbers and revenue. However, by implementing retention strategies, such as providing personalized onboarding and ongoing support, the company can stabilize its user base. This stability, in turn, allows them to forecast future growth more accurately and plan their resources and expansion accordingly.

Predictable revenue

Predictability in revenue is a significant aspect of sustainable growth, and customer retention is the cornerstone of this financial stability in PLG. Consider a mobile app that offers both free and premium versions. By focusing on customer retention, they can ensure that free users consistently find value in the app, eventually converting them into premium subscribers. This retention-driven approach secures a more predictable revenue stream than solely relying on sporadic user acquisitions.

With an ever-growing number of retained subscribers, the company can better plan for investments in product development, marketing, and infrastructure, knowing that a substantial portion of their revenue comes from a stable, loyal customer base.

This concept of revenue predictability relies heavily on recurring customer payments over extended lifetimes, referred to as **annual recurring revenue** (**ARR**). ARR refers to the total annualized sales from ongoing subscriber contracts. For example, a SaaS company with 100 customers paying $50 per month has an ARR of $60,000 ($50 * 12 months * 100 customers).

By retaining customers for longer durations, companies can count on these recurring revenue streams, which contribute to healthy ARR figures. This enables reliable financial forecasting, steady growth trajectories, and confident allocation of resources into future product enhancements, thereby catalyzing a positive cycle of compounding returns.

Amplified network effects

Network effects are a potent force in many PLG models, where a product becomes more valuable as more users join. Customer retention plays a crucial role in harnessing and amplifying these effects. As an example, consider a social media platform. By retaining engaged users and continuously enhancing their experience, the platform can foster a loyal community. These retained users are more likely to invite friends and acquaintances, actively participate in discussions, share content, and invite new users to join. Their advocacy and referrals amplify the network effect, leading to organic growth, as the platform becomes more valuable and vibrant with each retained user who remains active and engaged. This organic growth, fueled by customer retention, reinforces the platform's position in the market and solidifies its long-term success.

In the dynamic landscape of PLG, customer retention emerges as the linchpin for achieving stability, predictability, and amplified network effects, all of which are essential elements in the pursuit of sustainable growth. By mastering the art of retaining and nurturing your user base, you not only ensure the longevity of your product but also position your organization for enduring success in the ever-evolving market.

Cost savings and increased revenue from retained customers

Customer acquisition can be an expensive endeavor. It requires marketing, sales efforts, and (often) heavy discounts to attract new customers. On the other hand, retaining customers offers substantial cost savings, making it a highly profitable strategy. Here's how it works:

- **Reduced acquisition costs**: Acquiring new customers often demands significant marketing expenditure. Retained customers, on the other hand, come at a much lower cost. They are already familiar with the product and require less convincing to stay.

- **Upselling and cross-selling**: Retained customers are more likely to explore and adopt new features or upgrade to higher-tier plans. This presents opportunities for upselling and cross-selling, resulting in increased revenue without the need for extensive marketing efforts.

- **Lifetime value maximization**: By extending the lifetime value of customers, businesses can tap into an ongoing revenue stream. Customers who remain engaged over the long term are more likely to continue spending and even become brand advocates.

- **Volume pricing models**: Tiered pricing models need to balance breadth of adoption with depth of usage. While low entry prices attract new customers, volume discounts encourage organizations to consolidate workflows onto the platform. Graduated discount tiers reward higher utilization levels with better rates, thus incentivizing heavy usage and increased account expansion.

Case studies on successful PLG with high customer retention

Real-world examples often provide the most convincing evidence of a strategy's effectiveness. Let's delve into a few case studies that highlight how successful PLG strategies have significantly contributed to high customer retention rates:

- **Dropbox—the power of referrals**: Dropbox's "refer-a-friend" program is an iconic example of PLG. By offering extra storage space in exchange for referrals, Dropbox achieved remarkable customer growth and retention. This strategy turned satisfied users into advocates and significantly increased the product's stickiness.

- **Slack—simplifying collaboration**: Slack's user-centric approach focuses on streamlining collaboration. By making the workplace communication process easier and more enjoyable, Slack retained users by becoming indispensable in their daily routines.

- **Zoom—the role of a free plan**: Zoom's success lies in its freemium model, which not only facilitates user acquisition but also retention. The free plan allows users to become familiar with the product and experience its value before committing to a paid plan, resulting in high customer retention rates.

In each of these cases, customer retention strategies have played a pivotal role in propelling these companies to the forefront of their respective industries. They showcase how PLG, when combined with effective retention efforts, can lead to sustainable growth and long-lasting customer relationships.

In the sections that follow, we will explore strategies that growth product managers can employ to foster customer retention within a PLG framework. By understanding the importance of retention, defining it within the PLG context, and recognizing its role in sustainable growth and cost savings, you will be better equipped to steer your organization toward enduring success.

Strategies for improving customer retention

In the previous section, we delved into the pivotal role that customer retention plays in the context of PLG and explored the numerous benefits it brings to organizations that prioritize it. Now, let's shift our focus to specific strategies that can be employed to enhance customer retention within the PLG framework.

Strategy 1 – personalization powered by interoperability

Personalization is a cornerstone of effective customer retention that's enabled by rich user data and flexible integrations. By tailoring product experiences to individual needs and preferences, companies can create deeper connections. Netflix leverages algorithms to analyze behavior and serve personalized recommendations that enhance engagement.

Transitioning from one-size-fits-all requires understanding usage patterns, preferences, and feedback. Incorporating this data into tailored product experiences makes users feel valued.

To enable personalization, products must strike a balance between proprietary and open ecosystems. Open standards promote accessibility, but closed architectures allow tighter integration between suite tools. For example, custom merchandisers can conduct eCommerce on Shopify while leveraging Klaviyo for email campaigns thanks to open APIs. This interoperability provides modular capabilities.

Conversely, Amazon retains customers by enforcing compatibility across its properties, including Prime Video, Alexa devices, and Whole Foods discounts. This consistency comes at the cost of flexibility. Companies must assess the right strategic mix based on user expectations.

Overall, personalization sits at the intersection of data intelligence and ecosystem versatility, coming together to foster individualized experiences that deepen retention.

Real-world example – Netflix

Netflix, a pioneer in content streaming, excels in personalization. Its recommendation algorithm analyzes user viewing habits, ratings, and searches to suggest content tailored to individual preferences. This level of personalization keeps users engaged and minimizes churn, showcasing the effectiveness of understanding and catering to individual user needs.

Strategy 2 – onboarding and user education

The onboarding process is a critical juncture in the customer journey that shapes the initial user experience. A seamless onboarding experience not only enhances user satisfaction but also contributes significantly to customer retention. Slack, a prominent example, guides users through a series of interactive tutorials during onboarding, ensuring they grasp the platform's features and functionalities. This proactive approach minimizes confusion and encourages users to integrate the product into their daily workflows.

Effective user education extends beyond onboarding, incorporating ongoing resources such as webinars, tutorials, and knowledge bases. By providing users with the tools and knowledge needed to maximize product value, companies empower them to become proficient users, fostering long-term commitment.

Real-world example – Slack

Slack, a popular team collaboration platform, prioritizes onboarding with interactive tutorials. During the onboarding process, Slack guides users through key features and functionalities, ensuring a smooth introduction to the platform. This hands-on approach minimizes confusion, accelerates user proficiency, and sets the foundation for a positive long-term relationship.

Strategy 3 – loyalty programs and incentives

Loyalty programs are a classic yet powerful tool for retaining customers. These programs reward users for their continued engagement and can take various forms, from point systems to exclusive access and discounts. Amazon Prime, with its combination of fast shipping, streaming services, and exclusive deals, exemplifies how a comprehensive loyalty program can enhance customer retention.

Implementing a successful loyalty program involves aligning incentives with the unique value propositions of the product. By offering rewards that resonate with users, companies can create a sense of loyalty that extends beyond the core product features.

Real-world example – Amazon Prime

Amazon Prime's loyalty program is a benchmark for comprehensive incentives. Prime members enjoy benefits such as fast shipping, exclusive access to streaming services, and special discounts. This diverse range of perks caters to various user preferences, creating a compelling loyalty program that encourages users to stay engaged with the platform.

Strategy 4 – customer support and communication

Effective customer support is foundational to retention. Responding promptly to user inquiries, resolving issues efficiently, and providing clear communication are vital components of a robust customer support strategy. Zendesk, a leader in customer support solutions, not only offers a comprehensive platform for issue resolution but also emphasizes proactive communication through email updates and a user-friendly interface.

To enhance customer support within a PLG model, companies can integrate support features directly into the product, enabling users to access help resources without leaving the application. By facilitating seamless communication, companies foster a positive user experience and build trust.

Real-world example – Zendesk

Zendesk, a leader in customer support solutions, stands out for its user-friendly interface and proactive communication. Beyond providing a comprehensive platform for issue resolution, Zendesk emphasizes clear communication through email updates. This approach builds trust and ensures users feel supported, contributing to a positive user experience.

Strategy 5 – predictive analytics for churn prevention

Predictive analytics leverages data to anticipate user behavior, enabling proactive measures to prevent churn. Spotify, for instance, analyzes user listening habits to predict musical preferences, curating personalized playlists to keep users engaged. By understanding patterns associated with users who are at risk of churning, companies can implement targeted interventions, such as personalized offers or feature recommendations.

Integrating predictive analytics into a PLG framework requires robust data infrastructure and advanced analytics capabilities. By leveraging machine learning algorithms, companies can identify subtle signals indicative of potential churn, allowing for timely intervention.

Real-world example – Spotify

Spotify employs predictive analytics to enhance the user experience. The platform analyzes user listening habits to predict musical preferences and curates personalized playlists. By leveraging data to anticipate user behavior, Spotify proactively keeps users engaged and minimizes the risk of churn, showcasing the power of predictive analytics in a PLG context.

Strategy 6 – upselling and cross-selling techniques

Upselling and cross-selling are effective strategies for not only increasing revenue but also deepening customer relationships. Amazon's product recommendations, based on user browsing and purchase history, exemplify how upselling can be seamlessly integrated into the user experience. By suggesting complementary products or premium features, companies can enhance the value users derive from the product.

In a PLG context, upselling and cross-selling should align with the user's journey, offering additional value rather than imposing unnecessary features. By framing these opportunities as enhancements rather than mere sales pitches, companies can contribute to increased customer satisfaction and loyalty.

> **Real-world example – Amazon recommendations**
>
> Amazon's product recommendation engine is a prime example of effective upselling and cross-selling. By analyzing user browsing and purchase history, Amazon suggests complementary products, encouraging users to explore additional offerings. This strategy seamlessly integrates into the user experience, enhancing user satisfaction while driving additional revenue.

Strategy 7 – content marketing for retention

Content marketing is not solely a tool for acquiring new customers; it also plays a crucial role in retaining existing ones. HubSpot, known for its inbound marketing approach, provides a wealth of educational content that helps users maximize the value of their platform. Regularly publishing blog posts, whitepapers, and video content creates an ongoing relationship with users, positioning the company as a valuable resource.

To implement effective content marketing within a PLG framework, companies should align content with user needs and pain points. By addressing challenges users may encounter during their journey, companies position themselves as partners in their success, fostering a sense of loyalty.

> **Real-world example – HubSpot**
>
> HubSpot, known for its inbound marketing approach, provides valuable educational content beyond customer acquisition. Regularly publishing blog posts, whitepapers, and video content, HubSpot keeps users engaged by addressing challenges and offering insights. This ongoing relationship-building through content positions HubSpot as a trusted resource for users.

Strategy 8 – community building and user engagement

Building a community around a product fosters a sense of belonging and encourages users to stay invested. Salesforce, a pioneer in cloud-based CRM, has a vibrant community where users can connect, share insights, and seek advice. This sense of community not only enhances user engagement but also provides a support network that contributes to long-term retention.

In a PLG model, companies can facilitate community building by integrating social features directly into the product. This could include discussion forums, user-generated content, or collaborative features that encourage users to interact with both the product and each other.

> **Real-world example – Salesforce**
>
> Salesforce has successfully built a vibrant community around its cloud-based CRM. Users can connect, share insights, and seek advice, fostering a sense of belonging. By integrating community-building features directly into the product, Salesforce not only enhances user engagement but also creates a valuable support network that contributes to long-term retention.

Strategy 9 – referral programs and advocacy campaigns

Satisfied customers can be powerful advocates for a product, driving both new acquisitions and increased retention. Dropbox, for example, achieved widespread adoption by implementing a referral program that rewarded users for referring friends. By turning existing users into advocates, companies tap into a network effect that extends their reach and strengthens customer loyalty.

Referral programs within a PLG framework should be designed to align with the product's virality and ease of sharing. By making it seamless for users to refer others and providing meaningful incentives, companies can leverage the power of word-of-mouth marketing to drive retention.

> **Real-world example – Dropbox**
>
> Dropbox achieved widespread adoption through a successful referral program. By rewarding users for referring friends and acquaintances, Dropbox tapped into the power of word-of-mouth marketing. This strategy not only facilitated user acquisition but also turned satisfied users into advocates, contributing to both short-term growth and long-term retention.

These real-world examples highlight how successful organizations implement these strategies within a PLG framework, showcasing best practices that growth product managers can learn from and adapt to their specific contexts.

Lessons for growth product managers

Growth product managers play a pivotal role in steering PLG initiatives toward success, and the strategies discussed here offer valuable lessons they can integrate into their management approach. Let's discuss some of these lessons:

- **Customer-centricity is key**: Growth product managers must prioritize a customer-centric mindset. Personalization, onboarding excellence, and loyalty programs all underscore the importance of understanding and addressing the unique needs and preferences of users. By putting the customer at the center of decision-making, managers can drive sustained engagement and loyalty.

- **Proactive communication and support are non-negotiable**: As the bridge between development teams and users, growth product managers should emphasize the significance of effective communication and support. Zendesk's proactive communication and support strategies serve as a model. Seamless user experiences, facilitated by responsive support and clear communication, contribute significantly to customer satisfaction and, consequently, retention.

- **Harnessing data for predictive insights**: Growth product managers should harness the power of data for predictive analytics. Understanding user behavior through data-driven insights enables proactive measures against churn. Spotify's use of predictive analytics to curate personalized playlists is a testament to the impact of data in anticipating and meeting user needs.

- **Balancing monetization with user value**: Upselling and cross-selling strategies require a delicate balance. Growth product managers must ensure that these techniques align with user journeys and add genuine value. Amazon's product recommendations illustrate how a balance between revenue goals and enhancing user value can drive both short-term gains and long-term loyalty.

- **Building and nurturing communities**: Community building is not just a marketing tactic; it's a strategic move for fostering user engagement and loyalty. Growth product managers can take a page from Salesforce's book and embed community-building features directly into the product. Facilitating interactions among users not only strengthens the user base but also serves as a valuable resource for mutual support.

- **Advocacy as a growth engine**: Referral programs, when executed effectively, can turn satisfied users into advocates. Growth product managers should recognize the potential of user advocacy as a powerful growth engine. By making referral processes seamless and rewarding, managers can tap into the network effect, expanding the user base while deepening existing customer loyalty.

In navigating the complex landscape of PLG, growth product managers must view these strategies not as isolated tactics but as an interconnected framework for sustainable growth. By weaving these lessons into their management approach, growth product managers can drive user retention, fuel product-led growth, and position their organizations at the forefront of an ever-evolving industry.

The role of customer feedback in improving retention

In the preceding section, we explored a comprehensive set of strategies aimed at bolstering customer retention in the context of PLG. Now, we'll turn our attention to a critical component that underpins the success of these strategies: customer feedback. Understanding the importance of customer feedback and how to effectively collect, analyze, and act on it is paramount for growth product managers striving to optimize retention.

Importance of customer feedback in retention

Customer feedback serves as a powerful compass that guides product development and customer experience initiatives. In the realm of retention, it plays a dual role. Firstly, it provides valuable insights into customer satisfaction, helping organizations gauge the effectiveness of their retention strategies. Secondly, and perhaps more importantly, customer feedback unveils areas for improvement, allowing companies to address pain points and enhance the overall user experience.

By actively seeking and leveraging customer feedback, growth product managers gain a deeper understanding of user sentiments, preferences, and challenges. This knowledge becomes the bedrock upon which targeted retention efforts can be built, fostering a continuous cycle of improvement.

Different feedback collection channels

To harness the full potential of customer feedback, it's crucial to employ diverse collection channels that cater to various user preferences and behaviors. Here are some key channels:

- **Surveys and questionnaires**: Structured surveys and questionnaires provide a systematic way to gather feedback. Platforms such as SurveyMonkey and Google Forms offer convenient tools for creating and distributing surveys, enabling companies to collect quantitative and qualitative data.

- **In-app feedback tools**: Integrating feedback forms directly into the product interface allows users to share insights seamlessly within the context of their experience. Tools such as Intercom and UserVoice facilitate in-app feedback, capturing real-time sentiments and issues.

- **Social media monitoring**: Tracking social media platforms for mentions, comments, and direct messages provides an organic way to gauge user sentiment. This channel is particularly valuable for capturing spontaneous reactions and identifying emerging trends.

- **Customer support interactions**: Interactions with customer support, whether through chat, email, or phone, are rich sources of feedback. Analyzing support tickets and conversations helps uncover recurring issues and pain points, offering actionable insights.

- **User analytics and behavior tracking**: Quantitative data derived from user analytics tools, such as Google Analytics, Microsoft Clarity, and Mixpanel, complements qualitative feedback. By correlating user behavior with feedback, growth product managers gain a holistic view of the user experience.

Feedback analysis and categorization

Once customer feedback has been collected, the next step is analysis and categorization. Effective analysis involves both quantitative and qualitative methods:

- **Sentiment analysis**: When utilizing **natural language processing** (NLP) tools, sentiment analysis gauges the emotional tone of feedback. This helps categorize responses as positive, negative, or neutral, providing a quick overview of customer sentiment.

- **Thematic analysis**: Thematic analysis involves identifying recurring themes or topics within qualitative feedback. This method unveils patterns and trends, allowing growth product managers to prioritize issues that affect a larger segment of the user base.

Identifying root causes of churn

Customer feedback serves as a diagnostic tool for identifying the root causes of churn. By delving into this feedback, growth product managers can pinpoint specific pain points, usability issues, or feature gaps that contribute to user attrition. Understanding these root causes is essential for crafting targeted retention strategies.

For instance, if feedback consistently highlights difficulties in a particular onboarding step, it signals an area that requires immediate attention. Likewise, if users express dissatisfaction with a specific feature, addressing that dissatisfaction becomes crucial to prevent further churn.

Implementing feedback-driven changes

The true value of customer feedback lies in its transformative potential. Growth product managers must transition from analysis to action by implementing changes based on the insights gleaned from feedback. This involves collaboration between product teams, customer success, and development, ensuring a unified and agile approach to improvement.

Feedback-driven changes can range from minor adjustments to major feature overhauls. The key is to prioritize changes that directly address the root causes of churn and enhance the overall user experience. Implementing these changes demonstrates responsiveness to user needs, reinforcing customer trust and loyalty.

Feedback loops and iterative improvement

Achieving sustained improvement in retention requires establishing feedback loops and a commitment to iterative improvement. Rather than viewing feedback as a one-time diagnostic tool, growth product managers should embed feedback collection and analysis into the product development life cycle.

We spoke about iterative improvement previously; it involves continuously seeking feedback, making adjustments, and measuring the impact of changes. This cyclical process aligns with the dynamic nature of PLG, allowing organizations to adapt swiftly to evolving user expectations and market conditions.

Real-world examples of feedback-driven retention improvements

User feedback plays a pivotal role in guiding product improvements that directly impact customer retention. When organizations actively listen to their users and implement changes based on the suggestions and pain points that have been highlighted, they demonstrate responsiveness that bolsters trust and satisfaction. This fosters improved retention rates over the long run. Let's look at three real-world examples of companies that use feedback-driven development to enhance their products in ways that directly strengthen customer loyalty.

Example 1 – Slack's feature expansion

Slack, the team collaboration platform, consistently relies on user feedback to refine its product. Users expressed a need for more integrations with third-party tools, prompting Slack to expand its app directory. By actively responding to user requests, Slack not only improved retention but also strengthened its position as a central hub for workplace communication.

Example 2 – Trello's usability enhancements

Trello, a popular project management tool, prioritizes user feedback to enhance usability. Users provided feedback on the need for more customization options in task management. In response, Trello introduced features such as card covers and advanced checklists, addressing user concerns and boosting overall satisfaction.

Example 3 – Airbnb's trust and safety improvements

Airbnb places a strong emphasis on user safety, and feedback plays a crucial role in shaping trust and safety features. User feedback highlighted concerns around trustworthiness and security. In response, Airbnb implemented features such as verified profiles and secure payment systems, directly addressing user anxieties, and contributing to improved retention.

In each of these examples, organizations not only collected feedback but also acted on it strategically, resulting in tangible improvements to their products and, consequently, enhanced customer retention.

Turning customer feedback into growth intelligence

To wrap up our exploration of the role of customer feedback in improving retention within the PLG paradigm, it's essential to emphasize the critical considerations for growth product managers seeking to turn feedback into actionable growth intelligence:

- **Proactive listening and continuous engagement**: Growth product managers must adopt a proactive approach to listening. Regularly soliciting and encouraging feedback, even when things are going well, fosters a culture of open communication. Continuous engagement with users not only provides valuable insights into their evolving needs but also reinforces a sense of partnership, making users more likely to contribute meaningful feedback.

- **Holistic feedback integration**: Customer feedback should be viewed holistically, encompassing both quantitative and qualitative dimensions. By combining sentiment analysis, thematic categorization, and quantitative metrics, growth product managers gain a nuanced understanding of user experiences. This comprehensive approach ensures that feedback is not just heard but truly understood, allowing for more informed decision-making.

- **Timely and contextual analysis**: Timeliness is paramount in feedback analysis. Growth product managers should prioritize real-time or near-real-time analysis to swiftly identify emerging issues and trends. Understanding the context in which feedback is provided is equally crucial. Feedback that's received during onboarding, for example, might highlight distinct pain points compared to feedback from long-term users. Contextual analysis allows for targeted and relevant improvements.

- **Root cause identification and prioritization**: Identifying the root causes of issues is a fundamental step in feedback utilization. Growth product managers need to move beyond surface-level insights and dig deep to understand why users are experiencing challenges or expressing dissatisfaction. However, it is not always possible for GPMs alone to pinpoint the technical root causes, and working closely with engineering teams is essential to get to the source. Once identified, prioritizing these root causes ensures that resources are allocated to the most impactful improvements, maximizing the effectiveness of retention strategies.

- **Agile implementation of changes**: The agility to implement feedback-driven changes is a distinguishing factor in successful retention efforts. Growth product managers should streamline communication and collaboration between product teams, customer support, and development to facilitate swift implementation. The ability to iterate quickly in response to user feedback aligns with the dynamic nature of PLG, allowing for continuous improvement.

- **Establishing robust feedback loops**: Feedback should not be treated as a one-time event but as an ongoing process that's integrated into the organization's DNA. Establishing robust feedback loops involves creating mechanisms for constant user communication and maintaining channels for feedback collection across various touchpoints. Growth product managers should institutionalize these loops to ensure that user insights remain at the forefront of decision-making.

- **Balancing user desires with product vision**: While user feedback is invaluable, growth product managers must strike a balance between addressing user desires and maintaining the product's overarching vision. Not every user suggestion may align with the long-term strategy, and decisions should be made with a clear understanding of the product's mission and goals. A strategic approach to feedback ensures that enhancements contribute to both short-term retention and long-term product vision.

- **Monitoring and measuring impact**: Feedback utilization should not end with implementation. Growth product managers must continually monitor the impact of changes on user behavior, satisfaction, and retention metrics. This data-driven approach ensures that feedback-driven improvements are achieving the desired outcomes and guides further iterations as needed.

In essence, turning customer feedback into growth intelligence requires a strategic and holistic approach. Growth product managers who navigate the intricate landscape of PLG with these considerations in mind will not only enhance retention but also position their organizations for sustainable growth and resilience in an ever-evolving market. The journey from feedback collection to actionable intelligence is a dynamic and iterative process—one that, when mastered, becomes a driving force for product-led success.

Measuring and tracking customer retention

Having explored the vital role of customer feedback in enhancing retention, we'll now shift our focus to the essential aspect of measuring and tracking customer retention. In this section, we'll delve into key metrics, goal-setting practices, and data-driven strategies that growth product managers can employ to quantify and improve retention within a PLG framework.

Key customer retention metrics

To effectively measure customer retention, growth product managers must rely on a set of key metrics that provide insights into user behavior and satisfaction over time. Here are some crucial retention metrics:

- **Customer retention rate (CRR)**
- **Churn rate**
- **Net promoter score (NPS)**
- **Customer lifetime value (CLV)**

CRR

CRR measures the percentage of customers retained over a specific period. It is calculated by dividing the number of customers at the end of a period by the number at the start and multiplying by 100, to express the following as a percentage:

$$CRR = \left(\frac{\text{Customers at the end} - \text{new customers acquired}}{\text{Customers at the start}} \right) x \ 100$$

As an example, $(110- 20) = 90/100 = 0.9 \ x \ 100 = 90\%$.

Churn rate

The churn rate is the percentage of customers who stop using the product over a given period. It is calculated by dividing the number of customers lost during a period by the total number of customers at the start:

$$\text{Churn Rate} = \left(\frac{\text{Customers Lost}}{\text{Total Customers at the start}} \right) x \ 100$$

As an example, $10/100 = 0.1 x 100 = 10\%$.

Note that this is the inverse of CRR, so 90% in the preceding example as an inverse is 10%.

NPS

NPS measures customer satisfaction and loyalty by asking users how likely they are to recommend the product to others. Scores are categorized as promoters, passives, or detractors, providing a holistic view of customer sentiment. Scores can range from -100 to +100.

CLV

CLV estimates the total revenue a company can expect from a customer throughout their entire relationship. It involves predicting the average revenue per customer and multiplying it by the average customer lifespan:

CLV = Average Revenue per Customer × Average Customer Lifespan

Setting SMART retention goals

Setting **Specific, Measurable, Achievable, Relevant, and Time-Bound (SMART)** goals is crucial for effective retention management. SMART goals provide a clear roadmap for teams and ensure alignment with overall business objectives. Here's an example:

- **Specific**: Increase CRR by 10% over the next quarter
- **Measurable**: Achieve an NPS score of 60 by the end of the year
- **Achievable**: Reduce the churn rate by 15% within the next 6 months
- **Relevant**: Improve CLV by implementing a customer loyalty program
- **Time-Bound**: Increase customer engagement by 20% in the next 3 months

Cohort analysis and customer segmentation

Cohort analysis involves grouping users based on common characteristics or behaviors and tracking their performance over time. It provides valuable insights into how different cohorts interact with the product and how retention varies among them. Customer segmentation, on the other hand, involves categorizing users based on demographics, usage patterns, or preferences. Both cohort analysis and segmentation help tailor retention strategies to specific user groups.

Using CRM systems

Implementing a robust CRM system is pivotal for effective customer retention. CRM systems centralize customer data, enabling comprehensive tracking of interactions and engagement. Platforms such as Salesforce, HubSpot, and Zoho CRM facilitate personalized communication, timely follow-ups, and the seamless integration of customer information across teams.

A/B testing and experimentation for retention

A/B testing involves comparing two or more versions of a product or feature to determine which performs better in terms of user engagement and retention. Experimenting with variations in onboarding processes, feature designs, or communication strategies allows growth product managers to identify elements that resonate most with users, contributing to improved retention.

Data-informed decision-making

Data is a powerful ally in the quest for customer retention. Growth product managers should leverage user data to inform decision-making processes. Whether they're analyzing feedback, tracking user journeys, or assessing product usage patterns, data-driven insights provide a solid foundation for making informed decisions that directly impact retention strategies.

Benchmarking and industry standards

Benchmarking involves comparing a company's retention metrics against industry standards or competitors. Understanding how a product performs concerning the broader market helps with identifying areas for improvement and setting realistic goals. While benchmarks provide valuable context, it's essential to consider the unique characteristics and goals of the product in question.

Continuous monitoring and reporting

Effective retention management requires continuous monitoring and reporting. Regularly tracking key metrics, analyzing feedback, and assessing the impact of implemented changes contribute to a dynamic and responsive retention strategy. Automated reporting tools and dashboards streamline this process, providing real-time insights for prompt decision-making.

In essence, measuring and tracking customer retention is not a static exercise—it's a dynamic journey of continuous improvement. Growth product managers who internalize these insights, combining metrics with strategic goal setting, segmentation, experimentation, data-informed decision-making, contextual benchmarking, and continuous monitoring, will not only measure retention but propel their products toward sustained growth and unwavering user loyalty within the vibrant landscape of PLG.

Customer-centric retention – focusing on customer needs and expectations to build long-term relationships

As we navigate the concluding section of this chapter, our focus shifts toward maintaining high customer retention rates by embracing a customer-centric approach. Since we understand that the foundation of enduring relationships lies in comprehending and fulfilling customer needs and expectations, we'll explore various facets—from tailoring products to proactive engagement strategies. Let's delve into the crucial practices growth product managers can focus on to contribute to the sustainability of customer loyalty in the realm of PLG:

- **Understanding customer needs and expectations**: Building long-term relationships starts with a deep understanding of customer needs and expectations. It goes beyond merely meeting functional requirements; it's about creating an experience that aligns seamlessly with what customers value. Methods for gathering insights, including surveys, interviews, and user analytics, form the bedrock of this understanding. By actively seeking and listening to customers, growth product managers can decipher not only what features are essential but also the emotional and experiential aspects that contribute to sustained satisfaction.

- **Tailoring products and experiences to customer preferences**: The significance of customization cannot be overstated. Companies that excel in tailoring their offerings to meet specific customer preferences exemplify the impact of personalized experiences. By adapting product design and user experiences to align with diverse preferences, organizations can create a sense of ownership and resonance. This tailored approach not only enhances satisfaction but also positions the product as an indispensable part of the customer's journey.

- **Proactive customer engagement strategies**: Proactivity in customer engagement is a linchpin in maintaining high retention rates. Strategies that go beyond reactive problem-solving and instead anticipate and address customer needs throughout their journey foster a sense of care and commitment. Personalized communication, targeted promotions, and exclusive offers play pivotal roles in cultivating a relationship that transcends transactional exchanges. This proactive engagement transforms customers into active participants in the product's evolution.

- **Building emotional connections**: Emotional connections form the heart of customer loyalty. Beyond functional utility, customers seek products and brands that resonate emotionally. Successful companies recognize the impact of storytelling, brand narratives, and empathetic customer support in fostering emotional connections. By infusing human elements into the product experience, growth product managers can elevate the relationship from transactional to deeply meaningful, creating bonds that endure.

- **Customer success programs**: The concept of customer success is central to long-term retention. Effective customer success programs extend beyond initial onboarding, encompassing ongoing support, training resources, and strategies to help users unlock the full potential of the product. By ensuring that customers continuously derive value, these programs not only reduce churn but also contribute to the growth of product usage and advocacy.

- **Feedback as a continuous conversation**: Viewing customer feedback as a continuous conversation is fundamental to a customer-centric retention strategy. Feedback loops, where customers actively contribute to shaping the product's trajectory, create a sense of shared ownership. By actively seeking, analyzing, and incorporating feedback into iterative product development, growth product managers demonstrate a commitment to co-creating a product that evolves in tandem with user needs.

- **Surprise-and-delight tactics**: Surprise-and-delight tactics inject an element of delight into the customer experience. Unexpected gestures, personalized offers, or exclusive perks not only exceed customer expectations but also create memorable moments. These tactics not only enhance satisfaction but also contribute to positive word-of-mouth, fostering a community of engaged and delighted users.

- **Measuring customer satisfaction beyond metrics**: While traditional metrics provide valuable quantitative insights, measuring customer satisfaction requires a nuanced approach. Beyond the numbers, sentiment analysis and qualitative feedback offer glimpses into the emotional aspect of customer relationships. Understanding the emotional context provides richer insights for refining products and experiences in ways that resonate with users on a deeper level.

- **Long-term loyalty versus short-term gains**: In contemplating the trade-off between short-term gains and long-term loyalty, the path to sustained growth becomes clearer. Prioritizing customer-centric retention strategies may not always yield immediate returns, but the enduring loyalty and advocacy it fosters contribute significantly to sustainable growth over the long term. This strategic perspective requires a shift from quick wins to building relationships that withstand the test of time.

- **Cultivating a customer-centric culture**: The commitment to customer-centricity must permeate throughout the organization. Fostering a culture that values customer needs and feedback requires alignment across product development, marketing, and customer support. It's not just about individual interactions but the collective dedication to putting the customer at the center of decision-making. This cultural shift ensures that every aspect of the organization resonates with the principles of customer-centric retention.

- **Case studies of customer-centric retention success**: Real-world examples serve as powerful illustrations of effective customer-centric retention strategies. By showcasing companies that have successfully implemented such approaches, we draw insights into the specific tactics and initiatives that contributed to their success. These case studies provide tangible examples for growth product managers to draw inspiration from and adapt to their unique contexts.

Maintaining high customer retention rates goes beyond the transactional—it's about nurturing lifelong relationships. The journey involves understanding customer needs, tailoring experiences, engaging proactively, building emotional connections, and fostering a culture that places the customer at its core. Through continuous dialogue, surprise-and-delight tactics, and a commitment to long-term loyalty, growth product managers can transform their products into indispensable companions on the customer's journey, fostering relationships that endure and thrive within the dynamic landscape of PLG.

Summary

Customer loyalty stands precariously valuable in the fast-paced arena of PLG. While hordes of wide-eyed new users may enter the honeymoon stage, growth product managers understand that enduring relationships nurture sustainable success. This chapter outlined the playbook that growth product managers can use to shift from reactive retention tactics to proactive loyalty strategies.

At its core lies cultivating unwavering customer empathy—an intimate understanding of user needs to align experiences accordingly. Leadership must promote continuous research through interviews, analytics, and advisory panels to grasp changing expectations. Embedding users in the design process sparks insights to inform personalized engagement.

Education and communication form the cornerstones of self-sufficient yet supported customer journeys. Robust help resources coupled with responsive assistance channels minimize confusion, building confidence in exploration. Setting new users up for success requires tailored onboarding while continuous training propels proficiency.

Driving advocacy warrants care in enhancing, not encroaching on value. Incorporating referral prompts and usage-based upgrades calls for parity between revenue goals and user benefits. Trust lies in transparency—that is, conveying how each exchange adds value for the end user to nurture a symbiotic relationship.

Note that community sits at the heart of advocacy. In-product features such s forums and ratings that spark meaningful connections between users catalyze organic growth by tapping engaged champions' sphere of influence. Embedding community feeds reciprocity and shared success.

While historical trends provide context, goal calibration requires granular cohort analysis by usage characteristics. Consumption fluctuates across segments - new threats demand urgency, while loyal users call for patience. Custom benchmarking and predictive models assess leading indicators from ancillary signals to address emerging vulnerabilities.

In essence, cementing credibility requires setting realistic expectations before onboarding users onto new terrain. Ensuring pre-purchase messaging aligns with product functionality grounds initial impressions in reality. By leaning on research insights over marketing glam, teams can enable fulfilled promises instead of disappointed hopes.

Equipped with what was covered in this chapter, growth product managers can transform transient transactions into lifelong partnerships. Mature managers know disengaged users signify unmet motivations, not lost causes. Mending broken channels before bridge collapse requires enterprise-wide dedication but pays dividends for generations when powered by empathy.

Ultimately, the focus is on setting realistic expectations, aligning pre-purchase messaging with product functionality, and relying on research insights for long-term success. In the next chapter, we will delve into how you can optimize your **average revenue per user** (ARPU) by exploring strategies that can enhance revenue generation for each user.

Questions

1. What role does customer retention play in the context of PLG?

2. What are some best practices for crafting an effective onboarding experience that enhances customer retention?

3. How can growth product managers utilize cohort analysis of user segments to formulate targeted customer retention strategies?

4. What are some effective methods of capturing qualitative customer feedback to complement quantitative usage data?

5. How can growth teams build emotional connections with customers to improve retention beyond functional needs?

6. Why is it important to balance user desires with long-term product vision when acting on customer feedback?

Answers

1. Customer retention plays a pivotal role in PLG models as the ability to retain engaged, long-term users and nurture their loyalty directly impacts sustainable revenue and growth trajectories in PLG paradigms. Retention supports stability in user numbers, predictable revenue streams through recurring payments, and amplified network effects stemming from the advocacy of happy users.

2. Best practices include personalization to cater to user preferences, interactive and gamified tutorials to boost engagement, preemptively addressing common pain points, conveying value to motivate usage beyond sign-up, usage tracking to identify drop-off points, and contextual prompts to guide the next steps.

3. Cohort analysis involves grouping users based on attributes such as sign-up dates, usage frequency, or features used. By tracking metrics for each cohort over time, growth product managers gain insights into differences in behaviors, needs, and churn risks. They can address cohort-specific vulnerabilities through tailored messaging, life cycle campaigns, or in-app recommendations that have been optimized for specific segments.

4. Methods include in-product feedback surveys with comment boxes, analyzing app store reviews and social media complaints to detect recurring grievances, direct outreach via emails or phone calls to at-risk churn segments, and building user advisory groups/panels that provide qualitative, contextual insights into experiences.

5. Tactics include infusing brand storytelling across touchpoints, emphasizing shared values in communications, conveying company personality through words and visuals, delighting users with surprise perks/freebies, triggering nostalgia through user milestones celebration, and encouraging user-generated content and social connections to foster community.

6. While meeting user desires improves short-term satisfaction and retention, not all desires align with overarching product goals. Teams must gauge the requested capabilities against roadmaps, resources required, technical viability, and platform integrity. This balancing act ensures that the requested improvements contribute positively to both the user experience and long-term platform sustainability.

11

Unlocking Wallet Share through Expansion Revenue

In the previous chapter, we explored various strategies for driving customer retention and reducing churn, both of which are crucial for sustaining PLG. While retaining users represents one important lever, optimizing monetization for each customer also holds immense potential to propel revenue.

Capturing a greater customer wallet share represents a pivotal growth lever beyond baseline user acquisition. As cohorts of loyal users persist thanks to thoughtful retention efforts, opportunities flourish to increase their lifetime value. This chapter covers expansion revenue—that is, recurring income unlocked by optimizing monetization from existing customers—as a metric that quantifies the success of efforts to nurture enduring loyalty and value.

We will explore the components that are crucial to expansion revenue optimization:

- Metrics for tracking expansion revenue
- Strategies to increase wallet share
- Measurement frameworks to gauge impact
- Data-backed testing and personalization
- Avoiding potential pitfalls

Beyond baseline customer acquisition, unlocking wallet share enables compounding revenue lift. However, this requires balancing business goals with user experience preservation.

Equipped with the strategies outlined in this chapter, growth product managers will be able to nurture enduring loyalty and value expansion from customers in sustainable ways. Let's delve into the best practices that enable sustainable expansion revenue in PLG companies. We will start by studying some of the key metrics that will help guide your growth decisions and expand your wallet share from existing customers.

Metrics for tracking expansion revenue

Sustaining scalable growth requires maximizing the recurring value that's been extracted from existing customer accounts beyond baseline user acquisition. This relies on tracking metrics quantifying revenue expansion along multiple dimensions—from aggregate portfolio health signals such as renewal rates to usage-based indicators that point to granular upsell opportunities. Let's explore some key metrics that will help guide your growth decisions.

Annual recurring revenue

Annual recurring revenue (ARR) represents the annual value expected from predictable, recurring customer subscriptions. This core metric forecasts the sustainability of long-term subscription income that's immune to seasonal swings. For SaaS businesses, tracking ARR growth demonstrates scalability efficiency needing lower incremental sales costs to perpetuate revenue growth fueled primarily by renewals.

> **Real-world example**
>
> Cybersecurity leader CrowdStrike demonstrates the scaling power of ARR expansion through land-and-expand approaches to upselling additional endpoint protection modules and platform capabilities. By maintaining ARR growth rates above 60% annually, CrowdStrike is on track to hit $5 billion in ARR by 2026, despite supporting over 19,000 subscription customers already, underscoring substantial repeat revenues through renewals.
>
> Analyzing **incremental ARR (iARR)** from subscription upgrades or expansions indicates success in capturing greater customer wallet share. For example, DataDog generates over 40% of ARR from iARR channels, thus highlighting six-figure expansion deals within crowded Fortune 500 IT environments by interoperating across existing toolchains. This interoperability earns budget share gains from customer technology modernization initiatives.

Average revenue per user

Average revenue per user (ARPU) quantifies the average recurring income contribution from each user account over time. Growth signals, when applied judiciously, enhance monetization capabilities and help with avoiding compromising product-market fit. Top vertical SaaS firms such as Adobe, Autodesk, and Intuit demonstrate mastery in sustaining 20%+ net ARPU gains annually over decades while upholding 90%+ gross retention rates through heightened pricing power linked to differentiated value creation and loyalty cultivation.

Real-world example

Feedback collection platform SurveyMonkey has optimized packaging to balance broad self-serve access with encouraging paid conversions recognizing most value gains for enterprise users. They offer professional plans for $384/year, which provides researchers with advanced analytics such as benchmarking, image embedding, and data exports that lightweight advantage packages lack to spur 18% year-on-year ARPU jumps.

Analyzing usage patterns reduces customer churn risks when expanding monetization. Flagging accounts exhibiting declining engagement following price hikes allows proactive win-back campaigns to reverse potential losses. Meditation app Calm discovered a slight drop in sessions among long-tenured users after adjusting their annual pricing to $70, 26% higher than it was previously. By targeting high-risk subsets with one-time loyalty discounts, Calm restored retention levels while securing expanded budget share from devotees.

Renewal rates

Tracking renewal rates provides essential visibility into subscriber revenue retention, which is critical for predictable growth. While SaaS averages around 90%+ gross annual retention, which denotes seat-level persistence, net dollar retention rates accurately reflect adherence by factoring subscription value changes through expansions or downgrades. For leading platforms, this hovers closer to 110-120%, highlighting successful upselling and land-expand approaches to increasing wallet share.

Real-world example

Collaboration software firm Atlassian analyzes net renewal rates across products, cohorts, and territories to diagnose expansion revenue performance. Identifying churn risks from Jira license downgrades allows account managers to intervene, demonstrate the latest workflow enhancements, or bundle complementary tools such as Confluence wikis to showcase additional value from broader adoption. Such data-informed cross-sells have lifted Atlassian's net renewal rate to over 115%, helping them secure $2+ billion in highly recurring subscription income.

Expansion monthly recurring revenue

Expansion **monthly recurring revenue (MRR)** tracks growth driven by extra purchases from existing accounts such as discretionary upsells or add-ons. These signals reveal customer development efficacy, thus translating retention into high-yield recurring income streams.

Real-world examples

Marketing automation platform HubSpot closely correlates expansion MRR growth with the maturity of customer onboarding processes and account management prioritization frameworks being implemented across regional teams. Quantifying expanded deal sizes, shortened sales cycles, and enrollment into premium tiers over-index against benchmarks allows best practices to be diagnosed, which allows additional wallet share to be collected through prompt follow-on sales conversations during optimal satisfaction windows.

Collaboration tools provider Slack analyzes expansion MRR monthly to assess enterprise plan changes, reviewing sales pipeline growth and proactive support case trends to anticipate revenue expansion/contraction risks from large accounts.

Key lesson: Tracking expansion MRR provides precise visibility into recurring revenue gains from upsells and add-ons, enabling data-backed iterations.

Product usage data

Analyzing usage and adoption metrics helps in identifying underutilized capabilities and power users demonstrating deeper platform needs. These insights feed personalized expansion initiatives and premium packaging development.

Real-world example

By analyzing usage curves, content collaboration platform Notion uncovered an extremely engaged subset of users building internal wikis and knowledge management systems atop tools originally positioned for personal note-taking features. This revealed a clear appetite for enhanced permissions, access controls, and content organization capabilities for scaling usage across teams and business units. Notion responded by launching Team and Enterprise packages priced from $8 to $20 per seat to align value to usage. By doing this, they have converted over half of their highest traction accounts over the past year.

Account-based benchmarks

Account-based benchmarks empower the segmentation of customers by revenue tier or persona to define expansion goals tailored to wallet share potential, thus informing cross-sell prioritization. Comparing actuals against benchmarks signals accounts for management optimization needs.

> **Real-world examples**
>
> Monetization platform Patreon sets tiered 12-month expansion goals for creators that have been onboarded to basic versus pro tiers based on category earnings benchmarks. Identifying gaming streamers or podcasters scaling above analogous creator revenue thresholds informs account manager assignments to accelerate support resources and merchandising partnerships for those exceeding expansion benchmarks.
>
> **Key lesson**: Account-based benchmarking allows tailoring personalized expansion objectives grounded in cohort analysis.

In aggregate, these metrics supply a multifaceted view into optimizing recurring customer value. They constitute the analytics backbone, thus enabling data-backed growth. By maintaining a sharp focus on keeping customers happy and engaged, product teams can create space to drive more revenue from them through pricing enhancements, new premium offerings, and various monetization channels.

For companies whose products are sold on a per-user basis, it is critical to choose the right ARPU frameworks so that growth product managers can nurture a segment of brand devotees and turn it into a thriving source of recurring income. Let's dive deeper into this metric and its variants to understand how we can maximize our ability to monetize user engagement effectively and drive sustained revenue growth.

The significance of ARPU in PLG for user-based sales models

Optimizing **ARPU** has emerged as an imperative focus area for PLG companies to drive sustainability through maximizing user lifetime value. However, to strategically prioritize ARPU gains, growth product managers must first grasp how this metric quantifies user value across critical business dimensions.

This section will help you clarify ARPU's relationship with user acquisition costs, lifetime value projections, and underlying health signals, all of which are vital for data-backed growth decisions.

Key ARPU variants

As highlighted previously, ARPU represents the average recurring revenue generated per user across a defined customer cohort, typically calculated over a monthly or annual period. For software and other digital offerings, this closely relates to average pricing levels.

Here are some common ARPU variants:

- **Average revenue per annual/active/all user (ARPAU)**
- **Average revenue per monthly active user (ARPMAU)**
- **Average selling price (ASP)**
- **Average revenue per user (ARPU)** growth, which signals business health

As a leading indicator of customer value expansion, ARPU growth points to improved monetization capabilities and signals business health. ARPAU lifts indicate greater wallet share capture from existing customers. This may unlock additional funding due to perceived traction.

For example, a 20% annual jump in net ARPAU expanded Shopify's estimated market size, boosting their valuation despite no change in user base size.

ARPU quantifies retention potential

Higher ARPU signifies elevated switching costs for customers and likely satisfaction with offerings creating value. This directly bolsters retention and customer lifetime value. Users generating over 20% above the baseline ARPU have shown 60%+ higher retention rates for SaaS platforms.

ARPU impacts customer acquisition cost payback

With the **customer acquisition cost** (**CAC**) payback period calculated by dividing CAC by gross margin ARPU, boosting ARPU compresses the payback period. This improves capital efficiency, which is vital for scalability. For example, increasing ARPU by 20% directly shrinks CAC payback time, allowing for quicker growth.

ARPU benchmarks by industry

ARPU levels and growth vary widely across verticals. For US SaaS firms, the average ARPAU lies between $150-$250, though outliers such as Adobe at $600+ skew higher. Cloud infrastructure providers see ARPAUs over $1,000. Windows 365 quotes $166 ARPMAU for desktop subscriptions while music streaming ARPMAU hovers below $5. Benchmarks guide the goal setting.

This background on the different ARPU definitions ties to critical metrics such as customer lifetime value and CAC, benchmark levels across verticals, and the health signals that are sent by ARPU expansion, which equip growth product managers to aptly prioritize and measure ARPU gains.

The next section will build upon this ARPU context by arming growth product managers with actionable monetization frameworks to increase wallet share.

Core strategies to increase wallet share

Boosting wallet share requires thoughtful tactics to steadily capture a greater share of consumer wallets by delivering higher perceived value. This section explores a strategic framework encompassing optimization levers across six focal points:

- Pricing models
- Packaging tiers

- Add-on modules

- Upsell and cross-sell

- Promotions

- Loyalty

Astute growth leaders artfully test permutations across these avenues to expand monetization in adherent, customer-centric ways that deliver proportionate added value. Let's closely examine the leading tactics within each approach.

Pricing model selection

Finding optimal price levels involves balancing user willingness to pay against preserving attractive unit economics. Here are some common pricing philosophy frameworks:

- **Value-based pricing**: Pegging core pricing to a broader perceived end-user value, rather than relying solely on underlying costs or competitor benchmarks. For example, the project collaboration platform Asana substantiates increasing prices by quantifying members' productivity lift through time savings and visibility gains. They emphasize how usage significantly boosts internal coordination and output to warrant pricing escalation.

  Real-world example: Adobe frequently increases its Creative Cloud subscription pricing. This is grounded in them communicating quantified productivity gains such as the following:

  - 20% higher project output achieved through time savings from smoother design workflows

  - 57% faster asset creation enabled by AI-assisted automations to users, thereby monetizing generative features

  Key lessons:

  - Anchor pricing escalations directly to platform-created user value backed by empirical usage data evidence

  - Highlight productivity enhancers that are introduced through upgraded tools that warrant proportional wallet share gains

- **Competitive benchmarking**: Comparing pricing norms across rival solutions to address similar consumer jobs to be done helps orient reasonable expectations given the market landscape. For example, when mindfulness app Calm launched its paid subscription bundles, it closely analyzed incumbent meditation app pricing tiers before aligning around $70 annual and $400 lifetime packages. This signaled affordable options despite the highly differentiated content quality.

Real-world example: During its initial launch, Canva analyzed pricing tiers for design platforms such as Adobe and Dribble, as well as emerging competitors. This revealed an average pricing range of $9.99 to $49.99 for SMB use cases. Due to this, Canva anchored around a flat $12.99 monthly plan to signal an accessible entry point that targets a vastly underserved small business segment.

Key lessons:

- Evaluate pricing levels adopted by alternative solutions serving similar jobs to be done to ground expectations

- Identify and serve underpriced niche personas through accessibly priced packs conveying platform value

- **Cost-plus formulas**: Tallying precise product delivery costs first (for example, infrastructure, development, and support), then overlaying standard gross margin percentage targets, can ground responsible customer price points. For example, Roblox (an online gaming platform) candidly factors the required cloud utilization rates and engineering team expenses before settling on customer pricing for its gaming platform.

Real-world example: When determining pricing for its on-demand grocery delivery service, Instacart analyzed the costs of picking, packing and delivering orders, including labor, transportation, and store fulfillment fees. It then set a base commission rate to cover those costs and layered on a markup to reach target gross margins. Initial customer pricing was set at $3.99 per delivery, conveying affordability to compete with supermarket home delivery.

Key lessons:

- Map core operational expenses and base pricing to at least breakeven on delivery costs per order.

- Price competitively to established alternatives while conveying platform value via premium features like faster fulfillment.

- Test promotional offers like free delivery to acquire new customers and drive trial.

Testing combinations of these foundational pricing philosophies unlocks optimal balance points given unique market dynamics. However, pricing constitutes just one side of the equation.

Packaging segmentation

Carving distinct consumer groups into behavioral segments allows tailored product bundles that align expanded features, pricing tiers, and services to the precise value created for each cohort based on their specialized needs. This enables expansion through tiered offerings. Potent schemes capitalize on major needs-based dimensions such as the following:

- **User experience level good/better/best bundles**: Entry-level, intermediate, and premium packages that scale key capabilities, respectively (for example, Zoom's video call plans).

- **Business function role-based features**: Modules and features that apply to specialized sub-organizations such as sales, marketing, support, and engineers that are addressed through tailored pricing (for example, Salesforce add-ons).

- **Company maturity upgrade pathways**: Capabilities progressively expand as customers mature across Basic, Pro, Business, and Enterprise packages over time as organizational needs intensify. This is evidenced by Dropbox's tiering.

- **Vertical editions targeting industry-specific adaptations**: Functionality fine-tuned toward the unique needs, language, and workflows for micro-vertical niches such as software vendors, creative agencies, manufacturing firms, and more. As an example, Mailchimp specializes in features across verticals.

Real-world example

Slack offers specialized plans for large businesses with advanced controls versus smaller groups:

- An Enterprise Grid plan provides granular security, compliance, and administrative controls that apply to large, regulated businesses

- A Standard plan offers core messaging capabilities that cater to smaller teams

Key lessons:

- Profile distinct user personas to unveil core needs and specialized workflows

- Map segmented capabilities to tailored pricing plan configurations that match the demonstrated usage levels

---

Add-on modules

Offering supplemental add-ons and augmenting core packaged functionalities represents another scalable way to capture incremental revenue from existing user bases by precisely matching more specialized niche needs as they emerge.

Real-world examples

Both LinkedIn and Figma build thriving add-on marketplaces with third-party ISV partners:

- LinkedIn platform partners create niche tools for recruiting, sales engagement, creative content, and more that are targeted toward specialized business functions

- Single sign-on access and unified usage billing seamlessly blend external add-ons into the core platform

Adobe Capture enriches its baseline Creative Cloud with tailored add-ons:

- Add-ons cater to needs ranging from advanced font management and multi-layered photo editing to smoother organization-wide asset sharing

- Tight integration keeps users grounded in core editing tools while matching niche activity needs

Key lessons:

- API access and dev tooling fuel external innovator experimentation, thus matching unforeseen user needs

- Curation and single sign-on ease drive adoption across complementary external solutions

Niche modular add-ons augment platform value without bloating core application complexity.

Upsell and cross-sell

Actively encouraging current customers to purchase expanded capabilities through discretionary upgrades to higher-tier packages (upselling) or complementary solution offerings (cross-selling) constitute proven expansion formulas.

Usage metrics that indicate clients who are underutilizing available features can inform tactical targeted upgrade offers inside products, maximizing the likelihood of conversion. Collaboration leader Asana actively suggests higher-tier subscriptions to teams who are exhausting their current limits across dimensions such as storage and project scale, removing branding customization features.

On the other hand, suggestive cross-selling offers precision that matches contextual insights around existing spending or activity types, as well as smooth upgrade paths by minimizing search costs.

Real-world example

Freshworks prompts upgrades to larger SMB and enterprise plans:

- Analyzes when free users show behaviors indicative of them requiring expanded features and support levels

- Triggers in-app guides to scaled plans when usage thresholds are hit over time

Key lessons:

- Define data-backed triggers that map usage patterns to upgrade needs

- Directly prompt contextual plan upgrades at moments user goals exceed current capabilities

Promotions

While tactical pricing and packaging changes redefine longer-term value exchange, limited-time promotions such as discounts, credits, or extended free trials selectively reduce short-term friction that may inhibit initial purchases or upgrades, especially among prospects skeptical of product-market fit risks.

Real-world examples

Headspace offers free "Take 10" sessions to address onboarding barriers. This provides the following advantages:

- It allows prospective users to experience the core value before payment friction

- It lowers the risk for those unsure of real-world app utility

Slack offered expanded 14-day free trials amid the pandemic, which resulted in the following:

- Incentivized adoption by small businesses facing economic uncertainty who required tools to optimize their remote operations

- Targeted users at a point of an acute yet temporary need for openness

Zoom discounted annual plans during peak demand holiday surge, which resulted in the following:

- Tactically reduced user hesitation risks during the critical business purchasing budget availability window

- Prioritized market share gains over short-term unit revenue optimization

Key lessons:

- Address clear point-in-time user adoption barriers through timed friction alleviation, whether it's app uncertainty, economic hurdles, or seasonal budget cycles

- Offer incentives grounded in user experience obstacle reduction versus generic discounts lacking contextual relevance

- Balance targeted promotions that optimize conversion velocity against sustainable unit revenue health

Grounded and timed promotions that help users overcome adoption obstacles can effectively scale revenue trajectories if they're balanced through strategic intent beyond pure unit economics. Their situational applicability warrants evaluation within any customer journey.

Loyalty programs

Expanding ARPU long-term also requires nurturing enduring customer loyalty, which is likely to seed high-value repeat purchases and referral activity through formalized incentive programs offering exclusive tiered benefits, prestige, and special recognition tailored to evolving forms of demonstrated commitment over time.

Real-world examples

Sephora sustains engagement through compelling rewards tiered by commitment levels:

- **Insider**: Entry-level with free samples and birthday gifts

- **VIB**: Mid-tier status with free expedited shipping and makeup classes

- **Rogue**: Top-tier events such as first access to new products and beauty festival VIP passes

Adobe and Autodesk leverage prestigious partner network designations as retention tools:

- Technical support benefits, co-marketing funds allocation, and licensing discounts are conferred based on partner tier

- Stratifying partners incentivizes program investments and expands platform referencing abilities

Key lessons:

- Continually motivate progressive platform behaviors through the desirability of the next reachable status tier benefits and by recognizing community reputation

- Structure tier advancement criteria by balancing attainability for continuous re-enforcement against preserving the exclusivity of top elite tiers

- For B2B ecosystems, amplify participation through partner status designation to compound repeat customer incentives across multiple business entities

To summarize, effectively applying pricing models, packaging configurations, add-on modules, tactical promotions, and loyalty programs constitutes a powerful framework for optimizing willing consumer budget allocations in the long run. Weaving these expansion levers into the customer journey sustains compounding revenue lift.

With the core monetization components established, measuring iterative impact becomes the focus point. The next section highlights analytic techniques that can inform strategy testing effectiveness toward validating tactics that create a rising revenue tide for whole markets.

Key ARPU metrics

With an array of customer monetization levers explored, from tactical pricing adjustments to loyalty program design, the need emerges to quantify the financial impact of these strategies. This requires a sharpened focus on ARPU, a pivotal metric that encapsulates the average recurring revenue contribution of each user.

Optimizing ARPU is imperative for PLG companies to drive sustainability through maximizing user lifetime value. By deeply analyzing ARPU performance, opportunities to boost wallet share come into focus.

ARPU quantifies the average recurring revenue generated per user across a defined cohort, typically measured monthly (ARPMAU) or annually (ARPAU). For SaaS businesses, ARPU closely correlates to subscription pricing levels on a per-user basis.

Several variants provide unique insights:

- **Average revenue per annual user (ARPAU)**
- **Average revenue per monthly active user (ARPMAU)**
- **Average contract value (ACV)**
- **Average selling price (ASP)**

Let's take a closer look.

ARPAU

ARPAU calculates user revenue on an annual basis across various income streams such as subscriptions, transactions, and advertising. ARPAU lift over periods reflects positive pricing or monetization enhancements:

> **Real-world example**
>
> Music platform Spotify gradually increased ARPAU by 23% over 2 years after introducing personalized recommendation algorithms and targeted promotions, thereby driving conversions to premium tiers.
>
> **Key lesson**: ARPAU improvement signals greater wallet share capture through elevated pricing or impactful capability launches that users find valuable.

ARPMAU

Unlike ARPAU, ARPMAU specifically quantifies income from actively engaged monthly user cohorts. This provides engagement-centric visibility into pricing optimization and feature iteration impact.

> **Real-world example**
>
> Collaboration tools provider Slack analyzes ARPMAU monthly to assess enterprise plan changes, reviewing sales pipeline growth and proactive support case trends to anticipate revenue expansion/contraction risks from large accounts.
>
> **Key lesson**: ARPMAU prevents the overestimation of expansion revenue by eliminating inactive users and providing precise monthly signals that guide iterative adjustments.

ACV

ACV calculates the mean annual deal size across renewing and new enterprise subscriptions. ACV and iACV (incremental contract value) specifically diagnose enterprise customer expansion levels.

> **Real-world example**
>
> Cybersecurity leader Crowdstrike closely tracks ACV movements and recurring services consumption across cohorts to optimize expansion revenue from large corporations through value selling and strategic bundling.
>
> **Key lesson**: Enterprise software providers rely on ACV indicators to steer expansion initiatives that focus account manager resources on maximal LTV opportunities.

ASP

ASP measures the average revenue per individual transaction from checkout to checkout. This dial provides eCommerce platforms with granular revenue tuning adjustment visibility across promotions, pricing tests, and catalog merchandising changes.

> **Real-world example**
>
> Shopify's product teams assess ASP impacts from running limited-time discount codes for seasonal sales events or testing reduced shipping minimum thresholds to determine price elasticity.
>
> **Key lesson**: ASP reveals price sensitivity, which is essential for eCommerce margin optimization across various products and promotion types.

Analyzing trends by segment

Isolating ARPU performance across individual user segments, acquisition sources, and attributes reveals deeper optimization opportunities hidden at aggregate levels.

> **Real-world examples**
>
> **User cohorts**: An EdTech platform compared early 2022 registrants, showing a 12% higher ASP against 2021 cohorts. This indicated successful paid conversion campaigns.
>
> **Acquisition channels**: A mobile gaming app analyzed ARPAU by traffic source, finding a 20% lift from Apple Search ads versus social channels, thereby guiding future user acquisition budget allocation.
>
> **Demographics**: A streaming platform analyzed ARPMAU for teenage subscribers and found lower averages but higher overall retention, leading to youth-focused family plan bundles that drove account expansions.
>
> **Key lesson**: Microanalysis of ARPU trends uncovers specific personas and channels where pricing and packaging modifications have the biggest growth impact based on willingness-to-pay signals.

Having established the significance of ARPU growth for sustaining product-led company scaling and explored key ARPU metrics, including techniques to extract insights from trend analysis, let's transition to constructing comprehensive measurement frameworks that can analyze the impact of growth levers on ARPU to inform data-backed iterations. Robust reporting enables the diagnosis of tactic effectiveness and guides strategic optimizations for maximizing customer lifetime value through metrics that cover segmentation analysis, predictive forecasts, churn correlation techniques, and campaign ROI tracking. By continually synthesizing metrics into insights that then inform controlled experimentation, product organizations can create sustainable engines that convert retention risks into expansion revenue.

Measurement frameworks to gauge impact

Implementing quantification frameworks that provide visibility into key growth metrics is pivotal for product organizations seeking to sustain scale by scientifically optimizing business model levers that influence recurring revenue expansion.

In this section, we'll examine analytical techniques that provide visibility into performance lift across drivers of enduring customer lifetime value, including renewed subscription persistence, willingness-to-pay signals from usage patterns, and conversion efficiencies that quantify incremental wallet share capture from current subscribers, which is essential for growth forecasting.

Evaluating renewal rates, trends, and predictors

By tracking user cohort renewal rate trends across quarterly periods, product and customer success teams can spotlight potential subscription revenue retention vulnerabilities by revealing variability across market segments. Further subdivision by attributes such as customer tier and onboard cohorts and verticals unveils additional renewal influencer clarity.

Real-world examples

Collaboration platform Notion performs detailed monthly renewal prognosis analysis by assessing patterns among agency, healthcare, and financial services customers based on historical rates as contracts approach renewal deadlines. By also examining usage intensity correlations, they can calculate at-risk scores and predict non-renewals with 74% accuracy, allowing for preventative account management resource allocation.

Enterprise leader Autodesk goes further by overlaying real-time **net promoter score** (**NPS**) changes from re-subscribers approaching renewal deadlines to relate satisfaction scores causally to churn outcomes. Quantifying this predictive relationship steers customer success managers toward pre-emptive value selling for accounts exhibiting declining loyalty that remains highly strategic based on the current **annual contract value** (**ACV**). This program has consistently lifted enterprise retention rates by over 9%.

Another predictor companies leverage is **customer health scores** (**CHS**) – composite algorithmic metrics that incorporate signals from usage intensity, support case severity, payment promptness, and earned advocacy levels quantified to product embeddedness, referrals, and public app exchange peer reviews. Tracking CHS movement month-over-month provides an 88%-accurate leading indicator of subscriber upsell readiness.

Calculating and interpreting expansion revenue lift

Analyzing usage and engagement data identifies adoption obstacles and underserved subscriber needs, which are prime for expanded wallet share capture. For example, tracking quarterly active usage rates for recently added capabilities across customer cohorts highlights activation gaps indicates urgent expansion revenue opportunities that can be solved by making adjustments such as permissions flexibility or bundling to boost appeal.

Real-world example

Smartsheet tracks feature activation velocity and intensity benchmarked against historical subtype averages to quickly spot adoption lags. Looming enterprise renewals with teams exhibiting lower than 60% typical usage rates across core templates and forms functions trigger automated predictive churn risk alerts, resulting in over 85% faster issue resolution and 20% improved retention outcomes.

For products leveraging usage-based pricing models, examining usage differentials across client workflows also uncovers unwillingness-to-pay signals, which helps optimize package alignment to customer spending. This, in turn, boosts return potential. For example, AWS and Twilio incentivize developers toward higher usage tiers that have been priced attractively to capture a greater share of total workload revenue as data processing and communications needs intensify.

Product usage analysis by segment personas

Evaluating usage metrics across customer segments, buyer seniority levels, and usage intent patterns provides willingness-to-pay clues to optimize tiered plan configurations and pricing ladders for ability-to-pay levels.

Real-world example

Cybersecurity platform CrowdStrike analyzes usage differentiation across IT operations professionals, SOC analysts, incident responders, and board-level policy setters to design tailored plans that address specialized personas. High-level dashboard views satisfy CISO executives while daily activities necessitate extensive detection log filtering capabilities to streamline analyst threat-hunting productivity.

Understanding workflow discrepancies between collaborating users allows for modular plans that comprise common and role-based capabilities that closely fit specialized adoption habits that become evident through usage data signals. For CrowdStrike, this has improved in-product onboarding conversion by over 32% as it has simplified initial capability matching through tailored mix-and-match plans to nurture incremental seat expansions.

Comprehensive reporting frameworks

To enable organization-wide visibility for maximizing customer lifetime value, executives and line-of-business stakeholders should receive access to digestible dashboards that cover metrics such as the following:

- NPS trends by industry verticals
- Quarterly renewal and expansion snapshot
- ARPU movement by market sub-segment
- Feature adoption velocity across the buyer stage
- Campaign conversions to revenue impact

Real-world example

Music streaming giant Shopify builds integrated reporting that aligns with partner ecosystems' revenue health indicators, such as merchant sales velocity and bad debt rates. This influences their future ARPU against their Shop Promise customer satisfaction ratings such as support ticket quality surveys, which provide retention risk signals.

Correlating metrics this way provides comprehensive views to diagnose multilayered influence connections across drivers from partner health that impact product experience. These, in turn, affect revenue-locking retention feeding growth, which is crucial for sustainably scaling companies who are seeking to master growth recursion through cross-metric causal analysis and insight activation.

Data-driven optimization and personalization strategies

By drawing insights from robust reporting frameworks, product and growth teams can conceptualize initiatives that span tailored pricing, exclusive rewards programs, and targeted migrations. Launching instrumented releases and measuring true impact through controlled experimentation using tools such as Optimizely, Refine.dev, and Apptimize becomes pivotal.

> **Real-world examples**
>
> Properly gauging willingness-to-pay risks across segments requires gradual price testing by cohort against usage levels. Figma experiments with offering scaled pricing anchored to asset volume tiers for creative teams while keeping editor functionality constant. This balances enterprise accessibility against margin targets to scientifically derive optimal realization.
>
> Conversely, Calm's A/B tests expanded loyalty programs, granting offline perks such as branded retail partner discounts versus additional content access to quantify incentive configurations most persuasive for increasing paid conversion amongst free trial users in key global expansion markets such as India and Brazil, where median income differences may sway preferences.
>
> While metric analysis should inform strategy, allowing data to solely dictate decisions can result in over-indexing on doubtful signals. Instead, rely on empirically testing guided hypotheses that focus on improving key outcomes such as reduced churn, shortened sales cycles, and expanded deal sizes while leveraging tools that connect data directly to platform code.
>
> Prioritizing consonance between analysis and action is imperative to accelerating learning for growth.

Optimization practices

Optimization practices are informed by tracking frameworks, which execute controlled, data-driven ARPU experiments across engagement, pricing, and loyalty incentive designs using tools such as *Apptimize*, *Price Intelligently*, and *Mixpanel's* A/B capabilities. Let's look at some of these optimization practices.

Feature experience iterations for power users

Iterate features for power users to enhance their experience and potentially drive additional revenue.

> **Real-world example**
>
> A social media platform could experiment with different content recommendation algorithms for power users, aiming to increase engagement and ad revenue.

Promotional messaging performance

Test different promotional messages to understand what resonates best with your audience and drives higher conversions.

> **Real-world example**
>
> An eCommerce platform might experiment with various discount messages to determine which one results in the highest increase in average transaction value.

Pricing model testing

Experiment with different pricing models to find the optimal balance between value for users and revenue generation.

> **Real-world example**
>
> A SaaS company could test a tiered pricing structure to see if it encourages more sign-ups without sacrificing revenue.

Personalized premium offerings

Leverage user data to create personalized premium offerings based on usage patterns and willingness-to-pay signals.

> **Real-world example**
>
> A music streaming service could offer personalized premium playlists to users who have demonstrated a preference for a specific genre or artist.

Referral program ROI

Evaluate the **ROI** of referral programs to ensure they contribute positively to ARPU.

> **Real-world example**
>
> An eCommerce platform might analyze the impact of a referral program on both the acquisition cost and the lifetime value of referred customers.

Churn correlation analysis

Understand the correlation between ARPU and churn to identify potential areas for improvement in user retention.

> **Real-world example**
>
> A subscription-based service might analyze whether users with higher ARPU are more likely to retain their subscriptions, indicating the effectiveness of upsell strategies.

By relentlessly testing and optimizing campaigns informed by ARPU metrics, growth product managers can make customer-centric, data-backed decisions that deliver maximal business value.

The pivotal role of customer success teams

Customer success managers play a pivotal role in partnering with product teams to identify and convert expansion revenue opportunities. They do this by doing the following:

- Monitoring usage signals indicative of increasing platform needs
- Proactively guiding highly engaged accounts to upgraded tiers
- Addressing obstacles inhibiting the adoption of newly added capabilities
- Quantifying the business value of expanded offerings through ROI analysis

> **Real-world example**
>
> A B2B software company's customer success team tracks when free trial users approach storage limits or collaboration caps, which could signal a need for paid plans with greater capacity for sharing and workflow scale. By promptly contacting these accounts, they accelerated conversion rates by over 35%.
>
> **Key lesson**: Customer success teams serve as key partners in detecting and capturing expansion signals through account insights and timely interventions.

Pitfalls to avoid

While a diligent focus on metrics drives growth, certain risks can emerge. To empower growth product managers on their journey to success, it's essential to not only recognize these challenges but also understand how to adeptly sidestep them. Let's look at some of these pitfalls and how to avoid them:

- Vanity metrics – a deceptive mirage
- Data paralysis – breaking free from analysis inertia
- User experience sacrifice – preserving the core value
- Customer segmentation mistakes
- Poor timing of upsells
- Addressing critiques

Vanity metrics – a deceptive mirage

Pitfall: Tracking superficial engagement metrics such as clicks without tying them directly to revenue can be misleading, creating a deceptive sense of success.

Real-world example: A social media platform celebrates an increase in ad clicks yet fails to acknowledge the simultaneous decrease in revenue per user.

How to avoid: Prioritize ARPU data as the primary indicator of financial success. Ensure that your metrics directly align with revenue generation, providing a clear and accurate picture of your platform's economic performance.

Data paralysis – breaking free from analysis inertia

Pitfall: Endless analysis in pursuit of incremental ARPU gains can lead to inertia, hindering progress and missing out on revenue opportunities.

Real-world example: A marketing team spends weeks dissecting user behavior data but fails to implement changes, ultimately missing potential revenue opportunities.

How to avoid: Strike a balance between tracking and rapid testing. Set specific timelines for analysis and ensure that insights gleaned from data are swiftly translated into actionable strategies. Regularly reassess and adjust your approach based on real-time learning.

User experience sacrifice – preserving the core value

Pitfall: Relentless pursuit of upsells can inadvertently sacrifice the core value delivered to users, leading to a decline in customer trust and loyalty.

Real-world example: An eLearning platform introduces excessive ads to boost revenue, resulting in a decline in the overall user experience.

How to avoid: Prioritize user experience above marginal revenue gains. Ensure that any monetization strategies complement, rather than compromise, the core value your product delivers. Strive for a balanced approach where revenue optimization aligns harmoniously with user satisfaction.

Customer segmentation mistakes

Pitfall: Not clearly defining personas and mistakenly grouping dissimilar customers, resulting in less relevant expansion initiatives.

Real-world example: A streaming platform bundles casual viewers and avid fans into one "video lovers" segment and pitches high-end package upgrades to all users, disappointing casual viewers with irrelevant offerings.

How to avoid: Precisely segment customers into groups with aligned needs and willingness to pay. Tailor expansion initiatives to resonate with each group's preferences, without overextending into unsuitable territory.

Poor timing of upsells

Pitfall: Pitching add-ons or premium plans too early or late relative to the customer journey, missing the optimal window for conversion.

Real-world example: A mobile gaming app prompts users to upgrade to a paid subscription immediately after installing the app before they have experienced the core value, resulting in low conversion rates.

How to avoid: Identify the ideal timing to pitch expanded offerings by analyzing customer usage life cycles. This helps map promotions to peak value perception moments when customers are most receptive to upgrades.

By proactively sidestepping these pitfalls, growth product managers can pave a smoother path to sustainable ARPU growth. Avoiding potential setbacks empowers teams to maintain an intense yet balanced focus on revenue metrics without compromising long-term customer loyalty. This agile and resilience-oriented approach ultimately drives frictionless expansion.

Addressing critiques

Pitfall: Some argue relentless upselling optimized for short-term revenue risks eroding long-term customer loyalty and retention.

Real-world example: Constant prompts to upgrade plans or add more product modules could frustrate some users, making them feel nickeled-and-dimed rather than helping them focus on core value delivery.

How to avoid: Ensure expansion revenue efforts balance near-term monetization against nurturing trust and loyalty long-term. Tactics such as transparent pricing, frictionless upgrades, and loyalty rewards help maintain this equilibrium.

Through a proven strategic framework, rigorous analytical toolkit, and practical guidance on risks, this chapter has helped you sustainably nurture increased lifetime value from loyal user bases. As competition intensifies, capturing expansion revenue responsibly and grounded in customer needs differentiates resilient PLG firms.

Summary

Optimizing revenue growth from an existing customer base has become an imperative focus area for PLG companies striving to maximize customer lifetime value and drive sustainable scalability over the long term.

This comprehensive chapter provided you with an end-to-end strategic playbook so that you can sustainably scale revenue by nurturing greater wallet share from loyal user bases. It underscored the immense yet hidden value present within existing subscribers that can be responsibly unlocked through relentless improvement grounded in understanding customer needs.

We began by providing an analytical toolkit for diagnosing expansion opportunities and tracking iterative impact. The following key metrics were highlighted:

- ARR and iARR, which help gauge renewal performance and signal revenue growth efficiency
- ARPU, which quantifies pricing power and retention potential

- Renewal rates, which help with predicting longer-term subscriber revenue retention

- Expansion MRR, specifically tracking upsell income gains

- Benchmarks to tailor expansion goals by user segment

These metrics form the foundation of data-backed decision-making by exposing wallet share growth gaps. Trend analysis by attributes and micro-segments revealed deeper optimization insights.

Next, we provided a strategic framework that covers go-to-market levers to help close monetization gaps in adherent ways that deliver proportionate user value:

- Value-based pricing grounded in platform ROI gains for customers

- Intelligent packaging aligned with the workflows of distinct personas

- Discretionary add-ons that match emerging niche activity needs

- Targeted upgrade prompts during moments of peak perceived value

- Select promotions that smoothen adoption barriers

- Loyalty programs that continually reward evolving commitment

Carefully applying these expansion levers in balanced ways sustains compounding customer LTV expansion while mitigating risks of short-term optimization at the cost of enduring trust.

This chapter also emphasized building rigorous measurement systems while tying tactics to revenue impact, which steers controlled experimentation. Techniques such as cohort analysis, predictive modeling, and customer health scoring expose precise strengths, gaps, and opportunities that guide strategy and investment. Comprehensive cross-metric correlation highlights influence chains, which are required to fuel sustainable growth recursion.

To conclude, overexposure risks that undermine the sustainability of expansion efforts were highlighted. Mitigation tactics for pitfalls such as vanity metrics masking churn, analysis inertia inhibiting action, and relentless upselling eroding trust were underscored to nurture steadfast loyalty as the platform upon which to responsibly scale monetization and exceed user expectations in the long term.

Equipped with this 360-degree playbook which spans essential metrics, proven frameworks, measurement capabilities, and key considerations, growth product managers can unlock the immense hidden value present within existing user bases in a way that earns them enduring enterprise value while helping them stay true to customer-centric principles—the cornerstone for resilient and sustainable product-led company growth.

In our concluding chapter, we will crystallize what we've learned into a future-ready playbook for growth product managers in an increasingly complex market landscape. With user acquisition costs spiraling and retention becoming pivotal, we will highlight essential mindsets and capabilities for growth product managers to navigate uncertainty and spearhead sustainable innovation amid intensifying competition for customer wallet share.

The final chapter sets the stage for discussing the future-forward evolution of the growth product manager role while considering the strategies we've covered in this book to give you decisive insights so that you can thrive in challenging conditions.

Questions

1. What metric specifically tracks recurring revenue growth from upsells and add-ons to quantify expansion success?

2. Name two packaging segmentation strategies that align pricing to user willingness to pay.

3. How can growth teams mitigate the risks of optimizing for short-term revenue gains over preserving long-term user trust?

4. What predictive analytic techniques can steer account managers to preemptively retain at-risk accounts?

5. What pivotal role can customer success managers play in working with product teams to identify and convert expansion opportunities?

Answers

1. Expansion MRR tracks growth driven by extra purchases from existing accounts such as add-ons and upsells. Rising expansion MRR signals effectiveness in capturing wallet share.

2. Packaging by user persona aligns features with specialized workflows. Packaging by business maturity maps capabilities to needs evolution over time, from basic to enterprise.

3. Tactics such as transparent pricing, frictionless upgrades, and loyalty rewards help balance revenue optimization with nurturing long-term trust. Communicating ROI and value gained also grounds perceived fairness.

4. Usage intensity correlation analysis as well as real-time NPS and customer health scoring allow predicting at-risk accounts for preemptive retention campaigns when vulnerability signals emerge.

5. Customer success teams play a pivotal role by monitoring usage signals, guiding engaged accounts to expanded tiers, addressing obstacles inhibiting adoption, and quantifying business cases for upgrades. This captures expansion potential.

12

The Future of a Growth Product Manager

Product management has radically evolved over the past decade. The rapid pace of technological innovation and digital disruption has led to the rise of PLG, where the product itself is the main driver of customer acquisition and revenue growth. This approach centers around designing and optimizing products to solve customer problems and promote organic adoption.

As technology advances, competition continues to intensify, and digital transformation becomes a necessity. Due to this, PLG has become essential for business survival and success. Companies that embrace it react faster to market changes, build stronger customer relationships, and sustain long-term growth. This hyperfocus on products necessitates a new breed of product managers—specialized growth product managers who can strategize and execute data-driven product optimizations for business growth.

Our closing chapter embarks on a journey where we'll explore the critical facets of growth product management. We will delve into the key attributes that distinguish effective growth product managers, the dynamic landscape that shapes their role, and the imperative for continuous learning and skill development. As we navigate the following sections, we will not only uncover the essence of PLG but also highlight the skills growth product managers can expect to acquire on this transformative journey.

The following key topics will be explored in this closing chapter:

- The importance of PLG and essential skills for growth product managers
- The key attributes of a growth product manager
- The evolving landscape of growth product management
- Adapting to stay ahead of the curve
- The intersection of ethics and growth
- Case studies of spectacular product failure

- Growth product managers as change agents
- The future of work and skills
- Career paths and professional development opportunities for growth product managers
- The path ahead—growth product managers as conscientious innovators

As we navigate these topics, you will gain insights into the multifaceted role growth product managers play in driving PLG, equipping you to thrive in the evolving landscape of modern business. As customer expectations and business contexts continue advancing, growth product managers must constantly learn, adapt, and upgrade their skills. Our concluding chapter discusses the key attributes growth product managers need, the rapid evolutions shaping their role, and how they can skill up to remain competitive now and in the future. Let's dive in.

The importance of PLG for modern businesses

The concept of PLG has emerged as a transformative force since 2018, reshaping the traditional paradigms of customer acquisition and revenue generation. Defined by the centrality of the product in driving customer adoption and business growth, PLG has become a strategic imperative for companies navigating the complexities of today's highly competitive markets.

The definition and significance of PLG

PLG represents a departure from traditional sales and marketing-driven approaches, placing the product itself at the forefront of the customer experience. At its essence, this strategy entails designing and optimizing products to seamlessly address customer needs, fostering organic adoption and user engagement. The significance of PLG lies in its ability to create a self-sustaining ecosystem where the product becomes a powerful catalyst for customer acquisition, retention, and advocacy.

In contrast to traditional models that heavily rely on sales teams and extensive marketing campaigns, PLG leverages the inherent value of the product to attract, convert, and retain users. This approach not only aligns with the preferences of today's empowered and discerning consumers but also ensures a more cost-effective and scalable means of achieving business objectives. The product becomes a compelling channel for customer interaction, with its features and usability driving the customer journey.

Case studies illustrating successful PLG strategies

Examining real-world examples provides tangible insights into the effectiveness of PLG strategies. One exemplary case is Slack, a collaboration platform that disrupted the conventional enterprise communication landscape. Slack's success can be attributed to its intuitive design and features, which allowed individual users to adopt and champion the platform within their organizations. The product's inherent virality led to widespread organic growth, transforming it into a staple for businesses worldwide.

Another illustrative case is Dropbox, a cloud storage service that employed a freemium model to drive product adoption. By offering a basic, free version of its product, Dropbox encouraged users to experience its value firsthand. The seamless user experience and utility of the product led to widespread adoption, with users organically converting to premium plans as their needs expanded. These cases highlight the potency of PLG in not only attracting users but also in creating a scalable path to revenue.

The key role of growth product managers in driving PLG

Within the realm of PLG, growth product managers assume a pivotal role as architects and stewards of strategies that propel the product's influence. These professionals act as the linchpin between product development, marketing, and customer success, orchestrating initiatives that drive user acquisition, retention, and expansion.

Growth product managers are responsible for understanding the market dynamics, user behaviors, and competitive landscapes that influence the success of the product. By leveraging data-driven insights, they identify opportunities for optimization and innovation, ensuring that the product not only meets but exceeds customer expectations. They become the champions of a customer-centric approach, aligning product development with the evolving needs and preferences of the target audience.

Furthermore, growth product managers play a critical role in fostering cross-functional collaboration. They bridge the gap between product development teams and marketing, ensuring that the product's value proposition is effectively communicated to the target audience. This collaborative approach is essential for creating a seamless user experience, from initial adoption to long-term engagement.

Key skills and attributes for growth product managers

The multifaceted role of a growth product manager demands a diverse skill set that goes beyond traditional product management competencies. To navigate the complexities of PLG successfully, growth product managers must cultivate a blend of technical acumen, strategic thinking, and interpersonal skills. Let's examine these skills:

- **Customer-centric mindset**: At the core of a growth product manager's skill set is a deep understanding of customer needs and behaviors. This customer-centric mindset involves empathizing with users, anticipating their requirements, and continuously seeking ways to enhance their experience. By aligning product development with customer expectations, growth product managers contribute to the creation of products that resonate with the target audience.

- **Data-driven decision-making**: In the era of PLG, data serves as the North Star guiding strategic decisions. Growth product managers must be proficient in leveraging data analytics to derive actionable insights. By closely monitoring user metrics, product usage patterns, and market trends, they can identify areas for improvement and optimization. This data-driven approach ensures that product decisions are grounded in empirical evidence, enhancing the likelihood of success.

- **Results-oriented focus**: The success of PLG is inherently tied to measurable outcomes. Growth product managers must exhibit a results-oriented mindset, focusing on **key performance indicators (KPIs)** that align with business objectives. Whether it's increasing user acquisition, improving retention rates, or driving revenue growth, growth product managers play a pivotal role in setting, tracking, and achieving these outcomes.

- **Adaptability and innovation**: The landscape of PLG is dynamic, marked by rapid technological advancements and shifting consumer expectations. Growth product managers must possess a keen sense of adaptability, embracing change as an opportunity for innovation. This includes staying abreast of emerging technologies, industry trends, and competitive landscapes, ensuring that the product remains at the forefront of market relevance.

- **Communication and collaboration**: Effective communication is fundamental to the success of growth product managers. They must be adept at articulating the value proposition of the product, both internally to cross-functional teams and externally to the target audience. Collaboration is equally crucial as growth product managers work in tandem with product development, marketing, and customer success teams to align strategies and deliver a cohesive user experience.

- **Leadership skills**: As orchestrators of growth strategies, growth product managers embody leadership qualities. They inspire and guide cross-functional teams, fostering a culture of collaboration and innovation. Leadership skills are crucial for navigating the complexities of PLG, where decisive and strategic leadership can be the differentiator between success and stagnation.

Growth product managers are integral to the success of PLG initiatives. Their role extends beyond traditional product management responsibilities, encompassing strategic planning, data-driven decision-making, and cross-functional collaboration. By cultivating a skill set that aligns with the dynamic nature of PLG, growth product managers become catalysts for innovation and drivers of sustained business success. As we continue exploring the future of growth product management, it becomes evident that the intersection of skills and strategies is fundamental to thriving in the evolving landscape of modern business.

Successful growth product managers, such as those at Spotify and Meta, embody a customer-centric approach, prioritize data-driven decision-making, and maintain a results-oriented mindset. These attributes contribute to the development of products that not only meet user needs but also drive measurable and impactful growth for the business.

As growth product managers navigate the dynamic terrain of user-centric strategies, data-driven optimizations, and results-driven mindsets, it becomes imperative to explore the evolving landscape of growth product management, where emerging trends and challenges shape the future trajectory of this crucial discipline.

> **Real-world example**
>
> To continually improve the algorithms powering its personalized styling service, Stitch Fix makes client feedback integral to product design through surveys capturing detailed style preferences. This tight, structured feedback loop provides the company's growth product managers with rich insights into ever-evolving consumer needs and pain points.
>
> By relentlessly gathering and incorporating user perspectives—both through quantitative preference ratings and open-ended commentary—Stitch Fix's growth product managers can tweak style recommendation engines to boost client satisfaction. Stich Fix's growth as an eCommerce fashion leader, despite having no advertising, exemplifies customer-centricity at scale. The key insight for growth product managers is prioritizing user listening channels that yield actionable enhancement opportunities.

The evolving landscape of growth product management

The field of growth product management is undergoing a profound evolution. As consumer behaviors, technologies, and distribution channels continuously transform, growth product managers must actively adapt to spearhead innovation. By embracing agility, pursuing continuous learning, and leveraging advancing technologies, growth product managers can thrive amid volatility.

The technological imperative for adaptability

We live in a time of unprecedented technological change that compels adaptation. Emerging technologies such as **artificial intelligence** (**AI**) and automation are reshaping products and services. Netflix harnesses AI algorithms to deliver personalized recommendations, keeping subscribers engaged longer. Such innovations demonstrate how technology can transform user experiences when strategically implemented.

However, integrating innovative technologies into product design is complex. It requires growth product managers to expand their competencies to evaluate applicability and prevent adoption pitfalls. They must champion exploratory research, rapid prototyping, and cross-functional collaboration to capitalize on technological opportunities while mitigating risks.

The burden of upskilling can be demanding for growth product managers who are already balancing packed schedules. However, dedication to continuous learning is imperative to leveraging technology's potential. Leading firms such as Google foster skill development by allowing "20% time" for employees to self-direct projects. This policy sparks creativity and lets people expand their capabilities organically without the pressures of formalized training.

Apart from learning itself, growth product managers need frameworks to integrate emerging technologies into product roadmaps. Agile development, which is standardized across digitally native companies such as Spotify, allows for flexible responses to market changes. By emphasizing iterative releases and cross-functional teamwork, agile methods help growth product managers nimbly calibrate product-market fit as smart technologies unlock greater possibilities.

Harnessing the power of digital channels

Beyond advancing tools, growth product managers must also adapt their distribution and engagement strategies to emerging digital channels. Platforms such as mobile apps and social networks provide targeted access to users in their native environments. Integrating these channels is now essential, not optional.

> **Real-world example**
> Amazon leverages digital channels for an omnichannel experience that keeps customers engaged across devices. Their smartphone app features intuitive access to accounts, recommendations, and voice-activated purchasing through Alexa. This convenience helps Amazon dominate emerging mobile shopping trends as consumers transact effortlessly via apps.

To mirror such success, growth product managers should incorporate digital channels early in product blueprints to enable multi-channel consumption. This entails moving beyond channel-specific metrics by evaluating engagement holistically across the complete user journey. Growth product managers must also champion usability and consistency across channels to fulfill rising user expectations.

Fulfilling the promise of personalization

Personalization represents another epochal shift that growth product managers must harness to thrive. Consumers increasingly expect tailored recommendations and experiences. Global personalization spending is predicted to reach $15 billion by 2025, proving it is becoming a product differentiator.

Addressing personalization requires growth product managers to implement sophisticated data tracking such as analytics and surveys. This equips them to categorize users, map needs to features, and define customization parameters. Spotify also pioneers here with its personalized Discover Weekly playlists based on listening habits.

However, personalization also introduces ethical considerations regarding data privacy and transparency. Growth product managers must champion responsible data usage while balancing customization. Strict data governance helps earn user trust while unlocking personalization's advantages.

It is also vital to keep core product functionality consistent, despite greater personalization. Features that enable adaptation such as user preference menus should layer atop a solid foundational product. Striking this balance between customization and consistency across user segments will become a hallmark skill for growth product managers as personalization expands.

Understanding shifting consumer behaviors

Growth product management also requires understanding consumer behavior shifts to align strategies accordingly. The COVID-19 pandemic triggered lasting changes as people grew accustomed to remote transactions and virtual collaboration.

Growth product managers should continuously research emerging behaviors by conducting surveys, interviews, and ethnographic studies. Interactive prototypes can also capture user feedback to assess the appeal of the proposed functionality. Such efforts help growth product managers empathize with users to uncover underserved needs.

Notable innovations have successfully aligned products with new consumer habits. For example, the meditation app Calm tailored its programming toward remote workers struggling with burnout and anxiety amid lockdowns. Calm combined breathing exercises and ambient music to help people find Zen while working from home.

This exemplifies how observing consumer environments can unlock new market opportunities. Growth product managers must vigilantly work to comprehend both latent and explicit user needs to conceive relevant products as behaviors evolve.

But purely chasing trends can also lead products astray. So, growth product managers must balance responding to shifts in demand with sticking to overarching product vision. For instance, crypto startup TripleFi originally strayed from its core offering by expanding into NFTs and social tokens due to their surging popularity. But this deviation diffused focus rather than fueling growth. Grounding in long-term goals and user value helps guide wise product adaptations.

As we've explored, growth product management continues to be shaped by technological breakthroughs, changing consumer behaviors, and other dynamic forces. But with great power comes great responsibility. This brings us to a crucial related topic—the intersection of ethics and growth.

Real-world examples

When the COVID-19 pandemic forced workforce disruption and remote product development, the growth product managers at payment platform Klarna rapidly adopted digital whiteboarding collaboration platforms such as Miro to adapt their processes. This agile adoption supported continued co-creation and innovation rhythm despite physical separation.

By embracing new visual tools enabling remote brainstorming, Klarna's growth product managers ensured product velocity kept pace with consumer payment behavior shifts triggered by the pandemic. Their process adaptability and tool exploration fueled Klarna reaching over 150 million worldwide users. The key takeaway is that growth product managers must continually pilot innovative technologies to unlock efficiencies and sustain speed as changes arise.

Recognizing surging youth engagement on mobile, Nike's growth product managers launched the SNKRS app in 2015 to test harnessing mobile to drive product drops and scarcity-based demand for exclusive shoes. By limiting purchase eligibility for hot releases to the app, SNKRS merged convenience with exclusivity.

Triple-digit revenue growth for Nike SNKRS since inception highlights the potential of digital channels for increasing customer lifetime value. Growth product managers must strongly advocate for piloting high upside but initially risky innovations around emerging formats and use cases. As SNKRS head Carrie Just exemplifies, embracing uncertainty promises breakthroughs.

As growth product managers navigate the evolving landscape shaped by technology, behaviors, and ethical considerations, the imperative to stay competitive compels them to exemplify adaptability and leadership in times of uncertainty. Let's explore how growth teams can proactively skill up and shape product roadmaps to continue driving innovation amid exponential change.

Adapting to stay ahead of the curve

To remain at the forefront of market relevance and customer value, growth product managers must champion agility, exploration, and continuous learning as consumer preferences and technical capabilities rapidly transform.

The pace of change today demands that growth leaders embrace a startup mindset marked by hypothesis testing and rapid experimentation. Rather than rigidly sticking to initial assumptions or yearly roadmaps, truly adaptive growth teams interact regularly with real users in research sessions and usability labs to check product-market fit. They pilot early-stage **minimum viable products** (**MVPs**) prioritizing key user journeys to garner feedback. They also leverage frameworks such as design sprints to quickly ideate and prototype new concepts.

Equally vital is upskilling teams on emerging technologies using both internal training and external certifications. Rotational programs allow team members to expand competencies across domains such as data science, design, and AI ethics. Leaders should encourage reasonable innovation time for exploring new tools. Conferences, hackathons, and prototyping challenges further spark creative applications of advancing capabilities to drive differentiation.

However, adaptation cannot happen in isolation—it requires cross-functional orchestration. Growth product managers are central nodes that communicate insights from the market and shepherd product, engineering, and analytics teams to recalibrate accordingly. They frame problems, outline hypotheses, set testing metrics, and rally resources to fuel invention. With technology and consumer sentiments in flux, sustaining an innovation rhythm is central to both near-term gains and lasting brand loyalty.

As teams skill up and champion agility, aligning metrics that provide essential direction amid uncertainty is critical. An unwavering focus on core user and business outcomes allows product innovation to flexibly evolve while progressing toward the most vital results.

To stay centered despite volatility, growth product managers must crystallize the KPIs that signify success—whether it be user engagement hours per week, account expansion rates quarterly, or new market revenue annually. These measurable outcomes serve as decision guideposts when debating feature enhancements and technology integrations. If a proposed path fails to demonstrably advance these North Star metrics through testing, it warrants careful reassessment, regardless of its novelty.

However, adaptation cannot be open-ended. Innovation still requires a commitment to difficult multi-year tech integrations and adding emerging capabilities such as conversational interfaces. So, while North Stars provide real-time guidance, longer-term roadmaps should describe how building specific machine learning, blockchain, or quantum computing tools can unlock step function advances. Sustaining category leadership mandates rising to the challenge of complex, often unproven investments that incrementally keep raising the bar on user experience.

By balancing adaptable experimentation with a commitment to high-impact technological challenges, growth product managers spearhead sustainable innovation amid exponential change. As consumer behaviors and tools continuously transform, growth teams must champion agility while progressing toward ever-bolder outcomes.

With adaptability and leadership as core growth product management strengths, the path ahead promises abundant opportunities to responsibly harness technology for positive impact. Now, let's examine inspirational avenues for leveraging growth skills to advance financial access, accelerate diplomacy, and amplify social causes.

The intersection of ethics and growth

As growth product managers shepherd strategic development based on data and user engagement, they shoulder immense responsibility regarding ethics. Their decisions directly impact human experiences, reinforce or remedy inequities, and determine the trajectory of technological influence. This section will explore key ethical considerations for growth product managers navigating complex spaces such as privacy, accountability, and vulnerable populations.

Balancing business imperatives and user well-being

A core tension arises between priorities such as conversion rates, engagement metrics, and revenue growth versus user welfare. Data collection and persuasive design, which hook users quickly, generate results but can cause distraction or even addiction. As best-selling author on habits and product design Nir Eyal stated regarding such techniques, *"We have to ask ourselves, is this something we want?"*

Growth product managers must carefully evaluate when business growth imperatives undermine human flourishing. User experience testing helps assess whether certain optimizations feel coercive. Frameworks such as the ACM Code of Ethics and Google's People + AI Guidebook also offer standards for conscientious innovation. Growth product managers serve as user advocates, championing their dignity over marginal revenue gains or vanity metrics.

Data privacy and transparent consent

The maxim "data is power" rings especially true for growth product managers seeking personalized and predictive insights, from purchase histories to location tracking, surface-level and derived data fuel product enhancements. Yet such omniscient surveillance also repels users and regulators. Europe's GDPR guidelines reflect growing demands for data transparency and control, mandating explicit opt-in consent across properties such as WhatsApp.

While data collection powers innovation, growth teams must align practices to informed consent. Product tours should clearly articulate how analytics track experiences. Dashboards enabling data deletion also build trust. When new monitoring tools are launched, proactive communication keeps communities aware rather than ambushed. Growth product managers must shift from exploiting ambiguity to championing clarity regarding data utilization.

Inclusive and accessible algorithmic systems

As AI permeates growth tech for recommendations and personalization, ethical application is vital. Algorithmic bias that excludes underrepresented groups or locks in historical discrimination demands urgent redress. However, auditing for fairness is complex when multiple attributes intersect.

Thankfully, tools have emerged to stress-test our algorithms. For example, IBM's AI Fairness 360 platform mitigates biased data and models. Complementary policy approaches such as Algorithmic Impact Assessments also promote accountability. Inclusive algorithms will require diverse data sets and team perspectives. Growth product managers must proactively dismantle the myth of apolitical tech by championing AI ethics.

Human-centered design for all

Growth teams thrill at unlocking innovation and immense reach through digital experiences. Yet potential for exponential impact means a responsibility to carefully consider all constituencies touched by new products. Developing intuitive yet accessible interfaces often requires advocating for vulnerable communities internally.

An example is Apple's expanding accommodation tools, such as AssistiveTouch, which support mobility-impaired users. While small UX tweaks meet niche needs, they also unlock the magic of technology for more humans. Growth product managers can champion such opportunities by engaging advocacy groups early in design processes and harnessing inclusive design principles. The goal should be empowering technology utilization by as many people as possible.

By confronting ethical dilemmas, growth product managers evolve as conscientious strategists wary of overreach in pursuit of success. Leaders such as Tim Cook, CEO of Apple, urge the industry to apply care and wisdom so that crises of conscience need not arise. Growth teams, with their tight engagement feedback loops, must lead in fostering healthy digital ecosystems. The choices we make today will surely echo through history.

Real-world example

Uber's 2016 "Greyball" scandal offers an alarming case study of unethical product direction. When the rideshare giant aimed to avoid regulation and inspection in new markets, Uber's growth product managers working with the R&D team modified the frontend code so that authorities appeared unable to successfully hail rides, deceiving regulators.

The resulting $148 million settlement for intentionally deceiving parties via product manipulation highlights acute ethical challenges growth product managers may face regarding transparency. While innovation necessitates moving fast, integrity cannot become collateral damage. Growth leaders must champion social responsibility regardless of other priorities.

Case studies of spectacular product failure

While contemplating ethical implications may prevent potential crises, examining instructive cases of failure equally provides sobering lessons. Even hugely resourced teams and well-known brands can completely misread user needs and market realities. By analyzing where other products went wrong, growth product managers gain wisdom into warning signs that may undermine their launches. Let's explore illustrative examples of spectacular failure.

Quibi – misjudging the market

Just as ethical blind spots carry consequences, so does misunderstanding target users and their changing behaviors. The streaming service Quibi failed precisely due to this market misjudgment.

Quibi shows what happens when assumptions about user needs prove fatally flawed. Their core premise was that consumers craved premium short-form video content viewable in spare minutes. However, the realities of when and how people consume content did not fit Quibi's model. Viewers simply did not flock as expected to 5-10-minute clips on yet another service. Quibi's spectacular collapse despite star-studded shows and $1.75 billion funding should give any growth product manager pause on whether they fully grasp evolving user preferences.

Juicero – overengineering without purpose

While Quibi misread macro consumer trends, Juicero failed by overengineering a solution lacking true purpose.

Juicero demonstrated what happens when innovation becomes completely detached from meaningful utility. Their internet-connected juice press was utterly overdesigned, equipped with QR code scanning, proprietary juice packs, and the crushing force of two Tesla sedans! Yet its actual purpose—making juice—didn't require such complexity. When users realized hands did the same trick, Juicero was doomed. The lesson for growth product managers is that feature creep driven by what tech allows rather than user needs leads products astray.

Theranos – the perils of deception

Sticking to ethics provides the ultimate failsafe against disasters such as Theranos, where deception brought down a $9 billion company.

No saga better illustrates the need for unrelenting integrity than Theranos's. They captivated audiences by claiming revolutionary blood testing technology only needed finger pinpricks rather than vials of blood. However, their breakthrough analyzer simply did not work reliably. But rather than coming clean, Theranos crafted elaborate ruses to demonstrate fake precision, duping investors, and patients alike. Growth product managers must consider Theranos a clarion call for honesty, no matter how alluring the prospects of exaggeration seem.

Spectacular failures offer sobering lessons for growth product managers hoping to avoid similar catastrophes. Quibi, Juicero, and Theranos collectively warn against losing touch with users, prizing tech over purpose, and compromising ethics. By studying their demises, product teams gain wisdom to navigate inevitable storms ahead.

Growth product managers as change agents

While discussing ethics and examining failure informs responsible innovation, the immense opportunities for positive global impact through growth product management should equally inspire. Technology wields unmatched power to drive societal, diplomatic, and sustainability progress by empowering human connections, advancing access, and multiplying the impacts of purpose-driven organizations. Growth product managers in particular serve uniquely as change agents that guide product evolution through data-driven user feedback loops. Let's explore avenues for leveraging technology as a force for good.

Just as poor product direction negatively affects consumers, as shown through fiascos such as Theranos, so too can ethically led growth teams bring immense opportunity by connecting human needs with technology capabilities.

Advancing financial and social access

Connectivity stands as a prerequisite for access to the exponential benefits of technology penetration. Accordingly, growth teams play pivotal roles in overcoming divides across internet access, devices, digital literacy, and user experience design. The rapid adoption of mobile and cellular networks in developing countries has been instrumental in providing internet access to large segments of the global population previously lacking connectivity. Innovations such as mobile money, increased female smartphone ownership, and intuitive communication apps demonstrate how central digital inclusion is for societal advancement.

By continuously localizing, learning user contexts, championing accessibility, and elevating outside voices, product leaders remove barriers limiting human potential. Growth product managers set the trajectory for how organizations harness data and optimize rollouts to advance access. The proliferation of mobile-first digital economies built on cellular networks expands opportunities for technology to promote financial and social inclusion around the world.

Accelerating diplomacy and sustainability

Technology also serves a pivotal role in unlocking new pathways for conflict resolution and environmental protection. Satellite connectivity and sensors enable conservation initiatives to preserve biodiversity and detect violations. Encrypted communication apps also support journalists and whistleblowers in countering corruption.

Growth product managers guide product market fit and feature development by collaborating with public sector partners to pursue stability, transparency, and sustainability agendas. Their user insights and launch capabilities become levers for multiplying goods.

Amplifying social impact campaigns

Finally, growth teams shape how to craft compelling calls to action and initiatives for their communities. Product functionality guides effective storytelling, measurable outcomes, and impacts, which fuels major social campaigns on platforms such as Instagram and TikTok.

User dashboards continuously tune the funnel from awareness to engagement to donation conversion for maximum real-world results. Responsible data utilization remains key so that growth amid goodwill efforts does not inadvertently undermine social innovation.

While discussing ethics and examining failure informs responsible innovation, immense opportunity remains for growth product managers to responsibly harness technology's potential to empower lives. As stewards guiding product experience, they uniquely shape how positive visions turn into meaningful access, diplomatic progress, environmental victories, and impact at scale.

> **Real-world example**
>
> The growth product managers behind the free online learning platform Khan Academy personalized video lesson recommendations and progress dashboards at a massive scale to expand access to engaging education. Dedicated growth teams tailor the user experience for all ages in numerous languages, resulting in over 100 million registered learners globally.
>
> Khan Academy's impact provides inspiration for growth product managers striving to leverage data in service of positive human empowerment. Their journey highlights how continuous experimentation and analytics refinement can optimize product-market fit between emerging technologies such as AI and expanding access to life-changing services, education being just one domain ripe for transformation.

The future of work and skills

As the discipline of growth product management continues advancing at breakneck speed, so too must the capabilities that tomorrow's leaders cultivate to steer innovation responsibly. Mastering emerging domains such as ethics, sustainability, and public sector technology promises new avenues for positive impact, as McKinsey highlights: *"Tech for good is increasingly recognized as a promising new field of innovation."* This shifting landscape of required expertise prompts many questions regarding how growth product managers must prepare through perpetual upskilling. Let's examine the most vital knowledge areas on the horizon and promising paths to proactively skill up.

Emerging areas of expertise

As AI assistants, intelligent workflows and automation transform industries, growth product managers will increasingly curate next-generation experiences at the human-technology frontier. The following are some core emerging competencies to spearhead sustainable innovation:

- **AI ethics**: Ensuring fairness, interpreting machine learning models, and strengthening governance. Organizations such as the Institute for Ethical AI provide frameworks.

- **Systems thinking**: Understanding sociotechnical complexity and interdependencies across media, climate, and health, as the National Academy of Engineering emphasizes.

- **Sustainability**: Incorporating environmental impact into product roadmaps and feature scoping, as surveyed executives already prioritize.

- **Policy and regulation**: Navigating areas such as data privacy, content moderation, and accountability as legislation mounts.

This multifaceted expertise empowers responsible innovation while ensuring continued relevance as external pressures on digital experiences intensify. Forward-looking firms such as Microsoft already offer training across these topics in proactive upskilling.

The X-factor of high-EQ leadership

Beyond purely technical capabilities, stellar growth product leadership demands profound emotional intelligence to navigate uncertainty, balance tensions, and inspire teams to realize a product vision. These timeless high-EQ strengths that AI cannot replicate are as follows:

- Communicating compelling narratives
- Fostering psychologically safe cultures where, as advocated by thought leaders such as Amy Edmundson, team members feel safe to take risks and learn
- Exhibiting creative flexibility per McKinsey research linking leader agility to superior corporate performance
- Shepherding co-creation across functions
- Celebrating small wins and learning

By consciously cultivating these lifelong leadership soft skills early on, emerging growth product managers can separate transactional managers dependent solely on the process. Instead, they evolve into transformational mentors guiding teams through inspiration.

Owning your capability building

Rather than expecting companies alone to furnish training, growth product managers should pursue personal mastery as lifelong learners through channels such as conferences, online programs, certifications, and communities of practice. Organizations such as Product School exemplify this continuous learning ecosystem by supporting upskilling.

A diversity of ongoing educational avenues prevents stagnation while expanding possibilities to address new opportunities. Capability building keeps pace with accelerating technological and societal change and promises sustained employability for those change agents steering product experiences. The future favors the perpetually curious.

Career paths and professional development opportunities for growth product managers

Navigating growth product management's evolving terrain also involves capitalizing on expanding career opportunities. The field now offers diverse trajectories to senior product manager roles, company leadership, entrepreneurship, and beyond.

For example, Xiaodi Hou now leads product design at payments giant Stripe after holding product manager positions at Amazon and Microsoft. Her success shows how seasoned product managers can leverage experience into executive status at major firms.

Meanwhile, others chart their courses by founding startups. Ex-Facebook VP Julie Zhuo authored best-selling product management books before launching her own coaching company. Her path reveals entrepreneurial possibilities for growth product managers seeking independence.

To access these opportunities, growth product managers must actively strengthen their leadership abilities, strategic thinking, and cross-domain knowledge. Mentorships, unconventional assignments, and training programs such as Microsoft's Academy for College Hires all provide development channels.

Conferences such as ProductCamp or communities such as **Product-Led Alliance** (**PLA**) also enable essential networking to position for career moves by connecting with executives and recruiters. Mastery across product, technology, research, analytics, and business domains also broadens prospects. Malleable expertise insulates growth product managers from disruption while empowering major career pivots.

The growth product manager journey also offers a fulfilling purpose by solving meaningful problems for people worldwide. Their innovations support Elizabeth Mattis Namgyel's wisdom that "*When you have a sense of purpose and meaning, you can weather any storm.*" By always connecting products back to positive human impacts during times of uncertainty, growth product managers can stay centered while creating change.

The path ahead – growth product managers as conscientious innovators

As we conclude our exploration of the multifaceted landscape of growth product management, one truth stands paramount—with the power to profoundly impact human experiences comes a solemn duty to progress responsibly.

Growth product managers stand at the frontier ushering in new technological capabilities and digital experiences. Their decisions resound across vast networks, for better or worse. And their creativity fuels discoveries that can either uplift lives or infringe upon human dignity.

The brands that will thrive and contribute lasting value are those guided by growth teams who lead conscientiously. Those who see the ethical gaps and forge new standards, make inclusion a first principle, and temper ambition with wisdom, and those who find inspiration in serving peoples' needs rather than exploiting them.

The future remains unwritten. Its course will bend toward the visionaries who move progress forward for all people, not just the privileged. Armed with the passion, skills, and sense of purpose cultivated on the path to becoming growth champions, a new generation now enters this arena.

May you have the courage to stand for justice, the empathy to see every user as human, and the integrity to lift others as they rise. If so, the brightest days lie ahead. There is no challenge that innovation guided by conscience cannot overcome, no human potential beyond reach, and no height of positive global impact unattainable.

The power lies in you and the journey begins today.

Real-world example

A compelling model for progress that uplifts people can be found in startup Banking-as-a-Service solution provider Clusivi. When founder Cedric Lipsey faced a $8,000 dental procedure in 2017 not covered by insurance, he discovered the punitive 29%+ interest rates of healthcare credit cards like CareCredit that would kick in if the debt could not be paid back within 6-12 months. This experience planted the seed for a business that could "reimagine banking, savings, and access to credit" for healthcare, especially for lower-income families.

Even with Lipsey's good income and credit, paying for essential care was extremely challenging. He realized that if this hardship affected him, the struggles were exponentially greater for working-class and poor Americans, preventing many from getting critically needed treatment and other essential needs. Compelled by his firsthand account, Lipsey set out to create an equitable funding alternative through Clusivi.

In Lipsey's words, "Clusivi was born from my personal hardship, but forged in the commitment to alleviate rather than exploit. Progress in financial services must put people before profits. With our lending model and patient savings tools, we can help the underserved members of our communities get care and other essential needs without drowning in debt. This is the future we want to build."

Through Clusivi's responsible approach to finance, Lipsey has turned his own difficult experience into an uplifting solution now the masses can leverage to access credit when they cannot via the traditional banking solution that relies on FICO scores. This exemplifies progress fueled by ethical innovation.

Summary

This concluding chapter explored the indispensable and rapidly evolving role of growth product managers in the digital age as product experiences take center stage in customer acquisition and revenue growth strategies.

We discussed how the growth product management discipline has emerged to steer this transformation, coordinating cross-functional teams to optimize product-market fit. Growth product managers assume strategic leadership orchestrating user research, design sprints, development, analytics, and launch campaigns to maximize adoption and retention.

We outlined essential growth product management attributes, including unwavering customer empathy, data and analytics fluency, strategic vision, stellar communication abilities, adaptive leadership capabilities, and systems thinking to navigate complexity. These distinguish elite growth product managers driving product-led business success.

This chapter also delved deeply into the dynamic landscape growth product managers must traverse to continue innovating, from ethical tech challenges to merger and acquisition integrations. We explored crucial contexts, including technological advances, digital transformations, shifting behaviors, and ethical considerations that growth product managers must navigate.

Emerging technologies such as AI, AR, and VR compel growth teams to continually explore applications while upgrading competencies to harness them responsibly. As omnichannel consumption becomes imperative, growth product managers play central roles in ensuring usability and integrated experiences across devices and platforms. Growth teams must vigilantly study consumer shifts through primary research and data analytics to align product roadmaps serving evolving preferences. Finally, issues such as privacy, algorithmic fairness, and platform addiction require establishing governance so that innovation aligns with human well-being.

These intertwined contexts present both opportunities and challenges that demand growth product managers exemplify agility and leadership to steer products strategically amidst exponential change. By championing continual learning and cross-functional collaboration while optimizing customer experiences, they can unlock sustainable innovation benefiting businesses and communities. However, this also requires establishing ethical practices regarding data utilization, algorithmic accountability, and balancing business priorities with human welfare.

To remain competitive amid these exponential forces, growth product managers must exemplify agility and leadership ushering teams through uncertainty toward opportunity. We highlighted avenues for skill development including experimental rotations, continual upskilling, and embracing versatile career trajectories beyond traditional planning roles.

When guided by ethical codes and human-centered values, growth teams create outstanding products benefiting businesses and broader communities simultaneously. The future favors thoughtful, strategic product leaders progressing inclusively by uplifting diverse constituencies through innovation.

Questions

1. What is PLG, what triggered its emergence, and why has it become an imperative?

2. What are the key attributes and skills that set successful growth product managers apart as emergent organizational leaders driving business outcomes?

3. Considering exponential technological and societal changes, how must the role of growth product managers continue advancing to steer products strategically amid complexity?

4. What expanding career trajectories and professional development journeys can ambitious growth product managers embark upon to maximize their impact?

Answers

1. PLG is a strategy centered around the product itself as the main driver of customer acquisition, retention, and revenue growth. It emerged in recent years as digital transformation compelled companies to shift from traditional sales-driven models to product-driven self-service models aligned with the preferences of modern consumers. PLG has become imperative because companies that embrace it can react faster to market changes, foster customer loyalty, and sustain innovation and long-term growth in competitive markets.

2. Key attributes include a customer-centric mindset, data-driven decision-making, results-oriented focus, adaptability and innovation, stellar communication and collaboration abilities, and strategic leadership capabilities. Essential skills encompass empathy and user research competence, analytics and technical fluency, interpersonal effectiveness to inspire teams, and versatility to thrive amidst uncertainty.

3. Growth product managers must champion agility and constant learning to evaluate and integrate emerging technologies such as AI ethically. They must also continually study consumer shifts to align product roadmaps to new behaviors across digital ecosystems and devices. Furthermore, they must upgrade leadership talents to communicate compelling visions and unify cross-functional teams.

4. Expanding trajectories involves pursuing executive leadership roles directing product strategy, independent entrepreneurship founding new companies, and cross-domain transfers of product management talents to new industries. Growth product managers can maximize impact by strengthening strategic thinking via lateral job rotations, participating in continuous learning programs, building networks and personal brands, and leading targeted innovation initiatives.

Index

H

Packtpub.com

Subscribe to our online digital library for full access to over 7,000 books and videos, as well as industry leading tools to help you plan your personal development and advance your career. For more information, please visit our website.

Why subscribe?

- Spend less time learning and more time coding with practical eBooks and Videos from over 4,000 industry professionals

- Improve your learning with Skill Plans built especially for you

- Get a free eBook or video every month

- Fully searchable for easy access to vital information

- Copy and paste, print, and bookmark content

Did you know that Packt offers eBook versions of every book published, with PDF and ePub files available? You can upgrade to the eBook version at packtpub.com and as a print book customer, you are entitled to a discount on the eBook copy. Get in touch with us at customercare@packtpub.com for more details.

At www.packtpub.com, you can also read a collection of free technical articles, sign up for a range of free newsletters, and receive exclusive discounts and offers on Packt books and eBooks.

Other Books You May Enjoy

If you enjoyed this book, you may be interested in these other books by Packt:

Gamification for Product Excellence

Mike Hyzy, Bret Wardle

ISBN: 978-1-83763-838-3

- Explore gamification and learn how to engage your user with it
- Gain insights into the functionality and implementation of different gamification frameworks
- Master specific game elements and mechanics that can be used to improve user experiences
- Design a successful gamification strategy to test your hypothesis and develop a business case
- Implement and test the prototype you've created with users for feedback
- Say the right words to sell your gamification strategy to stakeholders
- Use design thinking exercises and game elements to improve the product management process

API Analytics for Product Managers

Deepa Goyal

ISBN: 978-1-80324-765-6

- Build a long-term strategy for an API
- Explore the concepts of the API life cycle and API maturity
- Understand APIs from a product management perspective
- Create support models for your APIs that scale with the product
- Apply user research principles to APIs
- Explore the metrics of activation, retention, engagement, and churn
- Cluster metrics together to provide context
- Examine the consequences of gameable and vanity metrics

Packt is searching for authors like you

If you're interested in becoming an author for Packt, please visit `authors.packtpub.com` and apply today. We have worked with thousands of developers and tech professionals, just like you, to help them share their insight with the global tech community. You can make a general application, apply for a specific hot topic that we are recruiting an author for, or submit your own idea.

Share Your Thoughts

Now you've finished *Growth Product Manager's Handbook*, we'd love to hear your thoughts! Scan the QR code below to go straight to the Amazon review page for this book and share your feedback or leave a review on the site that you purchased it from.

https://packt.link/r/1837635951

Your review is important to us and the tech community and will help us make sure we're delivering excellent quality content.

Download a free PDF copy of this book

Thanks for purchasing this book!

Do you like to read on the go but are unable to carry your print books everywhere?

Is your eBook purchase not compatible with the device of your choice?

Don't worry, now with every Packt book you get a DRM-free PDF version of that book at no cost.

Read anywhere, any place, on any device. Search, copy, and paste code from your favorite technical books directly into your application.

The perks don't stop there, you can get exclusive access to discounts, newsletters, and great free content in your inbox daily

Follow these simple steps to get the benefits:

1. Scan the QR code or visit the link below

https://packt.link/free-ebook/9781837635955

2. Submit your proof of purchase
3. That's it! We'll send your free PDF and other benefits to your email directly

Printed in the USA
CPSIA information can be obtained
at www.ICGtesting.com
CBHW051219210524
8846CB00016B/121

9 781837 635955